The Emergence
of a Senate Leader:
Pete Domenici
and the Reagan Budget

The Emergence
of a Senate Leader:
Pete Domenici
and the Reagan Budget

Richard F. Fenno, Jr.
University of Rochester

CQ
PRESS

A Division of Congressional Quarterly Inc.
Washington, D.C.

Cover design: Paula Anderson
Cover photo: R. Michael Jenkins

Printed in the United States of America

Library of Congress Cataloging-in-Publication Data

Fenno, Richard F., 1926-
    The emergence of a Senate leader : Pete Domenici and the Reagan budget /
Richard F. Fenno, Jr.
        p. cm.
    Includes bibliographical references and index.
    ISBN 0-87187-636-1   --ISBN 0-87187-592-6 (pbk.)
    1. Domenici, Pete. 2. Political leadership—United States. 3. Budget—
United States.   4. United States. Congress.   Senate.   Committee on the
Budget.   5. United States--Politics and government--1981-1989.   I. Title.
E840.8.D66F46   1991
328.73'07658—dc20   90-19164
                                                                          CIP

To *Zachary Dube Fenno*

Contents

Preface

This book is about eight years in the career of Sen. Pete V. Domenici, a Republican from New Mexico. They were years in which Domenici rose to a topmost leadership position in the United States Senate. They were years in which Ronald Reagan established his legacy as president of the United States. And they were years in which Domenici played a large part in shaping the Reagan legacy. As chairman of the Senate Budget Committee—the committee of first resort in the only chamber controlled by the president's party—Pete Domenici became both custodian and critic of the Reagan economic program.

Most of the book centers on the ways in which Domenici carried out that crucial assignment in governing the country. But the chairman's budgetary activity in Washington is framed by the senator's electoral activity in New Mexico. The analysis encompasses both activities and both settings. It has been enriched by personal observation—as I accompanied the senator in Washington in 1981 and 1982, and in New Mexico in 1978, 1980, 1981, and 1984. It begins with his electoral victory in 1978 and ends with the surrender of his chairmanship in 1986. A final endnote contains firsthand observations on his successful reelection campaign in 1990.

In the 1990s, a book containing a heavy dosage of budgetary politics may not be considered overly appetizing. The halls of Congress and the pages of newspapers have been so heavily burdened for so many years with budget wars, budget deficits, budget reforms, and budget fatigue that it has become increasingly difficult to maintain public concern or interest in such matters. There is a desire, if not a tendency, to think of budget politics as the certified bane of the 1980s and the certified bore of the 1990s.

For purposes of this book, however, several offsetting observations are in order. First, the politics of budget making was the central preoccupation of the Reagan presidency. While this book makes no overall judgment on Reagan-era budget making, it does present a new and different legislator's-eye view of what went on. It is quite a different perspective from that propounded by executives such as Budget Director David Stockman and others. Second, like it or not, the budget policies of the Reagan years are directly responsible for the deficit-driven agenda ("more will than wallet") of George Bush's presidency. Willy-nilly, therefore, budget problems remain at the center—and at the bottom—of most Washington debates in the 1990s. The long, highly publicized budget-making ordeal in the fall of 1990 makes that point abundantly clear.

Third, the focus of this book is on the political career of a U.S. senator, on the activity of a powerful committee chairman, and on the relationships of that chairman with his fellow senators and the president of the United States. Budgetary politics become the window through which these enduring aspects of legislative politics are viewed. In a word, the book is about some crucial political relationships in the processing of a crucial policy subject. It is a book about the behavior of a Senate committee chairman and about the impact of that behavior on the making of six federal budgets.

My debts to those who helped me in this analysis are many and large. Most of all, I am indebted to Sen. Pete Domenici for his friendship and for his willingness to let me tag along in New Mexico and Washington. Whether in a "let's roll" mood during a campaign or an "I'm worried" mood during a budgetary countdown, he would steal time from a hectic pace to answer, to reflect, and to educate. His attitude of helpfulness extended, contagiously, to the members of his staff. I thank three of them in particular for their especially generous and indispensable gifts of aid and comfort while I conducted my research—Lou Gallegos, Fran Langholf, and Angela Raish. I acknowledge my enormous debt, too, to staff members Steve Bell, Martha Buddecke, Poe Corn, Diana Daggett, Pete Davis, Ari Fleischer, Gail Fosler, Bob Fulton, Tony Gallegos, Darlene Garcia, Lee Rawls, Ernie Vigil, and Peter Wellish.

I also thank a number of my colleagues in academia. Three friends—Rick Hanushek, Chuck Jones, and Tom Mann—read all or parts of the manuscript and gave me valuable help. Fred Greenstein and David Vogler gave me the opportunity to practice my story. Pat Fett and Wendy Schiller provided first-class research assistance.

Janice Brown remained, as always, my strong right arm in preparing notes and manuscript. The editors at CQ Press, with whom I have worked so easily and happily in recent years, have once again taken great care, demonstrated great competence, and given great encouragement. I thank all of them—especially Dave Tarr, Joanne Daniels, John Moore, and Ann O'Malley. I also thank the Russell Sage Foundation for their indispensable financial help. My wife, as always, found most of the mistakes. I am to blame for those that are left.

Introduction

Politics involves the interaction of private ambition, public institutions, and agenda-setting events. Political scientists, therefore, study the goals of politicians, the process of decision making within institutions, and the impact of factors external to both. This book can be thought of, most broadly, as one more attempt to examine each of these elements, to explore their interactions, and to chart their effect on outcomes. Its conceptual underpinning is the idea of the political career.

The political career is a succession and an accumulation of experiences gathered by working in a series of public offices and/or by undertaking a series of public responsibilities. The idea of a career is both a developmental and a contextual one. It compels an emphasis on the passage of time and on changing circumstances. It requires the study of ambition, institutions, and events. And it allows for a focus on individual politicians or on collectivities of politicians within or across specific institutions.

Whether the subject is an individual or a group, however, the analysis of careers will eventually come to focus on the interaction between the politicians and the institutions of which they are a part—and to the impact, on both, of factors beyond their control. This book concentrates on a six-year committee chairmanship embedded in the long-term career of a United States senator.

There is nothing novel about the use of the political career to bring analytical purchase to the study of American politics. Political scientists have studied the motivations that propel people into politics and keep them there; the paths that politicians follow into, within, and among public institutions; the responses of politicians to job opportunities presented to them by external events; and the sequences of learning and adaptation, success and failure that mark the movement of politicians as they change offices, jobs, and responsibilities.[1] In these several respects, it is assumed, political careers display regularities that can be described and that, once described, will help us to form generalizations about American political life.

That is also the broadest claim of this book. It may not, however, be its most compelling claim. For the book is about one career segment of one person's political career. It does, however, contain all the ingredients of career studies in general—their developmental and contextual emphasis together with their admixture of private goals, institutional positions, external events, and emergent opportunities. Moreover, the contours of the particular career we shall examine are sharply delineated. They chart for us the experiences of an unknown politician who became a national leader in a fascinating period of time. Still, the book is only a case study, and claims for its generality cannot be easily made. It may strengthen such claims, however, if it can be thought of as a case that suggests a framework for the study of other careers—or career segments—as well.

The framework employed here is designed to be helpful in the study of the careers of our elected national legislators. It begins with the notion that some regular and recognizable stages mark the normal career path of a national legislator. The basic regularity is the sequence that begins with a period of campaigning in the home constituency, is followed by a period of governing activity in Washington, and is followed, in turn, by a reelection campaign back in the home constituency. Campaigning and governing are the two main activities of every legislator. And the campaigning-governing-campaigning sequence is the controlling sequence of every legislator's life.

Our sequential framework carries with it the notion that activity at one stage will have a cause-and-effect influence on activity at the following stage. It also conveys the idea that the anticipation of activity at the following stage will affect activity in the preceding stage. Most important, we would expect that activity at the governing stage will be affected by the results of the previous election and by the anticipation of the next election. In our framework, it is the legislator's postelection interpretation of his or her election experience that mediates the transition from campaigning to governing and, thus, affects governing activity. And it is the legislator's anticipation of the need to explain his or her governing activity to the home constituency that mediates the transition from governing to campaigning and, in that manner, affects governing activity. We expect these mediating influences to be strongest during transition periods at the beginning and at the end of the governing stage.

Within the governing stage itself, we can attempt a finer calibration by distinguishing several sorts of activities that can provide focal points for observation and analysis. There is an early period of adjustment to the legislature; there is the production of a record of accomplishment sufficient to end the adjustment period; there is the gradual development of a recognizable governing style; and there is the acquisition of a legislative reputation. These activities have a

FIGURE I-1 A Framework for the Study of a Career Segment

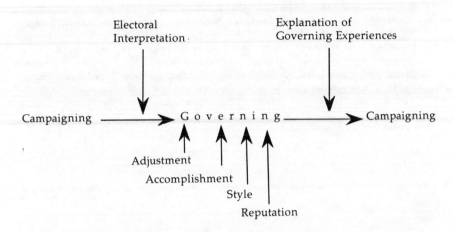

roughly sequential and developmental aspect to them, and they can be traced over time. They tend to begin with adjustment experiences and to cumulate in a reputation that, when publicized by the media and/or the candidate, has its effects at election time. These governing activities may take on a different meaning for a veteran legislator than for a newcomer—readjustment rather than adjustment, or a change in reputation, for example. Such differences are a matter for investigation.

Schematically, the controlling sequence, the transitional influences, and the governing activities of a career segment are outlined in Figure 1. When legislators are successful at retaining their jobs, we would expect this sequence to recycle, with longevity effects having their own independent impact as careers lengthened.

The case at hand focuses mostly on a single stage in the campaigning-governing-campaigning sequence. It analyzes the governing activity of a Senate committee chairman. But it treats the chairmanship as one point in a much longer political career. And it treats the entire governing period as embedded in a lengthier, ongoing sequence of campaigning and governing. Periods of governing and campaigning preceding his chairmanship will be examined. So will the experience of campaigning during his chairmanship. And the effects of these sequences on his governing behavior as chairman will also be examined.

There are, of course, many vantage points from which to study the behavior of a congressional committee chairman. Our perspective on Pete Domenici's chairmanship experience is a longitudinal, developmental, career-oriented one.

NOTE

1. Some congressional examples: Donald Matthews, *U.S. Senators and Their World* (Chapel Hill: University of North Carolina Press, 1960); Joseph Schlesinger, *Ambition and Politics: Political Careers in the United States* (Chicago: University of Chicago Press, 1966); Gary Jacobson and Samuel Kernell, *Strategy and Choice in Congressional Elections* (New Haven: Yale University Press, 1983); Burdett Loomis, *The New Politicians* (New York: Basic Books, 1988); Linda Fowler and Robert McClure, *Political Ambition: Who Decides to Run for Congress* (New Haven: Yale University Press, 1989); and David Canon, *Actors, Athletes and Astronauts: Political Amateurs in the United States Congress* (Chicago: University of Chicago Press, 1990).

1

Filtering Up:
Washington and New Mexico

CHANGING CONTEXTS, CHANGING CAREER

On November 4, 1980, a series of events over which he had absolutely
no control changed everything in the political career of Pete V.
Domenici of New Mexico. His party took control of the presidency
and the Senate. And in accordance with Senate rules and party
rules, he became chairman of the chamber's Budget Committee. This
chairmanship altered the entire structure of opportunities and constraints within which he acted in Washington. And these changes in
Washington radically altered the context in which he acted at home.
Contextual changes, in turn, induced behavioral changes in both
places. The unexpected nature of the Republican takeover of the
Senate imparted an extraordinary suddenness to the change. And
President Ronald Reagan's decision to place the budget front and
center on his policy agenda imparted an unusual significance to
the change.

For the media scorekeepers who watched Domenici during the
year that followed, the story line invariably featured the dramatic
alteration in his political career. A July 1981 *Newsweek* article, "Rating
the Senate Bosses," began:

> Few Senate Republicans have seen their roles enlarged more drasti-
> cally than New Mexico's Pete Domenici, an affable, chain smoking
> conservative who is now Chairman of the important Budget Com-
> mittee. Early last year, Domenici was the Committee's second
> ranking Republican behind the respected Henry L. Bellmon of
> Oklahoma, while Maine Democrat Edmund S. Muskie ran the
> show.... But Muskie left the Senate ..., Bellmon retired ..., and
> Domenici suddenly found himself in the forefront of the Reagan
> Administration's drive to balance the budget.[1]

Three months later the *Albuquerque Tribune* exhibited the theme's New Mexico perspective in an article entitled, "Constituents Proud of Domenici: Some Say Presidency Is Next Stop."

> In the last few years, Domenici has made the meteoric rise from local boy to U.S. Senate, from Albuquerque's Young Man of the Year in 1967 to Chairman of the Senate Budget Committee, from Chairman of the City Commission to confidant of a President. Until recently, Domenici was just another nameless face in the Senate. Then he shot to national prominence when President Reagan dropped his name during a televised speech on his new budget proposals. Suddenly Domenici was a hot item. He was interviewed by the major networks, and stories about him popped up on the national news wires.[2]

The theme was repeated endlessly.[3] A senator had been catapulted from the obscure periphery to the visible center of the governing process in the United States.

If it was Domenici's committee chairmanship that located him "at the center" of things, it was the 1980 elections that propelled him there. Official position may be the single most important resource a senator can command; but official position derives from a biennial concatenation of Senate classes and Senate elections that no senator commands. The recapture of the Senate by the Republican party for the first time in twenty-eight years forcefully reminded political scientists that party control is the fundamental ingredient in the opportunity structure of every individual legislator. After November 4, 1980, every Republican senator saw his or her chance to govern improve exponentially. Every Democratic senator's chances underwent a commensurate decline. Every senator's career underwent a huge change.

Pete Domenici was not the only beneficiary of the change in party control. But no one benefited as much as he. The other three Republicans whose newly acquired official positions cast them as prime movers of the majority party agenda—Howard Baker, Robert Dole, and Mark Hatfield—had worked before in the national political spotlight. All had served in the Senate longer than Domenici and all had held more responsible public jobs. So, the media's story line was entirely appropriate. Between November 4, 1980, and January 3, 1981, Pete Domenici underwent a greater increase in responsibility and public notice than any other member of the United States Senate.

These facts present an invitation to think of our story line in career terms, to think of our career segment in developmental terms, and to treat a succession of contexts. Accordingly, we shall emphasize the pursuit, achievement, and alteration of a legislator's goals over time; the opportunities and the constraints of a committee chairmanship; the unending demands of budgetary decision making across an ever-changing succession of external and institutional contexts; the gradual accumulation of governing lessons in dealing with committee members, Senate colleagues, and the president; and the measured emergence of a national policy maker in Washington and a celebrated representative in New Mexico. And we shall overlay these analytic interests with a framework that highlights the legislator's movement across the repetitious campaigning-governing-campaigning-governing career sequence.

In this chapter we explore Domenici's career in the period immediately preceding his chairmanship. Our focus is on the governing patterns he adopted during his first term in the Senate, his subsequent reelection campaign, and the effects of that campaign on his governing patterns. A look at this early governing-campaigning-governing segment of his career provides essential background for understanding his subsequent behavior as committee chairman. The chapter traces his early Senate career up to the point where he assumes that new position.

GOVERNING IN WASHINGTON

ADJUSTMENT

For the media scorekeepers, Pete Domenici's life before November 1980 was a blank. In 1979 his name had been mentioned eight times on the three evening network news shows. In 1980 he had been mentioned twice. But in fact for eight years he had been adjusting, accomplishing, and developing a governing style. The story behind the story line, therefore, is that he was hardly without a track record when he awoke one morning and found himself in a position of leadership. The career that suddenly changed so radically had been changing all along.

Domenici brought with him to the Senate in January 1973 a strong desire to govern. It was not that he had a lifelong desire to be in politics; it was that in whatever organization he served, he wanted and expected to rise to the top. "I am not one of those that planned for a long time to be in politics or to be a senator," he said, five months into his term.

> In anything I did in life, whether it was typical high school activities or a ball team or a civic group, I have generally *filtered up* to being president or chairman of the group or some such thing. That's an ingredient that has been part of my life. I guess I always had a yearning to be something in whatever I did.[4]

Calling himself "an accident" in politics, he repeated several years later that,

There was something there inside of me. In every organization I belonged to I was elected president.... From the third grade up ... always president. So there was something there. But I tell you that for seven years when I was practicing law, I didn't join a single organization. I just worked fifteen hours a day; I had six kids; I didn't give a thought to politics.

In his only previous elected office, the Albuquerque City Commission, Domenici had been chosen chairman—the equivalent of mayor—by the group in his second year of service. In the Senate, a member of the minority party cannot rise to the topmost positions in the organization. But he or she can "filter up" to become a legislator of more than average consequence. Domenici began with that modest goal. He wanted to achieve a distinctive degree of influence within the organization—to "be something" with respect to the governing activity of the Senate. Only gradually did he find ways to accomplish this goal. For eight years, he grew increasingly effective in achieving it. These eight years of gradual "filtering up" give us some necessary background for understanding Pete Domenici's performance as chairman of the Budget Committee.

His first six years in the Senate produced a goodly proportion of frustration. But the ratio of frustration to accomplishment slowly changed. His early adjustment period lasted, by his own accounting, for two years. And it was difficult. For one thing, he had to scale back expectations derived from previous experience. People who knew him first in Albuquerque and then worked with him in the Senate talked about his problems in "adjusting from" his previous job. One talked about his adjustment from good local press coverage.

He got such good press when he was on the city commission—the editor then was a man who liked city politics—that when he went to Washington he thought it was his right and his due. He spent the first few years thrashing around trying to get press and not getting any. He shouldn't have been wasting his time trying. The papers here thought, "He's a freshman senator, not worth covering." And they were right.

Another talked more generally about the adjustment from his local leadership position. "Pete does not make a good member. He never was a member of anything. He was always the leader. When he got to the Senate, he had a terrible time learning to be a member of the Senate." Even with a scaled-back set of expectations, his previous experience was of limited comparability.

In addition, he made a slow "adjustment from" his 1972 campaign. He overloaded his start-up Senate staff with campaigners from New Mexico. One senior staffer recalled,

We had a lot of people we felt we had to hire from the campaign. We brought a lot of them with us.... The big mistake we made was that we did not hire anyone who knew the Senate. . . . I had to check ten offices every time I wanted to find out how you did something. It was insane.

Another top staffer said that the senator solved his discomfiture in the Senate by keeping his energies focused back home. "When he was first elected, he kept wanting to go back to New Mexico. It was hard to keep him here. He was uncomfortable in the Senate."

He also faced the problems of "adjustment to" his new job. Halfway into his first year, in June of 1973, he talked about his adjustment to a set of institutional constraints not present in the small, nonpartisan city commission. "Two kinds of inhibitors," he said, were especially prominent—the party system and the seniority system. "Since a Republican is [in] the minority party you are obviously greatly inhibited in terms of committee chairmanships. You can't have those. So you don't determine how fast the committee goes [or] what it does. . . . " As for the seniority system, "The thing that is bad about that process is that you don't get the staff assistance from the committees. That is a serious regulator of what you can and can't do."

He accepted these constraints, but he found them frustrating. "The committee system has fantastic problems. It is delegating enormous power to committee staffs. . . . Its shortcoming is that the committee staff is becoming too strong and is really the voice."

He felt equally estranged from proceedings on the floor. "Our staff tries to get an idea of what's going on on the floor," he said. [But]

> There is a miserable part of this process. Mistakes of huge proportion can be made there. . . . [The floor] is not used for a bonafide, well-thought-out process of amending. . . . People use it to come in with philosophies, to build their reputations, and the like. It makes life very difficult to know what is going on.

The picture is one of a minority party newcomer experiencing some difficulty finding a way to participate satisfactorily in the institution's legislative business. His frustration was contained. But, for one person "yearning to be something," it was present.

I first met Pete Domenici near the end of his first reelection campaign in October 1978. Everywhere he went, he spoke about the difficulties of his early Senate years, and of the experience gap he had to negotiate. He told a Sandia High School civics class, "When I took the job, I knew nothing about it. The people elected me and plunked me down in the United States Senate. My position was the lowest in seniority. The first couple of years were tough." "There was," he told an Albuquerque women's group, "nothing good about my first two years. The first two years, if you had asked me if I enjoyed it, I would have changed the subject."

A year and a half later, Domenici described, in more detail, what he called his "very slow adjustment" to the Senate. "I don't want to over-psychoanalyze myself," he said.

> But when I went to the Senate, I was very reluctant to step forward. I look at people now who are at the same stage I was seven and a half years ago, and they are already stepping out to make a place for themselves in the Senate. I'm just as smart as they are, just as able to make a speech, frame an argument, or build a coalition as they are. But I faced the job with great trepidation. The rules of the Senate troubled me. I was afraid even to ask for a quorum call. It was a very slow adjustment. And then there was all the work of a Senate office. The letters started coming in; the problems they brought to the office imprisoned me. The half dozen bitches I would get when I went home bothered me when I came back to work. Gradually I broke free from those demands. I could come back to Washington, go to committee and not worry about what had happened.... Then, I began to get some amendments passed in committee. They are mini-Senates, where you can put the rules aside and deal with people face to face informally and get to know them. Your success in committee then carries out to the floor.

Domenici's success in committee and on the floor in "getting some amendments passed" was his earliest kind of legislative accomplishment.

A lot of his amendments came from his trips home. Even while he felt imprisoned by demands from home, he used them to his benefit. "There wasn't a trip home that I didn't pick up something that resulted in an amendment—sometimes just a word change. By the end of the term, the Library of Congress told us I had gotten more amendments passed than any other freshman senator." It was one way to participate. And, he experienced enough success at it to bring his earliest adjustment period to a close.

ACCOMPLISHMENTS

For a senator who wanted to help govern, these early accomplishments represented a threshold. They were a sign that he was not without some influence, but they did not bring him the distinctive degree of governing influence he wanted. His amendments were small in scope, local in orientation, and, above all, scattershot. They lacked a policy focus. "For Pete," said one of his associates, "the grass always looks greener in the other pasture. He has great enthusiasms and they change." Gradually, Domenici learned that the degree and kind of influence he sought could be achieved only by making qualitatively important contributions in a few policy areas.

Looking back in 1979, he said that,

> The biggest mistake you can make—and I made it—is that because the institution demands so much of you, you will shotgun and try a little bit of everything. The temptation is severe. For a representative in the minority, it's the sure way to failure.

Experience had taught him, he continued,

> to be more of a realist in terms of how much one senator can accomplish in the institution.... You understand that there are one hundred guys and you aren't going to do everything in other domains ... [and] that keeps you from being impetuous. You don't have to be out on the floor to prove you are ... for the military. Let Stennis and Tower cover that waterfront.

He learned further that,

> The most important quality up here is respect as a legislator.... [And] to earn respect, you've got to specialize and become knowledgeable and get it out to your fellow man. Be wise enough to pick an area, bright enough to learn it, and find the opportunity to apply it, both in committee work and floor work.... Act with honesty, decency, and camaraderie, and you will gain respect.

Just when Domenici began to make the shift from quantity to quality in his legislative efforts is not clear. By 1977, at least, he was explaining his legislative strategy in exactly those terms:

> You learn pretty quickly when you get to the Senate that you can be involved in an awful lot of things. So you have to pick something, or a few things maybe, and concentrate on them if you want to achieve anything.[5]

When called upon to defend his record of achievement in his 1978 reelection campaign, Domenici used both quantitative and qualitative arguments. He used the Library of Congress statistics on numbers of amendments passed by first-termers to rebut his opponent's blanket charge that he lacked influence in the Senate. But he placed much greater emphasis on the quality of his policy-making achievements.

These achievements came from actions taken in the latter part of his first term. One consistent campaign theme (albeit, as we shall see, the secondary one) was his assertion that he had, indeed, "made a difference" in the Senate. Debating his opponent on television, he said that "I didn't dream I would make a difference. But I did." This was, of course, exactly what he had always wanted to be able to claim for his Senate service. And he elaborated. "There are three successes I'm proud of." They were the compromise energy bill favoring the gradual deregulation of natural gas, the nondegradation aspect of air pollution policy, and the implementation of budget reform.

Regarding the first "success," he told a meet-the-candidates forum,

> I have enjoyed it, except for the first two years. . . . The last four years
> have been exciting. I didn't think I could come back and say I had
> made a difference. But I believe I can say that. . . . My hardest decision
> was to compromise on energy policy. I joined with three Republicans
> and six Democrats. If I hadn't, we would not have had a bill. It took
> tremendous intestinal fortitude and hard work. I didn't think I'd be
> put in that position so early. I'm glad I was and I was glad I could
> help.

He described his second "success" to a high school civics class.

> But for me, we wouldn't have nondegradation. Not me alone. Nine or
> ten of us formed a team. The way the cards were stacked, we couldn't
> have a bill. I made a decision that something was better than nothing.
> I took two members of my party with me, we joined with seven on
> the other side and produced a compromise. We worked late at night.
> It was almost as if we had won a football game. We stood up and
> applauded each other and hugged each other for completing fourteen
> months of effort.

Each success was grounded in his committee memberships—the Energy
Committee for natural gas, the Public Works Committee for air pollution. His committee-based concentration of effort represented the time-
tested, orthodox path to influence in Congress. It also represented a
distinct change from his scattershot pattern of legislative involvement.
And his new-found sense of accomplishment was palpable.

It is one measure of Domenici's desire to help govern that his
contributions to and his support for the energy bill entailed serious
political costs at home. The compromise bill phased out controls more
gradually than the New Mexico oil and gas industry wanted. And these
primary constituents of his were very unhappy with Domenici. "The
greatest political risk I took [in my first term]," he said during
his reelection campaign, "was my support of the compromise energy
bill."

> The oil and gas people of this state were mad at me. And they had
> been my strongest supporters. Up until the end, I voted with them;
> and the money was coming in. Every other member of the delegation
> voted against the compromise. The day after my vote, the money was
> shut off—just like that. They know I'm involved in making energy
> policy. But they'd rather have someone who committed himself
> beforehand to vote their way all the time than have a senator who is
> helping make policy.

Domenici's assertion of independence was costly—in terms of the short-
run loss of intense electoral support and in terms of the long-run
expenditure of resources needed to win back these groups. Three years
later, on a trip through oil and gas territory, he commented, "I've

worked awfully hard to build that support back up again. My reception in Hobbs reinforced my feeling that the movers and shakers of this area are back on board again . . . some of them in spades." His willingness, in 1978, to incur these costs to accomplish something in the Senate indicates the seriousness with which he pursued his governing-related goals.

In the case of his third "success," budgetary reform, his accomplishments were more gradual and less focused. But they, too, were based on his committee membership. And they were far more consequential in the long run. Almost from the beginning of his first term, he took an interest in the fiscal processes of the institution. At the end of a June 1973 interview, he said, "Now I don't want you to end your chat with a freshman senator after five months without [my] telling you what I really think are the two most significant things of a procedural nature that are wrong." First and foremost, he said, "the system of appropriating and funding, budgeting within the Congress must be modernized." He became an early supporter and worker for budgetary reform.

In a biographical sketch prepared for the information of interns working in the Domenici office in 1975, his staff wrote, "During his first two years in the Senate, he distinguished himself in leading a push by freshman class leaders for congressional budget reform, leading to the enactment of the Budget and Impoundment Control Act of 1974." Since this was the major accomplishment listed, it was, presumably, the legislative highlight of his first two years. Yet Domenici had not said a word during the three-day floor debate on the landmark legislation. He submitted a written statement for the *Congressional Record*. When the majority leader handed out the customary kudos after its passage, several Republicans were named. Domenici was *not* one of them.[6] It was, then, another indication of his slow adjustment to the Senate that his staff should have to claim this as his major two-year accomplishment.

But it was another measure of his early institutional and policy interests that he parlayed his active support into a seat on the new Budget Committee. It gave Domenici the base from which to indulge his budgetary interests. After one of the committee's earliest information seminars, a Congressional Budget Office staffer found himself in an elevator with Domenici and a liberal Democratic newcomer.

> Domenici bubbled on as to how interesting he found the work of the committee. The liberal Democratic senator answered politely, but afterwards made reference to what a fool Domenici was to waste his time on budget committee work.[7]

In time, Domenici's enthusiasms would be amply rewarded.

But even in his early years on the committee, he was able to achieve a modest measure of influence within the group. He joined with the like-minded members of both parties to strengthen and protect the new budget process. In the period 1975-1978, said one Democratic committee staffer,

> The Budget Committee was run by the big four: [Chairman Edmund] Muskie, [Lawton] Chiles, [Henry] Bellmon, and Domenici. They formed the centrist coalition; and that centrist coalition dominated the committee. Lots of deals were cut by those four huddling together.

As late as 1981, Domenici, too, believed that "The centrist coalition has been the main force on the Senate Budget Committee since its inception." [8] So, by the time of his reelection campaign in 1978, Domenici had tasted enough of that intra-committee influence to claim his participation in the process as one of "the three successes I'm proud of."

While his "three successes" did not indicate major accomplishments, they did give evidence of a senator who wanted to govern, who wanted to "make a difference," and who was in the process of "filtering up."

STYLE

These few instances reveal a pattern of legislative involvement to which Domenici was being attracted—a team-playing, consensus-building pattern. He was not a prima donna. He was not a self-promoter. He understood that if he, as a member of the minority party, was to become influential within a committee, he would have to negotiate with the Democrats. And this is what he did. In a legislative logjam in committee, he would act as an honest broker. In a situation where the majority party could not decide, he would lead some minority members in working out a bipartisan compromise. Where a key institutional procedure was at stake, he would work with whomever else was protective of it.

His top staffers saw policy brokerage and bipartisanship as elements of his natural operating style. In January 1979 one of them commented,

> He's not a political guy. He's the least political senator around. He's a policy senator. Most of his friends who come in the door are Democrats. He's not partisan. He has no interest in the political process other than his own reelection.

Added another,

> He's a policy guy and that makes him a consensus guy. "Let's get all this input from everybody." As mayor, Pete would always take a lot of people and bring 'em all in to consider a problem. That's why he was such a good mayor. He's continued the same style as a legislator.

His "mayor's" job, after all, did not give him superior power over his colleagues. He was one among equals. And that is the way he performed, as team leader, but also as team player.

Domenici is not—as we shall see—above partisanship. But he is not a natural partisan. He does not come from a partisan background at home. His city commission position was nonpartisan. He won his party's nomination for governor in 1970 as part of "a radical reform movement in the Republican party," and at a time when he did not even know who the state chairman of his party was. (His loss in the governorship race was to be his only electoral defeat.) He was denied a place in his party's delegation to the 1976 convention, and he had to personally argue his way onto the delegation in 1980. In a historically Democratic state, this independence from the organizational party was an asset.

In the Senate, independence helped to pattern his governing activity as a member of the minority party. He worked readily and easily across party lines. And that, in turn, brought him effectiveness on the inside. It did not, however, bring him credit on the outside. He accepted that result—for his first term at least—a result that goes with being a good team player. His primary goal as a legislator was (and always has been) to help produce legislation, not to prosecute partisanship.

In 1979 I watched Domenici engineer a compromise on the Energy Committee. I asked whether he did not find himself, agreeably and often, functioning as an agent of legislative compromise in committee. His answer revealed other elements of his developing legislative style. "Your observation is pretty accurate," he said.

> I find, as a member of the minority, that when two things are present, this kind of intuitive approach to resolve the issue comes into focus, and very often, works. It worked in the Clean Air Act. I have to feel personally comfortable with the subject matter. . . . [and] I have to have been working on a thing for a long time. I don't have to know the specific detail, just the general subject, to come into the breach. . . . I can do this easily when I have staff assistants who understand the issues and can make them understandable to me. . . . The ultimate clean air standards for autos ended up being my proposal . . . my compromise.

He concluded,

> You'll find senators with a more facile approach. They don't have to be well informed to appear well informed. Senator A can take a piece of paper and begin spouting as if he really knows. I can't do that. It's not in my nature. My staff pushes me. But something prevents me from doing it.

The comment is reminiscent of his "reluctance to step forward" in his early Senate days. Pete Domenici is a compromiser. But he is a very cautious compromiser. He wants to make sure that he feels comfortable about what he is doing, and that he knows what he's doing before he gets involved.

His comments also suggest a reliance on staff that affects and is affected by his behavior. Observation suggests the same thing. As a politician and decision maker, Domenici displays, we have noted, a drive to accomplish and a cautiousness in the process of accomplishment. From time to time, and by turns, his staff fuels the drive, dampens the drive, and counteracts the caution.

Pete Domenici is an active person. He is a worker, a talker, a worrier—all at the same time. He likes to be enveloped in activity. He works best when he has others around to feed him ideas, to help him develop his ideas, and to discuss implementing strategy. He is intellectually aggressive; he shifts gears easily from one subject to another; he thinks in dialogue with others. But he wants thoughts to lead quickly to action. He does not like to be alone or sit still. His staff helps meet this need for intellectual and political activity. One staffer said,

> We push him awfully hard. When he feels good, he thrives on it. He does best when there's chaos—so we have to create chaos. He doesn't want to be alone without anything to do. . . . Forty-five minutes in the office alone would drive him absolutely crazy.

He makes good use of staff, incorporating their ideas and information into his thinking quickly and broadly. His restlessness can, however, lead to impatience. On such occasions, the staff may have to slow him down or hold him back, as they indeed did in the campaign of 1978, and as they often did when he wanted the Budget Committee to "do something" or "get moving."

On the other hand, when caution becomes the regulating factor in Domenici's behavior, his staff acts to counterbalance it. Domenici wants, "yearns," to accomplish things. He wants his accomplishments to be substantive and constructive. He reserves his greatest scorn for "bullshit and demagoguery." So badly does he want to accomplish that he expends a great deal of his abundant nervous energy in worrying about whether he is doing the right thing in the right way. He tends also "to worry a great deal about myself, to worry about and second-guess my abilities and argue with myself about my basic capacities." [9] These worries manifest themselves in caution at the point of accomplishment. Here, the staff leans against the caution, "pumping him up" and urging him to act. On the matter of deciding whether to commit himself to a major legislative initiative, for example, Domenici recalled,

> It obviously wasn't going to do me any good among my fellow senators to work my head off on this and then get my ass whipped on

the floor. . . . So, for a long time, I was scared of this thing. The staff guys kept pushing me, and I was kind of saying, "You guys go soak your head." [10]

The Domenici staff "enterprise" has acted, in all these ways, as a regulator on his governing activity and an influence on his accomplishments.

Thinking further about the preconditions for his legislative involvements, Domenici added a final element of ideological flexibility. "I'm not [often] precluded from taking a position by ideology," he said.

Senator B has as much natural talent as anyone. But he would not be able to offer a compromise as often as I can. He would feel locked in by his ideology. . . . I wasn't locked on clean air. I was willing to argue with the auto companies and with Ed Muskie.

Pete Domenici is not a natural ideologue. He is an orthodox, budget-balancing, fiscal conservative. He is philosophically devoted to the free-enterprise system, especially to its Sunbelt strains of individual initiative and economic growth. He does not believe that the federal government is the best answer to many problems—other than national defense. He would prefer that state and local governments retain sufficient revenues to meet socioeconomic needs at that level.

He speaks, hopefully, about the refederalization of the system. When he was "mayor" of Albuquerque, for example, he pioneered the creation of an urban job training program. And some of his first-term amendments sought to improve the national Comprehensive Employment and Training Act (CETA) program. But he eventually decided to cut CETA drastically as a case of excessive and wasteful federal spending. CETA "was invented in my city," he told his Senate colleagues during a budget debate.

It worked, and we sent it up here. But the CETA program we knew then is a far cry from what it is today. . . . Even those who invented it, the very city that invented it, have now looked at it and said, "It doesn't work. Strings, rules, regulation, abuses, all kinds of problems are there." [11]

There is a pragmatic, case-by-case aspect to his approach that exists alongside his conservative orthodoxy. He recognizes economic and social problems as facts of life and is willing to use federal resources to help people in need. Often, in conversation, he distinguishes himself from the more strongly ideological conservatives within his region and his party. "I think I'm sort of a moderate to a moderate conservative," he said in a 1983 interview. [12]

Two influences, one early and one proximate, help to account for this ideological flexibility. One is his family background. When he talks

of family influences, he speaks of his Italian immigrant father's entre-
preneurship and frugality in starting a grocery business. "My dad
always believed there was a direct relationship between working hard
and growth. He felt he had to be worried about next week and next year
... had to put money in the bank...." [13] But he also speaks of his
mother's compassion. "She was an awful lot of what I'm about. She was
the generous one. She gave away everything. My father had to stop her
so we wouldn't go broke." His staffers describe him as a budget cutter
and "the biggest bleeding heart you ever saw." The tug-of-war between
two family influences—frugality and compassion—may help to explain
Domenici's flexibility and his willingness to compromise.

The more proximate, more tangible influence on Domenici's views
is the incredible diversity of his constituency—perhaps the most diverse
population with the most diverse set of interests of any of the fifty
states. "It's hard to represent New Mexico," he said. "We're not a simple
little state in the desert the way some people think."

> We have everything from agriculture to two of the most sophisticated
> scientific laboratories in the world and everything in between. Except
> for water, New Mexico is rich in natural resources—uranium, potash,
> coal, gas, oil, copper. The lab at Los Alamos and the one in
> Albuquerque are our two largest industries. The people there have an
> intellectual capacity that is unbelievable. We have three cultures—the
> Indians who are coming more and more into their own and make up
> 6-7 percent of the population, the Hispanics who make up 36-37
> percent, and the rest. We are changing from a liberal state to a
> moderate conservative state—not a conservative state, not yet.

The state is "hard to represent" in the sense that no single rigidly held
philosophy will serve such diversity.

Whatever its ideological makeup and however much a burgeoning
population is changing that makeup, the state has some well entrenched
old relationships with the federal government and some badly needed
new ones. The two research labs receive more than a billion dollars a
year from the Energy and Defense departments; the east side farmers
enjoy subsidies; and the southeast oil and gas industry enjoys tax
benefits. But the state as a whole is resource rich and income
poor—forty-second among the states in median income in 1979. New
Mexico needs economic development, and this cannot be done without
the federal government. Pending such development, the state's low
income population is in need of many social services. And this poorest
segment is highly visible. It is comprised primarily of Hispanics and
Indians. And these groups are both culturally distinct and geographically concentrated. Their problems—long-run development and short-
run assistance—get impressed on every statewide official. Their pres-

ence helps account for conservatives, such as Pete Domenici, who neither loathe nor fear the intervention of the federal government—and even welcome it on a case-by-case basis.

Pete Domenici is, then, by belief, by upbringing, and by the representative process, an orthodox, conservative Republican, with overlays of partisan independence, legislative pragmatism, and ideological flexibility. These characteristics help him to be a consensus builder in the Senate.

The impact of Domenici's first-term accomplishments registered mostly in committee. But in thinking about governing he always coupled committee activity with floor activity. He wanted success at every stage of the process. And he saw his own legislative proficiency growing on the floor as well as in committee. The most highly publicized of these efforts was his leadership in 1977 in the passage of legislation to require, for the first time in history, users of the nation's inland waterways to pay for that usage. The story of how Domenici shepherded that bill in committee and on the Senate floor has been well told—first in the *Washington Post* and later in a full-length book, *Congressional Odyssey: Saga of a Senate Bill*, by *Post* reporter T. R. Reid. And it was that performance, Reid's book makes clear, that earned Domenici respect inside the institution, among opponents as well as allies.[14]

Looking back on it, Domenici commented, "I fell into that accidentally, but once I was involved, I felt comfortable with it. I felt I was really accomplishing something—not bullshit and demagoguery." Of the day he won his floor victory in a head-to-head contest with veteran Senator Russell Long, he recalled,

> That was a great day. We even had champagne. Things like that don't happen around here very often. It was a great confrontation and was played up in all the Washington papers. We pass amendments; but we don't very often have a confrontation and a change of direction.

It was not a major piece of legislation. But it was a major legislative success for its sponsor. And it was a very different success than success in committee. It involved a head-on clash, the glare of publicity, a more complex arena, and an enlarged set of talents. It was the kind of accomplishment that rounded out Domenici's first-term "adjustment to" the institution.

Reflecting, in 1980, on that first-term adjustment to the Senate, Domenici talked about the meaning, to him, of success on the Senate floor. He was speaking generally. But he might well have had the so-called barge-charge bill in mind. "I think it's terribly important," he said,

> that every senator have one major floor experience. Not presenting some amendments where the fix is in—though that's a help—but

something that keeps you on the floor for three or four days, where you say, "I'm going to take as long as it takes to make an argument and persuade people that mine is the best way to do it." You may not win, but people will know you are a serious legislator. You need the experience of going up and down the aisle, nudging people and saying, "This is the way it is." And, eventually, after two or three tries you may win. You need that experience on the floor, to build your morale. You feel like a legislator.

The gradual accumulation of legislative experience—amendments carried, compromises arranged, legislation passed—moved Domenici out of his adjustment period and into the serious business of governing. It was a slow, gradual "filtering-up" process. In the course of it, he displayed some of the elements of a distinctive governing style—a desire to get a product, a skill at compromise, a leaning toward bipartisanship, a legislative pragmatism, a caution in action. Altogether, it was a team-oriented, consensual governing style. By the end of his first term, he had developed some sense of accomplishment and some growth of self-confidence. He had begun, with reason, to "feel like a legislator."

CAMPAIGNING IN NEW MEXICO

Tens of thousands of college students know Pete Domenici as the determined hero of the barge-charge bill. *Congressional Odyssey* is a widely read textbook account of how a bill becomes a law. But in New Mexico, few knew and few cared. T. R. Reid expressed the strong belief that this legislative achievement would help Domenici win reelection in 1978. It did not. I never heard the senator refer to it on the campaign trail; he did not list it as one of the "three successes I'm proud of"; it was not mentioned in any of his campaign literature or on any of his TV spots. In explaining why he took on the bill, Domenici had told Reid, "I knew I was going to run again, though, and it would help if I could go back and say to the Albuquerque paper or the Santa Fe paper, 'I had enough clout to get a tough bill passed.' " [15] So far as I could research in the senator's files, however, only one New Mexico newspaper (the *Albuquerque Tribune*) mentioned it in its endorsement of him. The bill was of considerable importance to Domenici's reputation in Washington. And it was of considerable importance in building his own self-confidence. But it cut no ice at home.

When, in 1980, Reid's *Post* articles were enlarged into a book, their publication was a nonevent at home. That summer, when I met the senator in New Mexico, he expressed pleasure with Reid's treatment. As for the book's impact, he commented,

> About the only effect it had here was that my mother went out and bought me some new clothes. See this suit? She read where he said I looked like a refugee from a Woody Allen movie, so she bought me three new suits. The great New Mexico press didn't print a single word about it.

He added, "The *Washington Post* did a nice review of it though."

It is my strong impression that his experience with the inland waterways case can be generalized. Although Domenici's legislative involvements were expanding in Washington, very little notice was being taken of them at home. It is the problem of working in two separate arenas, compounded by the problem of being a junior, minority party senator. In the period immediately preceding his chairmanship, Domenici worked to bring his two worlds into a manageable relationship to one another. It was a season of reappraisal for him. And the central, focusing event of that season was the reelection campaign of 1978.

The preemptive and preparatory stage of the campaign was dominated by the results of a June 1977 poll in which Domenici was paired against several possible challengers. The poll showed him to be only 7 points ahead of Attorney General Toney Anaya. For an incumbent, recalled one campaigner, that slim lead meant "we could be in big trouble." "So," he continued,

> we made a major strategic decision—to put an aura of invincibility around Pete Domenici. We collected money from all segments of the population of the state. We brought Domenici and his family back to New Mexico. We ran a spring primary campaign as if we had an opponent—a heavy schedule of personal campaigning and a heavy television campaign.

The idea, of course, was, as Domenici put it, "to scare off other people from running by showing strength" and, as a campaigner added, "to hold off anyone else's early decision."

The first prong of the strategy worked on Governor Jerry Apodaca; the second prong worked on Toney Anaya. The campaign aide continued,

> Apodaca flirted with it till he saw Domenici had $250,000 in the bank—mostly in small contributions. Anaya delayed because he couldn't do anything until Apodaca decided. Then everywhere he went he found people committed to Domenici. He was late in announcing.

Domenici's people raised $300,000 in 1977 and spent $200,000 on their "primary" campaign. In the spring of 1978, they ran five pro-Domenici TV spots. "We were the only ones on television at the time," said one adviser. "It was one of our key decisions because we got tremendous visibility. Anaya had no money to do anything at the time." They took their second poll in June 1978. One year after their first poll, Domenici led Anaya by 24 points. Their preemptive strategy had been successful.

The Domenici campaigners entered the subsequent period of comparison and confrontation with a large lead. Planning for the campaign against Anaya revolved around two questions. First, should they emphasize the senator's achievements in Washington or should they emphasize his achievements at home? Or how should they mix the two? Second, should they give a high-profile, high-intensity pitch to their campaign or should they give a low-profile, proincumbent, low-interest tone to their campaign? Or how should they mix the two?

Pete Domenici's 1978 polls revealed a favorable yet bland image among New Mexico's voters. In June, 70 percent of them could recall his name, and 80 percent gave him a favorable job rating. In September, when asked what came to mind when they heard his name, 20 percent mentioned his "past record" or "good job," 13 percent said they "liked" him, 6 percent mentioned his concern for the state and for people, 5 percent said he was trustworthy, and the rest were scattered or "don't know." When voters were fed a series of personal qualities and asked whether they fit Domenici, he received his highest scores on "cares about people like you" with 44 percent of the voters in agreement, and second highest on "honest" with 39 percent. These kinds of data are by no means clear or conclusive. But Domenici and his advisers read them as suggesting the wisdom of a low-profile, proincumbency campaign and a low-key, down-home image for the candidate. There was no visible record to run on; and they did not try.

In his joint TV appearance with his opponent, Domenici's managers wanted him to emphasize three main themes: first, that he had been an open, honest senator; second, that the Library of Congress study showed he had gotten more amendments passed than any other freshman senator; and third, that he had been bipartisan, working, for example, with President Jimmy Carter and Senator Henry Jackson on energy matters. They were pleased, afterward, that he had gotten each of them across. And the newspaper account (which featured the gubernatorial candidates) gave the most prominent mention to the first item. It stressed Domenici's claim that "when he entered the Senate, he gave up all his business interests and has devoted his full time to being a senator" and that "he has voluntarily disclosed his personal finances every year he has been in office." [16] These two "honesty" planks were also featured in his campaign brochure, as the most specific evidence that he had "kept his word" as a senator. And keeping his word was in turn "the biggest reason" suggested for supporting him.

When I asked the senator during the campaign why people would vote for him, he said, "Because they think I have done a good job and because they think I'm honest." After the campaign, when I asked him how it went, he said, "On all the things we tried to emphasize, we were right—honesty, interest in, sympathy with." In a state with a history of political corruption and of long-tenured, out-of-touch senators, a campaign based on "honesty, interest in, sympathy with," was an appropriate home-oriented theme. And the Domenici campaign wanted to make the strongest possible identification of the senator with home. A campaign aide explained:

> Our basic strategy for the campaign grew out of the first survey concerning what New Mexicans felt about their future.... New Mexicans had a very positive attitude.... So our television was designed to be optimistic and upbeat ... very, very positive. In our TV we tried to make people feel warm about Pete and about the state.

Domenici's own feeling about the state was that "At this point in time, New Mexico is very upbeat, people feel good about themselves.... With the one exception of water, it has an almost unlimited future, a fantastic potential for growth."

His longest TV spot captured this upbeat theme. With a guitar playing a measured, lyrical theme in the background, and against a backdrop of happy people and gorgeous scenery, Domenici called New Mexico "one of a kind." And he went on, "We have to keep this land beautiful; we need to protect our water, our land, and all of this for our children and our grandchildren. There's a lot about New Mexico that makes us proud. Every day there's new hope, excitement about our future; you can see it in people's faces. You know, we're a lot like the American frontier, so much lies ahead for us."

A related ad, with the same musical theme, played against scenes of farmers and ranchers, extolled the "important values" of "small-town America"—"self-reliance, an honest day's work, lending a helping hand." But it also stressed the state's need for water and the necessity for farmers and ranchers to "be treated fairly by the government." The theme of these ads was more on "the good state" than "the good senator." He sought to draw strength by associating himself with the appealing aspects of the state.

These two theme commercials were buttressed by an all-purpose, person-on-the-street testimonial ad emphasizing "the good senator"— "a very busy man who never forgets the people," "no harder worker," "fair, honest," "answers our letters," "down home," "good man all the way around for the people, raining or snowing," "brought roads to San Juan County," "we love him." In addition, he had two general, thirty-second spots devoted to noncontroversial issues—one endorsing a strong national defense, the other pledging to fight inflation by cutting government spending. They reflected the overwhelming sentiment of his electorate. They were designed to reassure, not to excite. The campaign theme was a good-man-for-a-good-state theme. The campaign was designed to be bland and reassuring, not jarring or attention getting. As one strategist put it, "We didn't want a high-interest campaign."

From my brief observation of the Domenici campaign in October 1978, his strategists got what they wanted. It looked very much, in fact, like a typical congressional incumbent's campaign—low-profile and home-oriented. It was a type of Senate campaign made more likely by the small size (about 1.3 million) of the statewide constituency.

My first exposure to Domenici's campaign style came on an afternoon flight to the northern part of the state—Spanish speaking, Democratic, low income. The first thing the senator said to me on the plane was, "I act like a congressman." And he continued,

> Not like the one whose district we're going to visit. My district is twice as large, and I like to get into the issues more than he does. But we do a lot of casework and we get around and visit people, senior citizens, people in the northern part of the state. I have never assumed that the Spanish votes were closed to me. I always knew that if I helped them, they would become supporters. I speak a little Spanish. I go visit with them. Now I might not get as many votes this time as I had hoped, because my opponent is Spanish. But against any gringo Democrat, I would have gotten an awful lot of Spanish votes.

Throughout the brief visit, he did "act like a congressman."

In the tiny town of Mora, he circulated among three hundred people at a Republican rally in the high school gym, shaking hands with them as they sat at long tables partaking of punch and cookies. And he took his turn among the large contingent of candidates—an introduction in Spanish, ruffles and flourishes from a three-piece combo, a three-minute speech in Spanish. At one point he left the festivities to drive with a local official out into the countryside to visit a legless man who lived alone, whose outhouse was 150 feet from his house, and who had just had his wheelchair taken away from him by the state bureaucracy. "We'll get the staff on it in the morning," he said later.

In the evening in the nearby town of Las Vegas, at a reception for the area's congressman, his short speech emphasized personal service.

> The first two years in the Senate were not easy. The people sent me straight from city commissioner to the United States Senate. The next four years I was able to accomplish some things—for senior citizens, for instance, in their Social Security, their housing, their way of life. I

have enjoyed it. I like my job. I have served New Mexico for six years.
I want to serve you for six more years.

Then he spoke in Spanish. When he lapsed into Italian ("Oops, I slipped!") he drew appreciative laughter. When he mentioned his eight children—"I have only eight children—no more. We haven't had any more children since I got into politics"—he drew more laughter from his fellow Catholics. Afterward, he took off his coat and tie, sat down at a table with a group of shirtless local politicos, and drank beer and gossiped for half an hour. "That was a great half day," he said later. It was altogether very much a low-key, incumbent congressman's presentation of self.

The campaign was not oriented toward the free media. Indeed the staff tried to drive the media away by insisting that their candidate's lead was insuperable and that only the New Mexico governor's race remained up for grabs. A single statewide reporter covered the two events I have described, but he was traveling with the gubernatorial candidate and featuring his appearances. Otherwise, there was no media presence at Domenici's activities that day. In two and a half days of campaigning a week before the election, he got no radio coverage and no television coverage. Although he did receive brief newspaper mention in coverage of the Mora and Las Vegas events, no reporters rode with us on any leg of the trip. He did appear on Albuquerque TV for a debate (actually a joint appearance) with his opponent; and, two days later, he gave an interview to the local paper in Grants. He spoke to military retirees, to uranium miners, to high school students, to suburban women, and he went handshaking in public buildings, shopping centers, and automobile dealerships—all of it out of the eye of the local media. And, it goes without saying, out of the eye of the national media, too.

In terms of their quarter-million-dollar expenditure on paid-for-media, the campaign was more typically senatorial than congressional. But in terms of the proportions of free media attention and person-to-person campaigning, it was more typically congressional. And that was precisely the way the Domenici campaign strategists wanted it. As they often said, "Domenici is a great one-on-one campaigner."

Assuming that campaigns emphasize a politician's strength, Domenici's strength at home did not depend on his governing activity in Washington. It is true that he campaigned on the theme that he had "made a difference." And it is possible that when voters evaluated his job performance or his "past record" they were thinking of his "three successes" in his committees or his barge-charge bill on the Senate floor. But not likely. More likely, his favorable job evaluations reflected general approval—or, better, the absence of strong disapproval—of his behavior in office. There was, simply, nothing to vote against. It was important to the candidate's posture as a successful incumbent and important to the candidate's self-confidence that he was able to claim that he had "made a difference." But this Washington-related theme was strictly secondary.

The driving theme of the campaign was home-related: "He is honest," "He cares about people," "He is one of us," "He is just plain Pete." His campaign advertising made no mention of the barge-charge bill; but one of his *Albuquerque Journal* ads *did* claim that "in 6 years in the Senate, his offices have solved more than 15,000 New Mexicans' problems with their government." That emphasis fits with everything I observed in New Mexico.

It also squares with everything I observed, later, in Washington. Pete Domenici will take a moment, no matter how weary he may be, to have a friendly word and a picture-taking session with virtually every New Mexican who comes to his Washington office. His campaign theme rested, therefore, upon a demonstrable personal strength. Domenici, in person, is an open, down-to-earth, warm, accessible individual. He comes across as a very humane, very vulnerable person—a highly sensitive "worrywart" incapable of even pretending that he possesses a hard protective shell. Eight years after his reelection, Washington observers still described him as "unskilled at masking his moods" and as "that rarest of creatures in Washington—a real human being." [17]

It is easy, therefore, to think of him as the man portrayed by his 1978 campaign—as an honest, caring, helping person, as "Pete," a person who is just like the rest of us. What you see is what you get; what you get is what you expected to get. Campaign image and real person fit. What you got, in 1978, was a United States senator who acted like a close-to-home congressman. New Mexico voters liked, perhaps even preferred—maybe even prescribed—that combination.

THE ELECTORAL INTERPRETATION

Pete Domenici won reelection in 1978. But the successful campaign did not bring rejoicing. It triggered, instead, a reappraisal of the campaign and of his future relationships at home and in Washington. The trigger was the election result itself. Domenici's June poll had showed him 21 points ahead of his opponent; his September poll had showed him 25 points ahead; two weeks before the election, a random poll of one-half of the September sample found him still 25 points ahead. Two weeks later he won by 6 points, with 53 percent of the vote. The closeness of the race created surprise bordering on shock.

"We were all very depressed after the election," said one campaign strategist. "We thought we would win by a much larger margin." Explaining the outcome to me, one campaign staffer began, "The reason we *lost* was. . . . " Another described the victor as "very disappointed and despondent for a while." In March, the winner greeted me with, "We should have beaten the hell out of them, but we nearly got racked." How did he feel on election night?

> To tell you the truth I wasn't particularly happy about it. For one thing I didn't think it would be that close. For another thing, I think certain things work on you subconsciously. I knew how much work I had done back here and how much had gone into my six years. I knew what I was coming back to, how much work there was to do. I wasn't overjoyed. My family wasn't overjoyed. It was a very mild reaction that I had.

He had been given a victory, but not with the kind of approving mandate he expected, wanted, needed, and believed he had earned.

Political scientist Marjorie Hershey tells us that, in the aftermath of every election, the winning candidate and his or her close associates will come into agreement among themselves on what happened and what it meant. They will do this because they must have some working interpretation of the election results on which to predicate their future behavior. Elections are, after all, the broadest and most consequential expression of citizen sentiment in a representative democracy, and they can hardly be left unexplained by those to whom or about whom the citizens have spoken. It is not that the victor's account will be objective or complete or authoritative. It is only that the account is demonstrably theirs, that they will act upon it and that students must understand this account if they are to understand postelection behavior. Hershey calls this "the constructed explanation" of the election, as it is accepted and articulated—and acted upon—by the winners.[18]

Because of the electoral surprise, the "constructed explanation" of Pete Domenici's reelection focused less on why they had won than on why they had done so poorly. In Domenici's retrospective view,

> I knew there was no way I was going to win by 25 points. In my gut, I knew that. . . . I don't think he [Anaya] gained all that much in the end. I think we miscalculated from the beginning. . . . Two things hurt us. First, we miscalculated his strength, the appeal he had as a knight on a white horse. Secondly, in areas where we are strong, the turnout was low.

Then he went on to factor in a general anti-incumbent climate.

> People are just depressed. And they blame any incumbent for their condition. "Domenici is up there in Washington and he hasn't done anything to make me better off." If you pick someone who has no

> record in the area he's running for and let him run against an incumbent, that incumbent will be in trouble.

It was a statement of the familiar proposition that senators, compared with House members, are especially vulnerable to the changing moods of the electorate.

In Domenici's case, this vulnerability may well have vindicated the decision to campaign more like a local congressman than as a national senator. Indeed his campaign manager took the view that "I'd do it again just the same way we did it. We didn't make any mistakes." "My political people tell me," said Domenici, "that if it hadn't been for a lot of hard work and a good record, I might have been another of the incumbents who got beat this year." That was the positive side of the "constructed explanation." The campaign had worked. He had won. But he worried about what happened and why. And his worries had a considerable impact on his subsequent behavior in Washington and at home.

Domenici's opponent, Toney Anaya, was a high-profile crusader. And Domenici's postelection thinking centered on the contrast between his own low-profile campaign and that of his opponent. A New Mexico reporter, writing in April 1978, compared the two candidates.

> Domenici, the acknowledged front runner ... is established, respected and, apparently, well financed.... Anaya's three and a half year administration of the Attorney General's office has been aggressive and public. Championing consumer protection and prosecuting government corruption, Anaya has consistently drawn the attention of the news media, and his name is probably as well known as any public official's in New Mexico.[19]

Domenici's polls told him a similar story. For example, on the voter agreement with suggested adjectives, Domenici's lowest agreement score, 21 percent, came on "publicity seeking." It was Anaya's highest score, 50 percent. But Domenici did not see the difference as a clear plus for his opponent.

> [In our polls] very few people said they disliked anything about me; but about 6 percent said they disliked the way my opponent had conducted his office. I have no sympathy for him on that. Every prosecution was conducted with any eye to maximum publicity and media exposure. There are ways to prosecute by working things out. He went after every one with a press conference, no matter how minor.

Anaya's campaign was largely a crusade against Domenici's $900,000 campaign chest and the "special interests" who contributed to it. It was an issue that rankled Domenici considerably. But, assuming a huge lead, he did not take out after his opponent. When I was with him he worried constantly about what Anaya might do. That is why he commissioned a final quickie poll. "I'm a worrywart." Still, his end-of-the-campaign assumption, reinforced by the poll results, was, "He can't turn it around. I don't know what he can do. And even if he says something, the media will not pay attention to him. They think it's over."

So, too, did many of Domenici's potential supporters. Their post-mortems focused heavily on the "apathy" and "lack of interest" among voters in Albuquerque's suburban Northeast Heights, in Bernalillo County generally—places where they had expected bigger turnouts and higher percentages. These general comments were punctuated with stories of people who said, "You're going to win; I don't care about the governor's race so I'll stay home." Or, "If you needed me, I'd vote for you, but you don't need my vote, so I'll give Toney a vote." Domenici's people felt that Anaya had had the last-minute momentum. Their post-election poll showed that 17 percent of the voters made up their minds during the last week of the campaign and 8 percent more decided on election day. "It is very probable," wrote one adviser, "that many of these votes went to Anaya." And he asked, "Why were we unable to capture a larger percentage of this already large undecided vote?" One answer lay in their low-key campaign. "Anaya still thinks he would have won if he had two more weeks to campaign," said one strategist. "Maybe he's right."

Whether Anaya began with his strength or picked it up at the end, the Domenici camp underestimated the strength of his style, as it resonated in the media. In explaining what happened, the Domenici strategists laid heavy stress on Anaya's media appeal. Said one,

> Anaya had a good image as a crusader. A lot of people gave him credit for his guts in taking on the bad guys. He had a lot more strength than we gave him credit for.... With Anaya everything is moral; and it's exciting to read about his attacks on this person or that business. He used the attorney general's office to get more publicity than anyone I've ever known.

In a postelection memorandum, another strategist wrote,

> We were often far too cautious during this campaign. We opted for a lower-key approach. While Anaya was out blasting our contributions, we issued a white paper on the economy. It is not that the white paper is a bad idea, but Anaya got more publicity with his charges than we ever got with the paper. Anaya managed to effectively manipulate the media ... not only in the course of the evening news, but also in his ads.

In sum, Anaya had been much more effective with the media than Domenici and his advisers had thought possible. Their interpretation of the election campaign, their constructed explanation, was that *they had lost the media contest* with Anaya, and that it was that loss which accounted for the electoral surprise. High media visibility accounted for Anaya's strength. Low media visibility accounted for the low turnout of Domenici supporters, and the loss of the late deciders. They were so reassured or so unaffected by his bland, front-running campaign that they stayed home, or threw a "sympathy vote" to Toney Anaya.

When I talked with the senator in the spring of 1979, it seemed clear that this interpretation of the election had affected his thinking. First, there was evidence to support it. One postelection memo told him quite bluntly that Anaya "did well" because "he was tough and forceful as Attorney General" and that "it seems to me that Domenici will, in the course of the next six years have to be tougher on the issues and more forceful." Second, the outcome reinforced some of Domenici's own worries about his campaign strategy. If he had had his preference, he probably would have wanted a more visible campaign; one more oriented toward his governing than his ombudsman activity.

On the matter of Domenici's misgivings, there is indirect evidence. One strategist recalled that "we argued for hours and hours, all the time" about whether Domenici should be "more aggressive," even though they always decided otherwise. A friend and adviser commented,

> We underestimated Anaya's appeal. And we were not aggressive enough in answering him. It was just about the time people's utility rates were going up and Anaya tagged Pete with that—"utility Pete," he called him. We didn't answer that so the man on the street could understand. Between you and me, some of his advisers had Pete scared of the little guy so that he wasn't as aggressive as he should have been.

Another adviser recalled two matters about which the campaigners and the senator had disagreed. On the low-interest strategy, in general, "Domenici did not necessarily agree. He would have preferred that his race dominate the media. The staff thought otherwise." Similarly, Domenici wanted to mount an organizational effort in the northern Democratic strongholds, but the staff held him back. "If we did that, they would organize against us and offset anything we could gain. If it's quiet, leave it quiet. Don't stir up the natives—the Democrats, that is." It is easy to imagine Pete Domenici wanting to "stir up" rather than "leave it quiet." He is a person who thrives on action, on motion. On the campaign trail, his command is always "Let's roll." It is not natural for him to come to rest or lay back on defense. So it is hard to imagine him with much inner enthusiasm for a low-profile campaign.

Despite whatever misgivings he may have had, Domenici accepted the advice of his campaign advisers. It was the advice of caution. And in accepting it he displayed a stylistic consistency—a degree of caution in the electoral arena to match his caution in the legislative arena. There seems to be a built-in conflict in Domenici's political style, between his restlessness and his caution. One side of him itches to get going; another side of him holds back. So he tends to be impulsive, expansive, and aggressive up to the point where a decision must be made. Then, caution prevails. But, having begun with a larger concept or plan or vision, he worries about the decision he has made. That is the pattern revealed in his campaign—before, during, and after.

READJUSTMENT, REPUTATION, AND MEDIA

In reaction to his own disappointment over the results of his low-profile campaign and, with his own misgivings reinforced by the interpretation of those results, Domenici had decided by the spring of 1979 to give himself a higher profile, both in Washington and at home. In Washington that meant continuing to expand his legislative responsibilities, increasing his involvement in governing. At home, it meant working to make certain that his Washington performance got adequately conveyed to New Mexico. The link between Washington and New Mexico was to be the media, which would translate an effective Senate performance into a dominant political position at home.

Domenici never said it, but my strong impression was that he was determined never again to be outdone in the media. From 1978 to 1984, he had five different press secretaries. They described his emphasis on the press in terms ranging from "top priority" to "insatiable" to "paranoid." Toney Anaya had shown what the aggressive use of one's office could do for one's prominence among the electorate. Domenici's constructed explanation of the election, that he had lost the media battle, had a major effect on his thinking about his second term.

When I asked him what kind of reputation he wanted to earn in his second term, he talked about his own enlarging sense of responsibility for national decision making.

> A couple of characteristics are important and don't change. I hope I had 'em after six years and I hope I'll have 'em after twelve years. [The first is] honesty and integrity.... The second is that I'm generally interested in people. Both were there in the last campaign. To take the two and move over to the next six years, I'd hope on the second one ... that my people see my concern about them but I hope I can convince them their problems are part of America's problems and there is a need for change. If I can come through six years and have people say, "He didn't vote for exactly what my group wanted, but he voted in the way that we now realize is good for the country,"

I'll be satisfied. . . . I want to be in touch, but we've got problems that might require national leadership. It may be in history that people will say, "Hey, Pete was right.". . . I'm hoping I can please constituents without being for everything they want.

There is a lot of pretty standard senatorial speechifying here. But there is also the self-conscious addition of a national policy dimension to the honesty and caring themes that carried him through the campaign of 1978. In that sense, he was hoping for a very different kind of campaign in 1984.

One enlarged responsibility he had clearly begun to anticipate at that point involved the Budget Committee. Ranking Republican member Henry Bellmon had scheduled his retirement for 1980. When, in March of 1979, I wanted Domenici to reflect on his recent campaign, he changed the subject. "We have some big challenges ahead in the Budget Committee. In two years, I'll be taking over the Republican side of the committee." At another point, he said, "When I become ranking member of the Budget Committee, I'm going to look into the basic budget law, not just to look into it because it isn't working." That spring, he read Bernard Asbell's book, *The Senate Nobody Knows*, about Edmund Muskie, the committee's chairman. "I learned," he said, "that Muskie is a good campaigner because he is a good senator."

In May I walked with him to a Budget Committee conference. "The main reason for my going to the Budget Committee, is so I can learn the process. I'll be taking over next year." On the way back, he said to a staff aide, "We're going to be running this in two years. I feel comfortable with the process. If we don't have a sharp recession, it will survive." His influence was slowly catching up to his long-time interest in congressional budgeting. He was anticipating a quantum increase in the scope of his governing responsibilities. And he could not wait to get going.

As a necessary complement to his eagerness for national responsibilities, Domenici displayed an eagerness for favorable media attention. As a result of their reelection reappraisal, Domenici's staff decided that "the press section will begin [in January] a weekly column in the New Mexico press under the senator's byline." They also decided that "one of the senator's goals is to publish more articles, not only in trade journals, but in the national media." Staffers were asked to contribute outlines for ideas for use in the column and were offered a "sabbatical" to write the articles.

In January a staff memo announced a similarly intensive legislative effort. The memo listed twenty-two bills being drawn up for introduction by Domenici between January 15 and March 22. "The following schedule for introduction," said the memo, "is predicated on introducing 2 or 3 bills a week—or the rate at which their content can be spoon fed to the press section." In March one of the top staffers stated flatly that "the number-one concern of this office is press." He went on, "The other day we prepared a memo to our staff in the field discussing their duties and so forth. In it we said, 'The number-one concern of this office is press.' When the senator saw it, he said, 'That's right . . . but we'd better take it out.' " The routines of the enterprise were being changed to accommodate the senator's desire to be more of a national leader and to gain recognition as such.

Domenici's main concern was with the job of translation being done by the media at home. One staffer commented,

> He worries all the time about the press—especially the Albuquerque papers. If something doesn't get in the Albuquerque papers, it just didn't happen as far as he's concerned. And he thinks everything he does deserves a story in these papers. Every day we get the clipped stories from them here in the office. For him, that is reality. I think we ought to keep those clippings from him. Today he thought he should have had four separate articles in the paper. I had to say to him, "Boss, put yourself in the position of a newspaper editor. How many of those stories would you print?" In my opinion, we need to develop some thrust, not just a lot of stories.

One day in the spring of 1979 Domenici sat down at his desk, picked up a news clipping from back home, and complained.

> We have a guy in our delegation who is a millionaire. So what does the newspaper make the headline of its story on finances—that Pete Domenici made $4,800 in honoraria, $4,800! That's a pittance. No other paper in the country would have made that their local story. If the *Washington Post* got hold of that story, they would never let up on the millionaire. . . . The best I ever get is a news story and then it usually has a little editorial zinger in there. That's what creates rumbles back home. People read this article and think I'm up here making millions. I suppose I shouldn't give a damn. I just got reelected and I have five more years. But I can't look at it that way. I'm convinced that if I were a Democrat—majority or minority—with all that I've accomplished, they would be writing glowing reports.

These are the standard complaints of Washington legislators—not enough local coverage and unfair local reporting. But they achieved unusual prominence in Domenici's life during the two years following his reelection.

The overweening concern with the Albuquerque newspapers has a very important political rationale. The senator perceives Albuquerque to be the swing segment of his reelection constituency. And he sees the media in general as the major force in creating and maintaining that constituency. But there is no New Mexico television presence in

Washington—only a newspaper presence. Hence, the swing importance of the Albuquerque newspapers.

Domenici's primary constituency—geographically speaking—resides in the counties east and south of centrally located Albuquerque. "They give me 30 percent of the state," he said. "It is a strong base. It is stronger, I'm sorry to say, than my hometown of Albuquerque.... Beyond that 30 percent I have to put together a coalition piece by piece." He continued,

> I never know what my hometown of Albuquerque will do to me. It may be my ego, but I just think people in Albuquerque don't know me as well as the people in the smaller towns do. When you go to two or three events like this one tonight [an ice-cream social in Portales] people get to know you.... You can't get people to come to meetings like this one in the big city.... And I get much better newspaper coverage in the smaller communities than I do at home. The last time people in Albuquerque really got to know me was when I ran for city commission. But the town doubled since then.... People don't get to know who I am.... Grab every media event.... That's the only way people will hear you, get exposed to you.... People in Albuquerque will only get to know me through the media.

In 1978, Domenici had run 4 percentage points and 14,000 votes behind his 1972 totals in his hometown.

The senator's preoccupation with media coverage might seem to be in conflict with his stylistic preference for team play. Most of the time, it was not. In the first place, he was concerned about media coverage at home and about team play in Washington. In the second place, he wanted media coverage that reflected his accomplishments. And he believed that the bulk of those accomplishments were the result of team play. He is not a showboating, flamboyant, prima donna-type politician—anything but. And he does not seek media recognition on personality grounds. As he once said, "If I had only wanted my name in lights, I would have opened a restaurant." He is a team player; and he wanted the media to recognize his performance in that capacity. But his was not the kind of performance that forced media attention. And his personal approach to his work—earnest, responsible, inventive, cautious—was not grist for media profiles. Hence, Domenici's frustration. Sometimes, in that frustration, he was willing to take media attention whenever and however he could get it.

When we talked, in the spring of 1979, his concern with the media accompanied nearly every legislative discussion. In March he was planning to propose to the Republicans on the Budget Committee a package of tax cuts to help capital formation. He saw it as a personal initiative. He was trying on the role of ranking minority member for size. And press coverage bulked large in his thinking. He told his staffers,

> We've got to get all the Republicans together in a room and get them to agree on a Republican package. If they won't do that, the hell with them. Everyone can go off and play his own game. If we don't do this, the Democrats will get all the credit for being the cutters. If we can get a Republican package ... we'll get the credit. We'll get the press.

Later that day he commented on his ongoing effort to defend Energy Secretary James Schlesinger against his critics. "We did a good job with Schlesinger yesterday but we got upstaged in the press when [New Hampshire Democratic senator John] Durkin called for his resignation."

In May, Domenici was working with Senator Pat Moynihan on a novel approach to water policy that would reduce pork barreling, and he was concerned about announcing it.[20] "I went over to see Moynihan yesterday," he told a staffer. "He seemed excited. He wanted to check with his staff man. He probably wanted to check with his New York State people. You can't blame him for that. We can wait to have the press conference. I want it done right." Four days later, he and two staffers discussed the subject again.

DOMENICI: Our press conference will get the eastern editors.... This water thing will be great.

STAFFER A: You may not get as much publicity from it as you think.

STAFFER B: I've got New Mexico all juiced up. You're going to hold a closed hookup news conference afterward—all major papers and the wire services.

DOMENICI: That will be the second time in history....

STAFFER A: Why don't we get Moynihan to do that with us, too. He's a national figure and he likes publicity.

STAFFER B: It would take the partisanship out of it back home.

DOMENICI: Let's get him.

His preoccupation with the press was striking.

In those early months of 1979, Domenici expressed some sense that he was still thrashing about, that he had not settled into any recognizable pattern of legislative activity. And that feeling may have contributed to his restless search for press. He was feeling the pressure of his legislative job and he was, characteristically, worried about its effects on him. "Bills introduced—down; bills passed—down; days on the floor—down; amount of anguish and tension—up!" he exclaimed in describing the working atmosphere. "I have decided that the Senate is like dancing with a gorilla," he said. "You dance when it dances; you sit when it sits; you stop when it stops." [Fenno: "You mean it rides you? You don't ride it?"] "I don't care how big and how powerful you are, you don't ride it. Maybe for one week, in your heyday, you can beat it and stick it. But it's going to ride you. And the faster times change and more complex the society becomes, the more certain it is that it will ride you." It was a picture of some discouragement. It was also a picture of a legislator waiting for recognition for his accomplishments.

THE PLAYER: WASHINGTON AND NEW MEXICO

Toward the end of 1979, Domenici got a healthy dose of what he had been waiting for. He was the Republican sponsor of legislation to fund and to speed the production of synthetic fuels. His cosponsors were Democrats Henry Jackson and Bennett Johnston. Domenici called it "the most significant" piece of legislation he had worked on in his Senate career. And when it was finally passed—as the Energy Security Act of 1980—House Majority Leader Jim Wright called it "the most important bill we'll have this year and, conceivably, in this decade." Domenici's participation in this bipartisan endeavor, first in the Energy Committee and then on the floor, had all the earmarks of his previous consensus-building legislative efforts. And he was sought after as a conferee with the House because "He's a player. He attends meetings, works at compromises, and lobbies his fellow Republicans." [21]

This time—in sharp contrast to the barge-charge bill—the New Mexico press noticed. The *Albuquerque Journal* and the *Albuquerque Tribune*—their interest whetted by the strong opposition of New Mexico's other Republican senator, Harrison Schmitt, to Domenici's efforts—followed the legislation and gave Domenici a lion's share of the credit for its successful passage. "Domenici is the quintessential legislator," wrote one political columnist. "He sees his role as helping to fashion programs to solve problems, albeit with less faith in government per se, than his colleagues on the Democratic side of the aisle." [22] After the bill's passage, President Carter called Domenici to thank him for making the bill bipartisan. "Carter's observation that it was Domenici who made the synthetic fuels bill 'bipartisan' is accurate," wrote the same columnist later. "In the end, 15 of the 37 Republicans who answered the roll call supported the bill; but Domenici played a major role in lining up a number of them." [23]

Commenting on the same Carter phone call, a second political columnist said the president "praised Domenici for spearheading a bipartisan effort" and "thanked [Domenici] for engineering the administration-supported-legislation through the upper chamber." [24] In a later column on the same legislation, he wrote that "it is almost unheard of for a Democratic president to invest such faith and trust in a Republican" and "Carter is nearly always available for a meeting with Domenici." With respect to the Domenici-Schmitt rift, he wrote, "Domenici simply has more clout." [25] Clearly, the second-term senator was getting a new level of recognition at home for his national legislative performance.

When I traveled with him in New Mexico, in the summer of 1980, the career change in Washington had affected his career at home. He was displaying the broader, national perspective that he had hoped would characterize his second term. To my first "How's it going?" query, he answered, "My career in the Senate couldn't be better. But I'm worried about the bastion of liberty, the republic." And for several days he talked about "the republic." In a variety of forums, he discussed farm problems, defense strategies, fiscal policy, unemployment, and energy. To an outside observer, they were intelligent discussions, reflecting both broad knowledge and broad concern.

The senator clearly felt differently about himself than he had in 1978. He was no longer a person who would settle for the low, constituency-oriented profile of his campaign.

> I want the people of New Mexico to know what I'm doing. I'm a player now. I don't go down there and vote no. That synthetic fuels bill is as much mine as the Democrats'. I want people here to know that. I don't want any fru frus, any bullshit and demagoguery. I don't want to say, "I cosponsored such and such a bill" when I'm forty-sixth on the list—the Dole-Domenici bill. No bragging, just straight. For the first three or four years, I couldn't do that. I was so far down on the totem pole. . . . That's when you have to fru fru. It's all you can do. Now, I'm an important person in the Republican party in Congress. I want the people back here to know what my colleagues know. It's not easy. It's my greatest challenge.

His words help measure the distance between the senator of 1978 and the senator of 1980. A lot of his campaign rhetoric had been heavier on talk than accomplishment. He had wanted to be able to present himself as a national policy maker, but he couldn't. Now, he could.

In place of "number of amendments passed" and "making a difference"—or "fru frus"—there now appears the sturdier notion of "a player." As Domenici discussed it, a player is someone who regularly gets into the middle of legislative projects in an area of his competence and works constructively to see them through. A member of the minority can be a player as well as a member of the majority. Partisanship does not count. The ability to get votes for your position—in committee, from both sides of the aisle—counts; the ability to argue a case and persuade others on the floor counts; the quality of mind counts. Success in filibustering, in saying "no," does not count. To be recognized as a player "involves some previous success" as a legislator. "To my way of thinking," he summarized, "there aren't many players, not more than ten or twelve senators." And he was, he believed, one of the players.

Domenici's view of relations with his constituents had broadened, too. No longer was he content to "act like a congressman." "I've got a reform for you," he exclaimed early in my 1980 visit,

> Abolish all casework from congressional offices. Make it illegal for us to take Social Security, draft, veterans, pensions. Set up a government office to do it. Casework gets in the way of our legislative records. It's one reason why people don't know what you do.

He toyed with this new theme throughout my visit. "I'm almost ready to say we ought to cut all that [casework] out," he said to a group of farmers in Portales.

> It would hurt me, too. Some of you would write and want me to do something on a veteran's check that you aren't getting. It'd be wonderful, to tell you the truth, if I could say, "It's against the law," and turn you over to the Veterans Administration. 'Cause I would really like to be up there taking care of the kinds of things we've been talking about.

"You pay us to be legislators," he told an Albuquerque talk show audience, "and not to run around doing personal favors so we can fake you out." Domenici was not advocating fewer links to his constituents. He had come home, he said, because "I don't think you can let a Fourth of July recess go by without letting the people of your state, if they want to, see their senator. And they do want to see you." But he now had a broader conception of the linkage. And he was at home in pursuit of that newer conception.

After a talk to the graduating class of a small Albuquerque business school, he sat and talked about the purposes of his visit. First, he had come home because it was a way of letting his constituents know or get the feel, from direct contact, that he was a player—a nonmedia response to "his greatest challenge."

> Even if you can get media, and even if the media are favorable to you, the biggest challenge is to let people know what you are doing. You have to see your supporters at least once a year to pull them up with your own enthusiasm and to show them that you have grown. You have to grow.

Second, he had come home because he did not want to get out of touch with his constituents.

> The job in Washington is so difficult that it will take all your attention if you let it. You have to keep pulling yourself back home—even when the temptation is to say, "Screw it." You tend to lose touch with the institutions of your state—its universities, its towns, its cities.

The value of staying in touch was, quite simply, that it undergirded your continued effectiveness as a player.

> In Washington, ideology is not enough. You need to bring the flavor of your state. The tendency is to centralize, to homogenize. But the beauty of the system is its decentralization. We were lucky that we had states. Part of my job is to explain why something that works in Connecticut won't work in New Mexico. Some of the strong conservatives in the Senate think all they need to bring to their job is their ideology. That's not enough.

Altogether it is a view that sees his constituent relations as crucially supportive of his governing-related goals and his effectiveness in the business of governing.

For three days back home, Domenici spent a lot of his time presenting, listening, reacting, ruminating, and, in general, thinking about public policy. One could observe a serious concern for public problems and an open mind at work on them. His discussion of constituency relations, for example, pushed to the surface some specific thoughts on the need to expand one's constituency horizons in order to grapple with national problems. "One thing that would do the Republican party a lot of good," he said,

> would be to put five or six western conservative senators on a bus and take them for a two-week tour of about ten of our largest cities. Let them drive through the slums of those cities between the hours of 10 p.m. and 2 a.m. Just let them see it ... bunches of men sitting and drinking, kids running up and down the streets.... Then they'd know we have a problem. They might come back spouting the same line about the system; but they'd have seen it. I, too, believe this is the greatest system; but if we don't do something abut the 10-15 million people who are left out of the system, we could be in a lot of trouble. These people just don't mesh into the system at all.

It would be a good start, he thought, if they were to take a ride around Detroit during the upcoming Republican national convention. He went on to say that he had made only one request of the Reagan campaign—that the candidate make a major speech on youth unemployment and that he talk about the subject several times.

Domenici's main policy concern during a day and a half on the agricultural east side of the state was the embargo on grain sales to the Soviet Union, originally supported by the farmers and himself, and now opposed by the farmers. He was weighing the value of steadiness in foreign policy against the farmers' view that they, not the Russians, were suffering from the embargo. He began the day in Clovis with a newspaper interview in which he said he had come to listen to the farmers' views, that he was "reviewing the matter in depth" and would soon be "meeting with other senators in Washington" on the subject. After a luncheon meeting with a group of farmers, he told a radio interview that "There was a unanimous recommendation to me as their senator that I join with other senators in stopping the embargo. I'm leaning very strongly in that direction." He moved gradually toward the farmers' position as the trip progressed. On the second day, he told a farm group that "I've concluded that it's very questionable whether it's working." But, with typical caution, he held back from the commitment they wanted. "I want to be awful sure," he told the latter group, "that we aren't changing direction again to our long-term detriment."

The larger question he was wrestling with here was that of Soviet-American relations. And that subject consumed nearly half of his hour-long conversation later that day with Gordon Greaves, the editor of the *Portales News-Tribune.* Greaves, "the dean of New Mexico journalism," came across as the model of the wise, thoughtful, well-read, well-informed small-town newspaper editor.[26] He engaged Domenici in a lively, probing exchange on Soviet intentions and behavior, on our defense policy options in the light of assumptions about the Soviets, on the tradeoff between domestic inflation and national defense, on Carter's view of the Soviets and of the presidency, on the kind of foreign policy Reagan might make if he were president, and so forth. They exchanged perspectives, worries, information, and scenarios. When the senator had to cut it off, the editor said, "I wish we had more time. I wanted to talk with you about China. I've just spent two weeks there." Domenici said he was going there after the election and they would cover that subject—much like a seminar topic—on his next visit. "Wasn't that exciting?" he enthused as we left.

Flying back to Albuquerque from the state's east side, Domenici reflected on his visit with Greaves. And it brought him back to the theme he had voiced at the beginning of my visit.

> The problem is letting people back home know what you are doing. I have that sort of problem, more so in my hometown [with the papers]. Their guys in Washington think I'm a dogged, hard-working legislator. They admit I'm a good legislator, but that's it. They don't think I've got good ideas. They don't think I'm smart, that I think about national problems, or that I can contribute to a solution to national problems. But Gordon Greaves does. He respects me for my ideas. I don't think there's another opinion leader in the state who does. He's the only one. Yet I'm one of only ten or so players in the Senate. I can get forty-two votes on nearly anything I care about, and

sometimes fifty-two or fifty-three. Not many can do that.

It was his new, second-term frustration.

But, he reflected, it wasn't all the fault of the media. He had not been aggressive enough. "Some of the fault is mine," he went on.

> I don't push myself as much as I could. I'm a little ashamed that I haven't been more active in shaping my party's program nationally. I should have more to do with the party platform. If I think we ought to tour Detroit, I ought to propose it. I didn't know how, I guess.

The dilemma was a continuing one for Pete Domenici—one in which a temperamental desire for accomplishment contests with a temperamental caution in the process of accomplishing. In 1981, it would present itself in an entirely new set of circumstances.

For two years, Pete Domenici had been planning to "filter up" to his first consequential Senate position—ranking minority member of the Senate Budget Committee. According to plan, he would assume, in January 1981, a middling amount of influence on a committee of moderate importance. When he awoke the morning after the 1980 election, he found himself slated to be the chairman of the committee; and the committee was destined to dominate the work of the Ninety-seventh Congress. It was a shock—the same shock that delivered the Domenici story line to the media. "I really didn't believe it," he said later.

> The night before, my staff kept telling me, "We're in, we're in. You're going to be the next chairman!" I went to bed that night thinking it wouldn't be. When I woke up, it was so. But it just seemed like it couldn't be so. It took a while for that feeling to go away.[27]

But not very long. For it soon became obvious that the Senate Budget Committee would serve as the legislative spearhead for the new president's economic program.

Domenici's filtering-up process was over. He had overcome those "two inhibitors" frustrating him when he arrived in the Senate—party and seniority. He had been carried to the topmost levels of senatorial responsibility. He would never again have to fret about being recognized as a player. Nor would he ever again be thought of as nonprogrammatic. He had been given the national scope of activity for which he had been "yearning." If, indeed, one chooses to construe the success of the congressional budget process as a measure of Congress's capacity to govern the country, then Pete Domenici's sudden elevation presented him with one of the sternest governing challenges the American political system can provide.

NOTES

1. *Newsweek*, July 7, 1981, 23.
2. Gene Barton, "Constituents Proud of Domenici: Some Say Presidency Is Next Stop," *Albuquerque Tribune*, October 9, 1981.
3. See, for example, the following profiles: Helen Dewar, *Washington Post*, September 9, 1981; Martin Tolchin, "Domenici Finds He's Man in Middle," *New York Times*, September 23, 1981; and Richard Cohen, *National Journal*, February 19, 1983.
4. This June 1973 interview was conducted by Norman Ornstein, Robert Peabody, and David Rohde. This and the following excerpt are reprinted with their kind permission.
5. T. R. Reid, *Congressional Odyssey: Saga of a Senate Bill* (San Francisco: W. H. Freeman, 1980), 12.
6. *Congressional Record*, March 22, 1974, S4316.
7. John Ellwood, "House-Senate Relations and the Budget Process," unpublished, 67.
8. *Congressional Record*, December 16, 1981, S15747.
9. Linda Vanderwerf, "Domenici's Star Burning Brightly," *Las Cruces Sun-News*, March 13, 1983.
10. Reid, *Congressional Odyssey*, 12; articles on one key staffer are in *Business Week*, May 10, 1982, and *National Journal*, February 19, 1983.
11. *Congressional Record*, April 1, 1981, S6015. Similar comments will be found in: Transcript of Proceedings on Senate Concurrent Resolution 9, Revising the Second Budget Resolution for FY 1981 to Include Reconciliation, United States Senate Committee on the Budget, March 18, 1981 (Washington, D.C.: U.S. Government Printing Office, 1981), 646-647.
12. Transcript, "The Lawmakers," WETA, Washington, D.C., April 7, 1983.
13. *Wall Street Journal*, January 25, 1982.
14. Reid, *Congressional Odyssey*.
15. Ibid., p. 12.
16. Jerry McKinney and Ollie Reed, Jr., "Skeen, King Collide Again," *Albuquerque Tribune*, October 30, 1978.
17. Elizabeth Wehr, "Pete Domenici—A Reluctant Revolutionary," *Congressional Quarterly Weekly Report*, May 3, 1986; Dorothy Collin, "When You Cut Pete Domenici, He Bleeds Black Ink." *Chicago Tribune*, June 29, 1986.
18. Marjorie Hershey, *Running for Office: The Political Education of Campaigners* (Chatham, N.J.: Chatham House, 1984).
19. John Robertson, "Anaya Treading Senate Road," *New Mexican*, April 16, 1978.
20. See Ward Sinclair, "Domenici and Moynihan Take Aim at Pork Barrel," *Washington Post*, May 25, 1979; Ward Sinclair, "Blasphemy: Senate Heretics Poke Fun at Sacred Dams," *Washington Post*, November 29, 1979; Bob Duke, "Domenici to Keep on Pushing States' Rights on Water Projects," *Albuquerque Tribune*, November 30, 1979; and Lawrence Mosher, "Water Politics as Usual

May Be Losing Ground in Congress," *National Journal,* July 19, 1980.
21. *Congressional Quarterly Weekly Report,* December 1, 1979.
22. Paul Wieck, "Schmitt Pushing for Reform," *Albuquerque Journal,* October 14, 1979.
23. Bob Duke, "Domenici Praises Carter on Synfuels Effort," *Albuquerque Tribune,* November 9, 1979.
24. Bob Duke, "Carter Praise for Domenici Synfuel Effort," *Albuquerque Tribune,* November 9, 1979.
25. Bob Duke, "Schmitt Learning Senate Lessons," *Albuquerque Tribune,* January 23, 1980.
26. On Greaves's career, see *Albuquerque Journal,* January 4, 1984.
27. *Albuquerque Journal,* January 11, 1981.

The Chairman: First Seasons

THE BUDGET COMMITTEE CHAIRMANSHIP

Every committee chairmanship can be thought of as an opportunity to govern. As an official position, it bestows legitimacy. With legitimacy come, automatically, certain procedural prerogatives—notably those pertaining to control over agenda and timing. With legitimacy, too, comes a privileged opportunity for the chairman to acquire other key resources. Most prominent among these are information (from staff), attention (from media), and respect (from colleagues). Still, these resources only help to define an opportunity. What any chairman makes of that opportunity will depend, to a degree, on his or her personal goals, special talents, and decisions. As Domenici envisioned it, "A chairman can develop substantial power, a lot of power, but he can also lose it by being a poor chairman. Life can be miserable for a chairman if he wields power poorly."[1] Since this was his first experience, he would have to spend time early on learning and testing the exercise of a chairman's power.

Yet we should avoid overpersonalizing any account of a chairman's activity. For every chairman works within a context of opportunities and constraints that shape his behavior. They include the most general conditions of the society at large as well as the special responsibilities that have become attached to the chairmanship itself. They include the interests of nonlegislators, the electoral and partisan configurations in the two chambers, the concerns of those members of one's own chamber from which majorities must be formed, and the individual and collective predispositions of one's own committee out of which another majority must be formed.

More than any other senator, perhaps, the Senate Budget Committee chairman is enmeshed in this familiar world of encircling influences.

For him, the manifold separate factors are interlocked and institutionalized in an elaborate structure known as the congressional budget process. And it is absolutely impossible to understand the chairmanship of Pete Domenici without understanding the budget process in which that chairmanship is deeply embedded.

When Domenici became chairman, it was—as it still is—a new process.[2] It was the most significant congressional reform of the 1970s, which was itself the most reform-minded decade in more than half a century. It embodies a complicated set of procedural arrangements that envelop a large proportion of the entire legislative process. But more than that, even, the process embodies an idea—the idea of a congressional budget. That idea reflects much of what Congress thinks of itself as an institution—an acknowledgement of its weaknesses, a plan to assert its strengths. So, the Budget Committee chairman is positioned at the very heart of the budget process; and the context within which he operates presses upon him a set of institutional imperatives. A legislature that cannot make tough, sensible budgetary decisions cannot govern, cannot wield its quintessential power of the purse, and cannot shape national programs and national priorities. The budget reform of 1974, in sum, reasserted Congress's intention to govern the country amid increasing indications that it could no longer do so.

Internally, the reform provided for the coordination of decision making among elements of the legislature that had proceeded, historically, without coordination. It tried to bring a centralizing procedure to a fragmented institutional effort. And it tried to routinize macroeconomic thinking among all legislative decision makers. *Externally,* the reform was intended to redress a legislative-executive imbalance in budgetary power. It sought to give the legislature an independent institutional capacity to make budgetary decisions. It sought to put the legislature on an equal footing with the executive—to cooperate if possible, to compete if necessary. The very pretentiousness of the reform frames the task of those given special responsibilities for carrying it out.

That task is, moreover, endless, for the budget is part of what Jack Walker called "the recurring agenda" of Congress.[3] The process must be followed to a decision every year, year in and year out. The procedures and the results differ from one yearly cycle to another. But the cycling itself never stops. In such a process, the Budget Committee's task is Sisyphean. Its members must spend their time rolling the budgetary ball toward the top of the hill, over and over again. They learn, of course, from these continuous iterations of budget making—learn how better to do their job and how better to deal with the other people involved. But learning is not easy. For while the task is never ending, the political and economic terrain is ever changing.

In his masterful budget study, Allen Schick writes that "perhaps the most frequently asked question about the budget process is: 'Is it working?' " [4] The question gets asked partly because the budget process is new, and partly because the process is so central to governing. It also gets asked because the process is so fragile. Above all, perhaps, the process *is* fragile.

It is fragile, in part, because congressional budget resolutions have no status in law. They are vehicles by which Congress talks to itself but does not bind itself on macro-level spending, taxing, and deficit decisions. They are blueprints subscribed to at one point in time by congressional majorities, and they are easy to change whenever new congressional majorities take shape.

The budget process is fragile, also, because the budget traditionally comes from the executive who has the ability to command more public attention than the Congress. And, while congressional budget resolutions do not require a presidential signature (they are passed by concurrent resolution), practicality requires presidents to acquiesce politically. They must sign any spending, taxing, or authorizing bills that flow from the congressional budget. The ease with which such relationships are formed depends upon ideological and partisan configurations existing across the branches, configurations not notably amenable to congressional manipulation.

The process is fragile, too, because it touches the traditional prerogatives of the appropriating and authorizing committees in ways that make them reluctant supporters if not rivals. When the process disappoints individual claimants for money through its spending restrictions, or when it restricts appropriations committees by imposing spending ceilings, or when it instructs authorizing committees to enact savings through its reconciliation mandates, it puts the parts in constant combat with the whole. Among the leaders of the Appropriations and Finance committees, especially, upon whose traditional prerogatives the Budget Committee has been superimposed, the very legitimacy of the process remains under challenge. And they have tended to view the process, therefore, as something of an experimental if not temporary intrusion.

Legislators weighing the benefits of the budget process as a whole against the impediments imposed by its decisions on the parts will never be consistently favorable to the whole. And they will not be made any more favorable by the cumbersome set of timetables and procedures in which the process ensnares them. For the process invades their time as well as their territory, crowding out and frustrating other legislative activities. As Schick points out, the budget process will "work" only if legislative politicians want it to work. Yet nowhere is there a dependable constituency supporting the process. The committee, moreover, is without tangible inducements with which to influence the skeptical and the opposed.

Finally, the process is fragile because its prescriptions, and the assumptions on which its prescriptions are based, all lie at the mercy of the national economic condition. As Schick has also written, the budget does not drive the economy. The economy drives the budget. In the year before Domenici took over, for example, a growing recession made hash out of the three fiscal 1981 congressional budget resolutions—changing their acceptable deficit numbers from zero in June 1980 to $27.4 billion in September 1980 to $54.9 billion by the following March. And the final accounting recorded a record $58 billion deficit.

For all of these reasons—weak enforcement mechanisms, presidential prerogatives, institutional jealousies, and economic impacts—the congressional budget process is fragile. And the omnipresence of the question "Is it working?" only adds to the fragility.

There is no single answer to the "working" question. Generally speaking, there are two kinds of answers. Procedurally, the process "works" if Congress passes the one (originally two) prescribed budget resolution each year. Substantively, it "works," if the resolutions make a measurable difference in spending, taxing, and authorization patterns. Substantively, however, it is important to note that the legislators who passed the Budget Control and Impoundment Act unanimously in 1974 set forth no prescriptions and mandated no outcome. The process was not created, for example, to reduce deficits. Different sets of legislators had quite different substantive expectations. Conservatives expected that the process would reduce overall government spending; liberals expected it to reduce defense expenditures but increase spending for social services. All were content to let the Budget Committee "work" through accommodation—establishing appropriate procedural relationships with other legislators, and exercising its substantive discretion only "at the margins." [5]

The senator to whom the "working" question gets addressed most often is the chairman of the Budget Committee. As the chairman's role developed, he became (in the absence of subcommittees) the guiding negotiator inside the committee and "the point man for the budget process" outside.[6] The Senate Budget Committee chairman (or chairwoman) is now expected to be the prime senatorial preserver, protector, and defender of the budget process. Whatever his other goals might have been, he has a new, institutional goal thrust upon him. Senator Edmund Muskie said that he stayed in the Senate an extra term to further that single goal.[7] For the chairman, more than anyone else in Congress, the primary task is to help make the process "work," to help keep the process "alive." And because of the newness, the pretensions, the recurrence, and the fragility of that process, the chairman lives daily with the question: "Is it working?" Privately, it adds a new layer of worries. Publicly, it adds a new level of scrutiny by the media scorekeepers. "Each time Domenici enters the committee chambers," observed the *Albuquerque Journal*'s correspondent in March of 1981, "he is surrounded by reporters from major Eastern papers and the networks, all wanting comments on the latest wrinkle in the budget cutting exercise." [8]

Whatever their short-run queries, the underlying question the scorekeepers reserve for the chairman is the institutional one: "Is it working?" The question is one of institutional maintenance—adherence to prescribed procedures and retention of some Budget Committee control over budget making. The institutional maintenance goal is thrust upon every Budget Committee chairman. For Pete Domenici, this required yet another change in his mix of goals. His ultimate personal goal remained that of gaining influence inside the Senate. But as chairman he would have to weigh, continually, the importance of this personally generated goal against the importance of the institutionally generated goal of maintaining the budget process.

Both goals are, of course, related to governing. The achievement of either one, or both, can bring the distinctive degree of influence he sought. And he wanted to pursue both at the same time. But it was not always possible. The achievement of one would sometimes come only by sacrificing the other. Under certain circumstances one could get a personally desired policy and lose the institutionalized process; or one could preserve the process at the expense of policy. The presence of such a conflict was one persisting theme of Domenici's chairmanship.

If there was a clue to his likely resolution of this dilemma, it lay in his past record. For Domenici came to his chairmanship with a six-year record of concern and support for the new budget process. The House and Senate Budget committees had emerged as the "guardians" of the process, the group of legislators who worked out the requisite accommodations and kept the process "working." The Senate committee under Muskie's leadership had been particularly successful in this endeavor. Indeed, John Ellwood concludes in his excellent essay on cross-chamber differences that the new process "has caused a shift of power from the House to the Senate on budgetary questions." [9] He traces the aggressiveness of the Senate committee in expanding committee power under the act. From their fellow senators—for whom the new process meant an opportunity to gain institutional parity with the House in budgetary matters—came a good deal of support for aggressive committee action. For its part, the committee developed the kind of bipartisan, consensual decision-making procedure thought most likely to enhance committee influence while protecting the process.

Consensual decision making and bipartisanship came naturally to Pete Domenici. And he became, as we have noted, part of the "centrist coalition" inside the committee that launched and stabilized the process in the Senate. Though never uncritical of the process, Domenici voted for every budget resolution produced by the committee.[10] His support was especially important in the year before he assumed his chairmanship. In that year both wings of the broad supporting committee coalition splintered, and only the strong support of the centrist coalition enabled the committee to report out a resolution and keep the process alive. As a member of the Budget Committee, Pete Domenici displayed and developed his natural team-playing, consensus-building, governing style. He brought that style with him to his leadership position.

The year 1980 was a gloomy prelude to Domenici's succession. That year the question "Is it working?" brought disappointing answers. Budget makers chased the economy and other decision makers all year, adjusting here and there but having no perceptible influence. Media scorekeepers had a field day. "This week's next year's budget is better than last week's next year's budget," wrote one, "but I wonder what next week's next year's budget will look like?"[11] "The congressional budget process," said another, "which almost no one takes seriously anymore, seems to be headed for new heights of farce."[12] Another described the events as "a depressing signal of Washington's inability to govern, a deadly threat to the congressional budget process."[13] Others described the process as "total chaos," "collapsed," "in jeopardy," "a sham," "a charade," and "hypocrisy."[14] With Henry Bellmon still the ranking Republican, Pete Domenici did not break into public print nationally on the question until September, at which point he commented, "I'm not at all confident that this budget process will continue. The process is barely keeping its head above water, but I'm not willing to abandon it."[15]

Nor was he willing to abandon his strongly held policy goals. These were, in ascending order, reductions in federal spending, a balanced federal budget, and a growing economy. He had spent four years on the Budget Committee concentrating on spending reductions, in the belief that they were a necessary condition for the achievement of the two broader goals. On the cover of his 1978 campaign brochure he had made only one claim: that "this man has helped save you and the rest of America's taxpayers $100 billion during the past four years." He would compromise his efforts to cut spending when he believed that other ingredients were also necessary to advance the goals of budget balancing and a growing economy. And he would compromise on budget balancing when he believed that became necessary to a healthy economy. But he gave ground grudgingly.

His primary policy thrust was always to reduce excessive spending and to balance the budget. That may not have been the objective of all who supported the Budget Act in 1974. But it was Chairman Domenici's objective. He worried about deficits long before worrying about deficits became fashionable. The Budget Committee gave him a strategic position from which to pursue these policy goals and gave him, therefore, a personal stake in the preservation of the committee's influence. The "four years" of effort that he advertised during his 1978 campaign were directly tied to, and made credible by, his service on the Budget Committee. By any ultimate reckoning, therefore, both the policy goals developed by the senator and the institutional goals thrust upon the chairman would require that Pete Domenici keep the budget process "working."

Looking back on his thinking prior to the election, he said afterward that,

> I had planned to work with [Chairman Fritz] Hollings to protect the budget process. I wanted to push harder than [ranking minority member Henry] Bellmon had for fiscal restraint. But I wanted to keep the process alive. I never fed into my calculations the fact that we would have a president so committed to fiscal restraint. *That turned everything around.*

He would now have to think about protecting the budget process, not just as chairman, but also as a Republican chairman working with a Republican president. He was simultaneously introduced to a new policy context, a new leadership context, and a new partisan context.

As a result he faced three major questions: First, how would he work with the president? Would they be mutually supportive in their pursuit of good public policy? Second, how could he work with the members of his committee? Would he lead in the bipartisan tradition or would he lead by relying on the committee's Republicans? Third, how would he work with other members—especially the other budget-making leaders—of the Senate? Would he, under the changed conditions, be as supportive of the institution's budget process as he had been in the past? Domenici's first efforts as chairman would be heavily devoted to a slow, largely experimental search for answers. He would have to cope, over time, with a variety of situations. We have chosen to encapsulate these elements of sequence and context in the idea of budget *seasons*.

THE CHAIRMAN AS THE PRESIDENT'S LIEUTENANT:
DECEMBER 1980—AUGUST 1981

THE ELECTORAL INTERPRETATION

In Chapter 1 we described the substantial impact that an electoral interpretation can have on the subsequent governing activity of an individual legislator. This chapter illustrates the enormous influence an electoral interpretation can have on an entire party—and an entire government. Political scientists are accustomed to thinking about this phenomenon in terms of the existence (or nonexistence) of an electoral "mandate." [16] When the results of an election are interpreted as constituting a mandate, the winning party and/or its leading officials will be energized to enact the policies they espoused during the preceding campaign. And their enactments thereby will gain a strong measure of legitimacy.

When scholars, pundits, and politicians agree, there is little difficulty discerning a mandate. But what happens in cases of disagreement—as in 1980—when scholars and pundits can find no mandate and politicians lay claim to one? Whose interpretation matters then? If the impact on governing is what interests us—as in our framework, it does—then it is only the politicians' electoral interpretation that matters. And there is no clearer illustration of this linking mechanism at work in recent American history than in the aftermath of the 1980 elections.

The winning Republicans interpreted the presidential results as an approving mandate for Ronald Reagan to pursue the policies he had advocated in the campaign—reductions in domestic spending, increases in defense spending, lower taxes, and a balanced budget. They interpreted the Senate election results (the Democrats having won the House) as providing crucial, clinching support for their policy mandate interpretation. Had Reagan lost both houses of Congress, the mandate interpretation would have lacked both the breadth and the institutional base to make it credible. And the country would have taken a different course. But with the presidency and the Senate under their control, the Republicans could make a credible claim to a mandate. And they had a strategic advantage in implementing it.

The president could use his foothold in the Republican Senate to give him leverage in dealing with the Democratic House. And that is what he did. When he sent his first budget message to both houses in March, a banner headline read, "Reagan Sends Budget to Hill as 'Mandate for Change.'" [17] And when, three months later, he held his first press conference in support of that budget, he "called upon Congress to respond to 'an overwhelming mandate' by the nation's voters last November." [18] He won all his budget victories first in the Senate; and from that position of strength he successfully pressured the House. As the Republican Senate was absolutely necessary for the creation of the mandate interpretation, so would the Republican Senate be absolutely necessary in carrying out the mandate.

Republican senators accepted the mandate interpretation. Majority Leader Howard Baker's top aide described the party leader's attitude. "I'll never forget," he said,

> something Baker said to me just after I first came to work for him. We were talking about something I knew he didn't want to see passed, and I was goddamned sure I didn't want to see it passed. I said to him, "Why are you doing this?" He said to me—and I'll remember it as long as I live—"It's their turn." He believes that the 1980 election gave the administration a mandate. And he sees himself, with some nuances, as the administration's point man up here.

Among Republican senators there developed a *strategic corollary* to this mandate interpretation. It was the belief that Republicans as a party had to *demonstrate their capacity to govern*. They had not after all, held power in either chamber since 1954. Again, to quote Howard Baker's aide, "That's a large part of what my boss thinks the Senate has to do—show people we are able to govern." This corollary became the strategic premise of Senate Republican action.

The members told each other that they could prove their ability to govern only if they stuck together with near unanimity. Several conditions were conducive to that effort. They had a base to build on. Of their behavior in the previous Congress, it had already been written that "they have achieved more internal harmony and Senate influence in the past two years than at any time in the previous quarter-century." [19] They had a precarious majority of 53-47. The costs of individual defections were both very high and very visible. Furthermore, every Republican senator was freshly placed in a position of responsibility—a chairmanship or a subcommittee chairmanship. So, on the individual level, each one was thrown into a situation where he or she had to govern, and had no experience in doing so. The virtues of sticking together would thus be brought home to each of them individually. Finally, of course, they were members of the president's party and would be favorably predisposed toward his governing initiatives. In Baker's words, "We are a team, the president is the quarterback and we are his blockers, and we can't say now we don't like the plays." [20]

EARLY CHOICES

In this postelection context, and throughout his first budget season, Pete Domenici was a model Republican senator. He was thrilled at the prospect of working constructively with "a new president with a courageous and consistent plan to balance the budget in three years and a Republican Senate committed to make that economic plan work." [21] He accepted the notion of a mandate. "There is an American mandate," he said, ". . . that the size of the budget cannot grow as fast." [22] And he said that the budget process would survive "if the Republican Senate meets the public mandate." [23] Even more important, he accepted the strategic corollary—that the Republicans had to prove they could govern. He did not have to stretch to apply it to his committee for its work was central to the business of governing. To him, the meaning of the corollary was to make the budget process work.

His first strategic step as chairman was to establish close working relationships with those other Republicans he would need as allies in budget making—Howard Baker, the majority leader; Bob Dole, chairman of the Finance (or taxing) Committee; and Mark Hatfield, chairman of the Appropriations (or spending) Committee. As the scheduler of floor action, Baker would be essential to the maintenance of the elaborate budget timetable. From the time of Baker's election as party leader, Domenici was politically allied with him and personally close to him. In tandem, they worked to fold in the others. [24]

Domenici understood the natural strains and the sense of his own illegitimacy that existed within the group. Appropriations and Finance were the traditional budget makers in the Senate. They accepted the new committee on the block. But at the same time they could be expected to guard their jurisdictions jealously. And, in extreme cases, they could threaten Budget Committee influence and control. Domenici expressed optimism. "In the past," he said in January, "there hasn't been any kind of a commitment from Appropriations and Finance to make the budget process work. The attitude has been, if it doesn't work, that's just too damn bad." [25] He predicted that "the budget process will work if the major committee chairmen want it to work and are part of it from the beginning." Early on, he was able to say that "Senators Hatfield and Dole have told me and the majority leader that they are behind it, 100 percent." [26] "We have," said Domenici, "a mutual commitment to work together from the very beginning." [27]

The Budget Committee chairman thought of himself as a member of this four-person leadership team, and he worked with this team whenever he could. As he said later that year,

> You've got to have guys like Domenici and Dole if you are going to govern the country. It isn't how good we are individually. It's how good we are working together. The Republicans are governing. We've got to stick together in legislating and explaining to the country what we've done.

Throughout the first budget season, these four leaders of the Republican Senate—together with the president's friend Senator Paul Laxalt—backed each other to the hilt. In public at least.[28] That would not always be the case. But Domenici began his chairmanship by functioning self-consciously as a member of this team.

For the first eight months of 1981, he threw in publicly with the new president. A natural team player, he thought of himself now, not as a member of the committee team but as part of the administration team. With respect to administration-congressional relations, he said in January, "They don't plan to just announce an economic game plan that surprises those who have to carry it out up here. They intend to put it together as a *team*." [29] And he would work to implement it in that spirit. "I'm certainly part of the *team* that is in control," he told his Las Cruces constituents in February. "We should match our zeal for tax cuts with our zeal for budget cuts. It will be my responsibility to make Congress take the hard medicine first." [30]

He made two other strategic decisions in carrying out that responsibility—to move immediately and to move with a total *package* of budget cuts. He believed that immediate action "within the first 150 days" [31] was necessary to capture the momentum of the electoral mandate. "If we don't do this with an early package that employs the mandate given the new president, the new Senate majority and the more conservative [members of the] House, you can kiss it goodbye." [32] On the matter of packaging "the hard medicine" cuts, he expressed the view that,

> If these have to come to the floor one at a time ... the special interests will prevail. ... In my opinion, the answer to this is to find a way to get a package on the floor of the Senate where the special interests can argue about their part in it but our President and those of us who are worried about future jobs and future inflation can continue to focus on a package, with the ultimate vote on a package.[33]

The logic behind the package approach, as a way of resolving conflicting interests, would remain central to the chairman's strategic thinking throughout his tenure. In his earliest days, the packaging mechanism he utilized was called "reconciliation."

As planned by the architects of the 1974 reform, reconciliation legislation would be used, at the very end of the budget sequence, to "reconcile" existing laws with the spending ceilings and the revenue totals prescribed in the final budget resolution. Whereas budget resolutions do not carry the force of law, a reconciliation bill would change the law and would, thereby, provide solid enforcement of budget decisions. The reconciliation procedure called for the Budget committees to "instruct" each standing committee to report legislation that would implement budgetary prescriptions within its jurisdiction. Then, each Budget Committee would package the prepared legislation, without change, into a single reconciliation bill.

In practice, reconciliation came too late in the process to be implemented, and, in the early years, almost none of the permanent savings contemplated in budget resolutions were ever enacted into law. In an effort to change this result, the Budget committees decided in 1980 to include reconciliation instructions to committees in their first budget resolution. This procedural innovation produced the first reconciliation bill, and, ultimately, legislated savings of $4.6 billion. It created a precedent to be exploited by the new Budget Committee chairman a year later.

Pete Domenici's contribution, in concert with Office of Management and Budget Director David Stockman, was to apply reconciliation in so muscular a manner as to prompt budgetary analysts to speak in terms of revolution.[34] He removed the reconciliation bill entirely from the first budget resolution and pressed for its passage by Congress before the first budget resolution. His committee's instructions to the relevant Senate committees called for a package of legislative savings totaling $35 billion. With this procedural and substantive enlargement in hand, he shepherded a three-part budget package of fiscal restraint to completion.

First, he passed the landmark reconciliation instruction. Its quick and early passage in the Senate pressured the Democratic House to follow a similar course to nearly identical results. Domenici then steered the regular first budget resolution through from committee to conference. (See Appendix, Table A-1.) And finally, he moved the huge omnibus reconciliation package—ratifying the savings enacted by various committees—through the Senate and conference.

That capstone measure was the product of the Budget committees' instructions to fifteen House and thirteen Senate committees to reduce 266 separate budget accounts (appropriations and entitlements) and to change 250 bits of authorization legislation to bring current law into line with budget figures.[35] Fifty-eight separate subconferences involving 69 senators and 184 House members were required to bring about the conference committee results. The results promised savings of nearly $150 billion. The bill, said one wise observer, had a broader scope than any measure in congressional history, and it concentrated "enormous power in the Budget Committee." [36] And, that, in turn meant power for committee leaders.

During this first budget season, from January to July, it was Ronald Reagan's strongly held set of beliefs and his sense of economic priorities that carried the day. Reagan led and Domenici followed. Whatever his private doubts, Domenici was publicly loyal. He was neither a supply sider nor a dedicated Reaganaut, but he was excited over the prospects of large spending rollbacks and a balanced budget. So he accepted the idea of tax cuts, accepted the administration's optimistic economic assumptions, and promulgated the message of economic recovery. He did not often speak at length in the committee, but when he did, he spoke as the loyal lieutenant. "I am very willing—I am very willing—to place my confidence in the new President of the United States with reference to balanced budgets and new policies for this country." [37]

From the outset of negotiations over budget cutbacks, for instance, he argued strongly that "you have to restructure the entitlement programs." [38] (An entitlement program is one that guarantees a certain level of benefits to every person who meets the requirements set by law, leaving Congress no discretion in appropriating money for that program. Examples are Social Security, veterans' benefits, farm price supports, and Medicare.) In public and in committee Domenici urged the enactment of a slowdown in the indexed cost-of-living adjustments (COLAS) for burgeoning pension programs, on the grounds that the budget could not be balanced otherwise. When the chairman persisted in this vein during committee proceedings over reconciliation, the president journeyed to Capitol Hill to argue against Domenici on political grounds. The chairman desisted. "I plan to support the president," he announced after their meeting. And the two men were photographed smiling at one another as Howard Baker looked on.[39]

A month later, during negotiations over the budget resolution, Domenici resisted administration budget arithmetic on the grounds that it disguised the deficit. Again, the president called him with the message, "Get back on the team lest the Republicans prove they aren't fit to govern less than four months after taking power." [40] Once again, the chairman desisted; once again he proved himself to be a team player. In the wake of these presidential persuasions, Budget Director Stockman described the Senate Budget Committee as "a rubber stamp," as "pliable," and as "a domestic budget-cutting machine." [41] But Chairman Domenici's view was more tentative. As he explained his own decisions later, "Here we have a new President, a new team, a new theory, a new set of chairmen. We just had to go along and say, 'We'll try to work with the President. Let's give the President a chance.' " [42]

By springtime, Domenici had begun to worry about the size of the impending deficit. It was a concern that would dominate his economic thinking for the next five years. In May he wrote a confidential memo to Majority Leader Baker about the size of the president's tax-cut proposal. "I am deeply concerned," he wrote, "because of the impending deficits in 1983 and 1984 if we go entirely with the $302 billion cut. . . . My private recommendation to you is that we go with a tax package that is between 95 and 100 billion less than the President's. . . . These levels would be much more likely to allow us at least an outside chance of a balanced budget in 1984." When Domenici let it be known that he was thinking of proposing such a cutback in the Senate, he was called to the White House and asked by aides to desist in return for promises of a second round of budget cuts in the fall. For the third time, he swallowed his misgivings and remained loyal to the team.

Characteristically, he worried about it. Stockman writes that Domenici "begged the President to let him vote against the tax cut." [43] An aide commented afterward that his decision was made "despite every urging in his body and from his staff." Another aide said, "I think it'll haunt him for the next ten years." [44] But he did not act. "We thought there would be a chance to correct the first resolution later," he explained, "but there never was." [45]

Even more revealing of the relationship between Ronald Reagan and the Republican Senate was the manner in which Domenici ran the Budget Committee. Throughout his previous six years on the committee, he had worked in a bipartisan manner. But loyalty to Reagan and the Republican team, in effect, turned a naturally bipartisan senator into a practicing partisan. He gave continued lip service to bipartisanship, but the force of the strategic corollary led him to run his committee by relying on his twelve-person Republican majority. An early leadership test occurred on the first budget resolution when three conservative Republicans joined the Democrats to vote against reporting out the first budget resolution in April, embarrassing the chairman with an 8-12 defeat. Two of them were among six newcomers whom Domenici did not even know. In the manner of contemporary first-year senators, they were not bashful. Claiming to be concerned above all with the integrity of the Reagan tax-cut program, the three objected that the resolution did not show sufficient savings to guarantee a balanced budget for 1984.

Domenici, too, had worried about the deficit implications of his figures, but he had been persuaded to stay on the team. He took the position with his committee that it was impossible ("baloney") to accurately project savings for 1984, and that blocking the first budget resolution "does not help the prospect of the president's tax-cut package ... it makes it harder." [46] He pushed the first committee vote even though he knew he would lose. "This is the president's program," he said, "and my job is to get it through the Senate substantially intact." "Republicans are still pursuing their individual views," he continued. "They haven't realized their role is to support the president." [47] He pressured the defectors by casting them as opponents of the president's budget and by depicting their defection as "a pretty serious setback" [48] for the president's program. "I can't construe it any other way than they do not have confidence in this president." [49]

In adopting this posture, Chairman Domenici went as far as he ever had—or ever would—in allying himself with the president's policies, asserting that he "had faith in the positive economic effects of the president's policies and, indeed, faith that the president's policies would lead to a balanced budget and a rejuvenated economy." [50] He pressured the administration to lean on the three defectors by toying publicly with the strategy of building a bipartisan committee majority on the basis of a scaled-down, stretched-out tax-cut program. He had his staff prepare just such a proposal.[51] The three "strays" returned to the fold under the cover of some "smoked-up" budget-cut projects with which they could profess satisfaction.

The chairman had survived his first intracommittee test. He had done it with the full support of the president, with the full support of the majority leader, and with an electoral mandate at his back. He had not done so in the traditional manner by recruiting bipartisan Democratic support. His move toward the Republican extremists, rather than toward the bipartisan centrists, confirmed Domenici's fundamental decision to govern with a partisan majority, as did his use of the presidential stick to isolate them. After that episode, Domenici remained a partisan, despite his previous pattern and despite the drastic change it brought to the way in which the Budget Committee carried out its governing responsibility.[52] His partisanship demonstrates the long, long reach of the 1980 elections through the mandate interpretation and its strategic corollary into the inner workings of the Senate.

The conference on the reconciliation bill was his only public disagreement with the administration. It was, however, of considerable symbolic and psychological importance for Domenici's chairmanship. Budget Director Stockman asked Domenici to accept the House version of the bill and not to go to conference. The president made the same request of Howard Baker. Domenici insisted that his committee's work and that of other Senate committees deserved an equal chance in a conference. He took his case to Baker and to a meeting of the other Senate committee chairmen. His strong defense of Senate prerogatives carried the day.

Domenici was described as "a folk hero" for facing down the administration at the height of its power. One of his staffers commented, "When he first took over the Budget Committee we all wondered a little bit how he would handle it. But he has been in charge. When he said to Stockman, 'You run the Office of Management and Budget and I'll run the Budget Committee,' that was just what we wanted to hear." Stockman recalls that a "furious," "red-faced" Domenici told him, "It's about time you learned this is a democracy. . . . You can shove [your] pile of paper back in the OMB garbage can where it came from. From now on we're doing it our way." These actions helped to consolidate his claim to legitimate committee leadership.[53] But they were procedural, not substantive, differences with the administration.

From the standpoint of those who controlled it, the budget process never worked better than it did in 1981. The previous year's forebodings vanished in the face of an almost benumbed awe on the part of the media at the unbroken string of legislative victories.[54] From a procedural standpoint, Domenici was particularly pleased with the success of his packaging vehicle, the reconciliation legislation. He had found a way to bring committee spending into line with a projected budget resolution. "The budget process, as a tool of restraint," he said, "is pretty damn weak. With reconciliation, it will have a lot more teeth in it." [55]

From a substantive standpoint, too, the process "worked." Massive spending cuts of $35 billion and income tax cuts of $450 billion were enacted; defense budgets were increased; and the road to a balanced budget in 1984 was constructed. Its success was magnified even more when measured against the low expectations produced by the previous year's failure. Domenici's emphasis was on the extent of spending cuts. "It's clear to me, without any doubt, that this Congress has succeeded in the single most heroic effort at controlling federal spending in this nation's history." [56] For the conservative chairman, there was a heady sense of accomplishment. It was a season of budgetary euphoria.

It was a time, too, in which credit for legislative achievement was distributed to the principals. First, of course, to the president and then to various legislative leaders. Domenici was credited as one of a half-dozen Senate "players" in the national drama. He blossomed onto the front pages of national newspapers, onto the nightly national newscasts, onto the daily or weekly national interview programs, and eventually into a major nationwide presidential address. He was invariably written up as a success story—an unknown and untried legislator who had been "catapulted" out of obscurity, who had been thrown into a pivotal position in the political big leagues, and who had demonstrated a marked ability at governing. He received credit for being the chief architect of the fast-track reconciliation package strategy, for working cooperatively with administration and Senate leaders, for assembling and energizing a talented committee staff, for steering legislation around both Republican and Democratic roadblocks within his committee, for effective work on the Senate floor, for preserving the prerogatives of the Senate in procedural disagreements with the administration, and for negotiating effectively from strength with the Democratic House.

"In my experience here," said Majority Leader Baker in April, "I have never seen a senator grow as Senator Domenici has grown in his role as chairman of the Budget Committee." [57] For a person whose earliest legislative efforts had been scattershot, the job required a tremendous concentration of legislative effort. "I get all my personal satisfaction from the Budget Committee," he noted later. For a person who "yearned to be something" in whatever organization of which he was a member and who had spent eight years filtering up—and growing—it was a time of immense personal satisfaction.

The national media scorekeepers, observing his governing style as chairman, found it characterized by fairness, level-headedness, and determination. After he shepherded the reconciliation measure through committee, the *New York Times* correspondent wrote that,

> The senator impressed most observers with his calm and patience. He continually assured roll call committee members that they would be heard, and eventually developed a consensus that ended with a 20-0 vote.[58]

A *Washington Post* reporter, beneath the headline, "With Budget, Immigrant's Son Becomes Senate Star," described him as "a Republican loyalist . . . who works hard and is proud of it . . . a solid if unpretentious achiever who inspires rather more affection and confidence than reverence and awe." [59] Altogether, then, his first-season performance as chairman reflected many of the characteristics of a team player and a consensus builder—the extension of a governing style developed earlier. The new ingredient was the degree of influence and notoriety. But it was as a member of the Republican Senate team that he had achieved these things. So, if there was a large lesson to be learned, or confirmed, from his season as the president's lieutenant, it was the value of team play in the pursuit of legislative accomplishment.

THE CHAIRMAN AS INDEPENDENT ACTOR: SEPTEMBER—DECEMBER 1981

THE CHANGING CONTEXT

When I finally went down to see Chairman Domenici in the fall of 1981, his most sensational triumph was behind him. The most severe tests of his leadership, however, lay ahead. He was preparing to guide the second budget resolution through the legislature. But the confluence of external conditions that had floated eight months of legislative-budgetary success were slowly changing. In those first eight months he had been the beneficiary of an extraordinary political tide, inside and outside Congress. And that favorable tide was beginning to ebb. It had reached its high watermark when Congress broke for its August recess. Up to that point media scorekeepers had been painting an almost hyperbolic picture of policy revolution, presidential prowess, Republican cohesion, and Democratic disarray.[60] While some of them speculated, sotto voce, that these conditions could not last, their major theme was one of total wonderment.

When legislators, with a dose of constituency reaction behind them, returned from their recess, they brought with them the message of a changed context. They found, in their first extended period at home, a visible lack of recovery, punctuated by rising interest rates—the most sensitive of all political numbers. Some also found a sentiment that cutbacks in social spending had been pushed to the limit. The effect became known, in Howard Baker's phrase, as "the shock of August."

The national media picked up the theme, in headlines such as "After 'Shock of August' Reagan Faces 'Show-Me' Attitude on Hill," or "The Massacre on Main Street," or "Honeymoon Nears End for Reagan and Congress," or "Reagan 'Fall Offensive' Casualties, Not Victories." [61] "Congress left on a political high in early August," wrote one observer, "but as members fanned out to lakes, mountains, foreign junkets and early-bird forays for the 1982 elections, the euphoria dimmed." [62] Democratic willingness to follow the president began to decline, as one might expect. But Republican willingness began to erode, too. There was, for them, the simple matter of budget fatigue. The troops had followed their leader on a "forced march" and through several bruising battles. Now they wanted time to "catch their breath." [63] There was also a lessening of devotion to the administration's economic program.

The congressional recess of August 1981 marked the turning point in the Reagan domestic presidency. Before August, all was triumph; after August, all was struggle—from blitzkrieg to trench warfare. In the fall, with no economic recovery in sight and with no sign of change in the economic program, Chairman Domenici found himself less wedded to it and a bit more inclined to speak with an independent voice. But, given his caution and his team-playing instincts—only a bit more. All in all, committee negotiations with the administration promised to be somewhat more difficult and somewhat more adversarial during the second budget season than during the first. Domenici's success in the first budget season had come as Ronald Reagan's loyal lieutenant. That role seemed less likely in the upcoming one.

Conditions inside the Budget Committee were changing, too. Primarily, there was an increase in partisanship. Domenici had begun his chairmanship by following his personal inclination toward bipartisanship and by observing the bipartisan traditions of the committee. He had won the support of the senior committee Democrat, Fritz Hollings, for his early reconciliation strategy; and he had carried the reconciliation measure (instructing fourteen Senate committees to enact $36.9 billion in savings) unanimously in the committee. He had held the support of two "centrist coalition" southern Democrats (but not Hollings) on the 14-7 vote passage of the first budget resolution. Both measures had won bipartisan majorities in the Senate—as did the third leg of his triumph, the final reconciliation package.

Democrats, from Hollings to Minority Leader Robert Byrd, had proclaimed the bipartisanship of the effort. But, because the Budget Committee was being used by the administration to spearhead a sharp programmatic change, bipartisanship inside the committee had never been grounded in positive policy agreement. Committee bipartisanship was always more a matter of form than substance, a gloss polished by Domenici's personal attributes of sincerity and fairness. From the beginning, the Democrats had disagreed with the administration's economic assumptions, on which all the budget numbers were based. And while they acquiesced in the idea that large savings should be made, they disagreed with the Republican majority over where they should be made.

A Domenici staffer recounted at length the slow decline of the early bipartisanship within the Budget Committee.

> The first resolution was the result of an agreement by Baker and Domenici to give the president some momentum on his savings. Our first reconciliation resolution was an instruction to the committees to cut spending. And we produced it within two weeks after Reagan had sent up his package. That decision was a bipartisan decision. And up to that point we had bipartisanship. The resolution carried 88-10.
>
> Then we began work on the regular first budget resolution for 1982. At that point, we made a fundamental decision that was, in retrospect, I think, a mistake. We decided to proceed wholly on the basis of the administration's economic assumptions and ignored the CBO's [Congressional Budget Office's] assumptions. We told CBO to compute all their numbers on the basis of the administration's figures. That was wholly a staff decision. It was not made in committee. . . . It was made on the basis that there was not enough time to do otherwise.
>
> When that decision emerged in the committee context, the Democrats asked that we look at CBO's assumptions. At that point, Domenici turned his back on Hollings. He said that we would go with the administration's figures. And the committee voted to do that by a straight party-line vote. That was the beginning of partisanship on the committee. Then, of course, there was the matter of taxes. The two parties differed on that.
>
> Then, in order to bring along . . . [the last three Republicans] we had to generate some more savings, which we had to make up pretty much out of whole cloth. The Democrats did not like that either. We

> got a good deal of Democratic support after that inside the committee, on the floor, and on the conference report. But there always was the feeling underneath that, "You did it your way. Don't ask us for help. You would cater to the Republicans on the committee by changing your figures, but you wouldn't change any of your figures for us."

There was cross-party cordiality, but increasing policy and partisan polarization. It was in this sense that the election of Ronald Reagan, and the interpretation of the election and its strategic corollary, "turned everything around" for Pete Domenici. It propelled him from his natural bipartisanship to a responsible partisanship.

While increased partisanship inside the committee clarified Domenici's coalition-building tasks, it did not necessarily make them any easier because there was increasing policy fragmentation among committee Republicans. In his excellent study *The Fiscal Congress*, Lance LeLoup found that the personal goals of Senate Budget Committee members have emphasized the making of good public policy. Senators do *not* go on the committee to protect the budget process; and that goal does not motivate them once they are on it.[64] A lack of concern for the process was probably exacerbated in 1981 by the fact that the committee's twelve-person Republican majority contained six Senate newcomers, most of whom had to be persuaded to join the group as their last committee choice. They were likely to have a different view of priorities than the chairman. We have already emphasized the fragility of the budget process. Add to this the fragility of the committee members' loyalty to the process and a highly vulnerable committee comes into view. Its special vulnerability underscores the task facing the chairman.

The chairman's April difficulty with the three Republican recalcitrants presaged the possibilities of a fragmenting policy individualism within his majority. A Republican committee staffer worried that Domenici had won that victory with a fair-weather majority.

> This idea that all the Republicans marched in lock step with the administration is nonsense. Sure, as long as everything's going well, they sign on. But just let things go bad and they'll be all over the place. Each one will look out for himself [and] we'll have trouble getting anything out of committee.

Should the Republican majority disintegrate, the process itself might be the victim.

Those committee Democrats who were devoted to the budget process expressed exactly that worry—that the new partisan majority might not be so willing to hang together to protect the process as the old bipartisan majority had been. "No one is working to protect the process now," complained a veteran Democratic staffer in the wake of the three-member "revolt."

I'm not blaming Pete Domenici. He was always a part of the committee leadership that protected the process. He worked with Bellmon. The administration is pressing him hard to make the budget process carry some very heavy baggage. And the Republican members of the committee are very ideological. They want to make the numbers come out right for them. So Domenici has to fiddle with the numbers in order to keep them in line. He has to appeal to them by making ideological concessions to them; he can't appeal to them to save the budget process. If he decided to work with the Democrats, he would lose too many Republicans. So he has not been bipartisan. I think that hurts the process.

To some degree, these comments reflect a minority party in disarray. Unable to find a dominant policy voice, they repaired to procedural-institutional grounds for disagreeing with the majority.

House Democrats found a similar unity in the procedural argument that the president had seized control of the budget process and used it to run roughshod over congressional prerogatives—in effect turning the very instrument designed to produce congressional equality into an instrument to ensure their inequality. The willing acceptance, by congressional majorities, of presidential budgetary leadership belies the argument. But these arguments about process served primarily as umbrellas under which Democrats could gather while they learned to be a minority.

Bipartisanship, it seems, depends somewhat on how you define the issue facing the committee. If the issue gets defined as preserving the budget process, bipartisanship is possible. If the issue is defined in strong policy terms, bipartisanship is not possible. If the issue is defined in weak policy terms, bipartisan compromise may be possible. In 1981 the issue inside the committee gradually came to be drawn in strong policy terms, and partisanship resulted.

This raised the interesting question for the Senate of whether the budget process, as an institutional weapon, could best be protected, as it always had been, by a bipartisan majority or whether a partisan majority could serve just as well. Or, to put the question somewhat differently, would a partisan majority push their substantive policy views so single-mindedly that they would sacrifice the process if need be to accomplish their policy goals? And, if the chairman were pressed to choose between policy-oriented and process-oriented goals, which way would he go? Chairman Domenici carried these questions with him into his second budget season.

SIGNS OF INDEPENDENCE: NEW MEXICO AND WASHINGTON

In the fall of 1981, the economy tumbled officially into a recession. Washington headlines read: "Economic Situation Darkens: Growing

Recession May Push Deficit to $100 Billion," "Economy Is in Recession, President Acknowledges," "Unemployment Rate Is Highest Since '75," "Goodbye to the Balanced Budget." [65] High interest rates continued and triple-digit billion-dollar deficits were projected. The political question was who should do what about it, and when. For Budget Chairman Pete Domenici, the question was whether he—and his committee—should continue to follow the president's policy lead or exercise a little leadership of his own. And, if the latter, in what form and at what point. It was a question of substance and of timing.

The context for Domenici's decision was the impending *second budget resolution*—designed to be the final, binding statement, in September, of congressional budget totals for the next fiscal year. (It would turn out to be the last time the statutory provision for a second budget resolution was invoked.) August's euphoria had been only momentary for Domenici. During the week of August 21, he sent a memo to Majority Leader Baker predicting an $80 billion deficit in 1984—the year of the promised balanced budget—unless budgetary changes were made. He suggested "cuts in defense and a 3 percent cutback in entitlements for three years." [66] On "Face the Nation" September 13, he said that defense should be cut $30 billion over three years—nearly three times the $13 billion the president had said he would be willing to cut. And he also emphasized the need to curtail the uncontrolled growth of pension programs and other entitlements.[67]

Two days later he presented these same suggestions to President Reagan, urging him to move quickly and telling him that "You can run but you can't hide." "The balanced budget is long gone," he said. "It's the whole economic recovery and the Republican future that's at stake." To which the president's initial response was, "I'm with Pete Domenici. Anybody who thinks we can live with these deficits is dreaming. So let's stop making excuses about all these miserable domestic programs and start cutting. That's the only answer." [68]

It was not the only answer Domenici wanted. And the House Republicans did not want even that much—especially on entitlements. Domenici privately urged the president to "hang tough" with respect to entitlement cutbacks.[69] But the president, in a pattern that would become familiar, went along with the House position. Domenici's bicameral reaction would become familiar, too. "You can forget Social Security and the COLAs," he told Stockman. "Your spineless House Republican friends have poisoned the well. Nobody over here is going to fall on their swords if they're going to cut and run in the House." [70]

On September 24 the president launched his promised "September offensive" by asking for substantial second-round cuts in nondefense spending and lesser reductions elsewhere.[71] (See Appendix, Table A-2.)

In this nationally televised address, he quoted Domenici favorably on his "run-but-can't-hide" warning —confirming, beyond doubt, Domenici's new reputation as a national figure. The president again promised a 1984 balanced budget if "a firm steady course were followed." [72] Domenici huddled with the other Senate Republican players—Baker, Dole, and Hatfield. And in early October he announced:

> There is great consternation that the President's mix won't work. There is an evolving consensus that we need big 1982, 1983, and 1984 cuts, but made differently than the president has proposed. . . . The most dramatic turnaround is the consensus that we have to raise some more revenues." [73]

Under the protective cover of his fellow Senate players, Domenici was moving cautiously from policy followership to policy leadership. One media scorekeeper called it "the first open rift between the White House and Republican Congressional leaders over the budget. . . ." [74]

During a visit to New Mexico in mid-October, Domenici's public posture was an unsettled admixture of optimism and gloom, of general devotion to the president's moves toward smaller government, plus worries that strong correctives might be necessary to keep things going in the right direction. Privately, he was mostly worried. A staffer accompanying him on the trip commented, "I can't wait to get back here where they don't worry about the deficit all day every day. Sometimes he's so down about the deficit, so gloomy, so worried that I just crawl out under the door at night." Privately, too, Domenici was thinking through a package of budgetary proposals of his own. At New Mexico State University he told a group,

> I don't think it's worth going through what we have to in the next 40 days unless we get a package that will bring deficits down for '82, '83, and '84. . . . We will have to cut more out of defense. . . . We have to address entitlements in some way. . . . We need an $80-$85 billion reduction in the next three years. . . . I may be dumb, but I'm ready to face Social Security now. But Congress isn't. The president isn't. So we probably won't. . . . That's what I asked the president to do, but we'll have to wait a while.

Later, in Hobbs, he put the chances of success with this kind of package, "a mix different from the president's," at "no better than 50-50." In terms of his chairmanship, Domenici's problem in mid-October was whether or not to start his committee working on the second budget resolution before a consensus package could be worked out among all interested parties. He decided to hold off, lest he take the lead, be repudiated, and harm the budget process.

At a couple of points during the trip he explained privately that,

> The leadership wants us to go ahead with a resolution and select the committees we want to instruct. Dole wants to go ahead and have his committee set some parameters on tax increases. They are asking me when I can get started, and I'm saying within eight or nine days after we return. But I'm telling you that I'm going to renege on that. I'm not going ahead and then let the House torpedo everything we've done. My strategy now is to seek an accommodation with Jones [Chairman James Jones of the House Budget Committee]. I want to see what the House will do, and then ... we'll pass whatever resolution the House passes. But they may just waive the budget process, just waive it. If they do, we may lose the process altogether.

He explained,

> We'll have to get a second budget resolution through. I don't want to pass one that will end up getting waived at the end of the year. That would be the end of the process. If I thought the president had any chance of getting another Gramm-Latta [large spending cuts plus reconciliation] through the House, it would be worth the effort. But I don't think they can. So I'm taking the position that we will do anything we can to help—after someone else sets some parameters, Dole on the revenue side, for example. We are not going to get out front, carrying the whole burden and then watch the process get killed. I want to protect the process until such times as we can amend it. It needs it, badly. But we certainly can't do that now.

The president, of course, would be no help with the process, calling it at that very time "a kind of Rube Goldberg thing." [75] For the chairman, the situation called for a familiar balancing act, weighing the substantive policy benefits against the costs to the process. It was also a familiar posture for the individual, one side of him wanting to charge ahead; one side calling for caution. For the time being, the process and the caution side of the argument prevailed.

While Pete Domenici revealed himself, during this October 1981 trip, to be the same inveterate worrier as always, he also revealed himself to be a more self-confident and increasingly independent-minded worrier. It had been fifteen months since I last traveled with him in New Mexico. On that previous trip, he had (as we have seen) been reaching for national policy influence and for the recognition commensurate with it. Now he had achieved both. And the achievement seemed to have assuaged some of his self-doubts. He seemed, too, to be fairly self-conscious in thinking about the matter of his independence—at home and in Washington. Perhaps his budget dilemma triggered his home reactions. But he clearly did assert himself more strongly than he had in 1980. And he seemed satisfied—even liberated—in doing so.

The first event of the trip was an open forum before a friendly crowd of four hundred people, covered by local TV, at Del Norte High

School in Albuquerque. At the beginning of the question period, he fielded two fairly sharp criticisms of his Washington activity; and he did so with considerable assertiveness. One questioner rose to express disappointment that the senator's "conservatism index" had declined and to complain specifically about his vote to raise the ceiling on the public debt. "I don't know what that index measures," Domenici replied. As for the debt limit vote,

> Reagan came personally and begged us to vote for it.... I'm not going to stand up there and shoot down the national government in the first nine months of Ronald Reagan's term on something like that.... I won't vote against it as long as I'm part of Congress and we have a president I think is doing everything practicable to bring government spending under control.

Another questioner complained about congressional perquisites and asked, "Did you vote to raise your salary?" The senator answered, "Yes, and I make no apology for it." He explained his personal financial situation, saying, "I'm going to make speeches, and make as much as you will let me. If I earn $200,000 and I come home here, you can throw me out." And he concluded,

> It's very expensive to move a family to Washington and raise eight children. I have three in college. I'm not complaining. I'm going to do what I have to do to raise those children and I'm sorry if it bothers some of you. But ... we'll be up for reelection in three and a half years and if you don't like it, you can vote that way.

Those two unfriendly questions made the greatest impression on him; and both gave him a chance to assert a degree of independence.

When we met the next morning, his greeting was: "Were you there last night? Of course you were." And he continued,

> What did you think about that stuff about congressional salaries? Wasn't that awful? I don't give a damn about those people. They can come and get me if they want to. But I'm not going to give them one inch. And attacking me on the debt limit. That guy lost the audience, didn't he? What business have they got putting the debt limit vote on their conservatism index? That was a vote to help the president with his program. If they give a damn about this president, they'll take votes like that out of their survey. What kind of a survey is it anyway if I come out with 57 percent? If they think this senator is going to get any more conservative they can go climb up a tree. That knee-jerk conservatism is not what the president is going to win on.

His private assertion of independence was much stronger than the public one. But he was clearly pleased with his unyielding public performance.

He returned, spontaneously, to the same subject later in the trip, in a moment of self-examination. "What am I doing this for?" he mused one evening in Hobbs.

> In most parts of the state, people don't think I'm worth $3,000 more. Over here, they don't think I'm worth four cents more. I know now that I could run any business. I'd have to learn their specialty, but I could make $200,000 easily in business. I didn't used to think I could. Now I know I could.

The answer to his question was surely that he had something to contribute. "One of the great things about this system," he continued, "is that people like me can get elected and do what I've done—me, a man from little New Mexico taking charge of the federal budget." These few moments at home revealed a new degree of self-confidence, one sufficient to embolden his actions in Washington as well.

On the way back to Washington, he talked about the trip home and the task ahead. Referring back to the Del Norte meeting, he ranked it as the fourth most "enjoyable" (out of twelve) events of the visit. "It was a good turnout. A lot of my friends came. Even though there was some criticism, we had a good dialogue. I have been yearning to get some of those things off my chest—about congressional salaries." He was pleased with his independence. But moments later, as he looked ahead to his budgetary tasks, he expressed a sensitivity to the limits on his independence. "I have always felt the pull to take more of a leadership role than the citizens will support," he said.

> I yearn to be courageous. But I tend to think of my support in pieces and I'm always worried about losing it piece by piece. Each vote may lose you another piece of support. Reagan's economic program has made leadership easier. The issue is framed as a package. So it's easier to be courageous. Maybe that's not the way it should be. But it's the reality I think.

A more self-confident, more independent-acting senator was nonetheless expressing the characteristic conflict—one we have described previously—between his yearnings and his caution.

With respect to his Washington activity, caution was prevailing. In anticipation of an eventual committee decision, however, Domenici began to formalize his own version of what the proper three-year package of spending cuts and tax increases would look like—a package designed to achieve a balanced budget by 1984. He caucused with the potentially unruly Republican members of the committee to hear their views and to solicit their help in developing a position that would command their support.

When he circulated his package early in November to committee Republicans, it became known as "the Domenici Plan." In one form or another, this "plan" would be his budgetary benchmark for the remainder of the Ninety-seventh Congress—indeed of his six-year chairmanship. And the success of his leadership would depend on the kind of support he could get for his plan. The basic concept behind the Domenici Plan was that of a package—a mix involving all the elements that might help bring about movement toward a balanced budget.

From early October to early November, Domenici and the other Senate players tried to persuade the administration to accept a budgetary mix closer to the Domenici package—larger tax increases, larger defense cuts, larger entitlement cuts, smaller nondefense cuts, and, overall, greater deficit reduction—with all major impacts scheduled to fall in 1983 and 1984. Gradually the Domenici Plan became the negotiating position of the Senate Republicans. [76] It was the only full-blown alternative in town.

House Republicans, on the other hand, were urging the president to do the best he could to extract the additional savings he desired out of the appropriations bills as they moved along, but to make no other recommendations until his regular budget submission in January. A second budget resolution, with three-year Domenici-like numbers in it, stood no chance of House passage, they said. One of the media's closest budget observers commented, "House Republicans, all of them facing reelection next year, are only too glad to see tax increases and other painful measures fade off their immediate agenda. But, senators, with their six-year terms, tend to take a longer view." [77]

Chairman Domenici kept postponing his committee's markup meeting awaiting a definitive administration response to Senate and House entreaties. On November 6, speaking for a united Senate group, he tried to persuade the president to reconsider and to act. "I don't like to be the guy with the bad news," Domenici said. "We're all behind you. . . . But I've got to talk numbers with you. . . . You're just going to have to have some more revenue to make up the difference, to pay for all these things we want or don't have a prayer of getting rid of." To which the president replied, "Damn it, Pete, I'm just not going to accept this. . . . I don't question your concern with the deficit and all. . . . [But] we can't solve it with more tax and spending." [78] Later that day the president abandoned his promise of a balanced budget by 1984.[79]

On November 10 the president announced that he was postponing all decisions on budgetary matters until his budget message in January. On November 12 Domenici went to the White House and was asked personally by the president "that the second budget resolution not be used for policy changes in the '83 and '84 time frame . . . that he be given the time to submit [his next budget] to the Congress." [80] Senate Majority Leader Baker supported the president in that request. Domenici had been brought to a crucial point of decision.

He had his package ready to propose to his committee. Republican committee caucuses showed a great deal of support for that course. But exactly how much, he could not be sure. Three of his members went immediately to Howard Baker to demand leadership support for it. Privately, committee staffers said that "Domenici seemed like he didn't know which way to go." There were several days of confusion. On November 9 Domenici said, "If the president says absolutely not, we'd rather wait, it's his prerogative. It's certainly not our intention to move inconsistent with the president." [81] But when Reagan asked the leaders not to move, Domenici replied that "I haven't decided and can't decide for the committee. But I will carry that request to them." [82]

A November 10 story in the *Albuquerque Tribune*, headlined "Domenici: All Budget Plans Off," stated, "Senate Republican leaders, bowing to White House pressure, have agreed to shelve a controversial budget balancing plan until January, Budget Chairman Pete Domenici said today." On November 11, he was quoted as saying, "I don't think we could do it if the president of the United States wasn't comfortable with it." [83] Majority Leader Baker, supporting the president, was quoted as believing that Domenici had "lost control of his committee." [84]

On the policy side, Domenici was as impatient as any member of his committee. He believed that governmental silence in the face of worsening economic conditions was harmful. He believed that his committee could "send a signal" to the financial markets that there was a sustainable, long-term plan for bringing about a balanced budget—or, as he came to phrase it—"moving dramatically toward a balanced budget." He believed that timely committee action could effectively establish the next year's budgetary agenda. But on the matter of when and how to proceed, he was characteristically cautious.

The very act of presenting his own plan, or "mark" would be a radical departure from his previous behavior as chairman and from committee tradition.[85] That, by itself, inspired caution. Furthermore, he knew that the chance of ultimate passage of something like the Domenici Plan was virtually nil. He had not persuaded the president or the majority leader. And he was, after all, a team player. He did not yet have unanimity among his committee Republicans. And he could expect no help from the ever more partisan committee Democrats. They were exploiting Republican disagreements, which were being exacerbated at the time by David Stockman's *Atlantic* magazine revelations of Reagan administration budgetary legerdemain and ignorance. Besides, there was very little time left. The drawn-out negotiations had pushed the committee two months behind the statutory schedule for the second budget resolution; and the Christmas adjournment date was but a few weeks away.

Still, Domenici wanted a second budget resolution of some sort, to preserve that part of the budget process. He did not want to embark on so independent and so quixotic a course that the process could not produce any resolution at all. He had learned that, in the House, Chairman James Jones planned to settle for a pro forma second resolution that simply reaffirmed the first resolution. So he knew that he could, if he wished, hold to his October strategy, follow this "puny resolution" of the House, and thereby preserve the budget process—at least in a technical sense. There was, in other words, a face-saving alternative available to him should he decide to throw in, once more, with the president.

ACTS OF INDEPENDENCE:
THE SECOND BUDGET RESOLUTION

This season, however, Chairman Domenici decided not to throw in with the president—not completely anyway. The president had asked him to wait. He decided not to wait. And by not waiting he was, for the first time, staking out a position that was independent from—though not necessarily incompatible with—the president's. Characteristically, he worried about his decision. On the day he presented it, he asked a western colleague, "You don't think I'm doing wrong, do you, in what I'm doing with the president? ... The administration can't pull itself together to do anything. And we've got to do something. ... It doesn't play well in my state because it looks like I'm against the president. But that's all right." For reasons of process and reasons of policy, Domenici decided to proceed.

He believed it was his committee's responsibility to act at that time to preserve the budget process; he believed that timing was crucial in establishing a set of policies that would provide reassurance for the present and guidelines for the future; and he believed he had worked out the correct set of policies for those purposes. No other congressional Republican had either the same responsibility to act, or a comprehensive plan of action. So Domenici presented his plan to the Senate Budget Committee for its consideration "as a basis for marking up the budget resolution" and for its formal vote. (See Appendix, Table A-2.) His strategy was to push it as far as it would go through the normal budget process, retaining the House's pro forma alternative as his fallback option. At this point in time, he was sufficiently concerned about substance so that concern for process was temporarily relegated to a second priority.

"I offer it," he said to the committee, "with no illusions. Only a miracle, I think, would allow this plan ... to be adopted this year by the entire Congress, not speaking of our committee, but by the Congress."

"Speaking of our committee," he said privately,

> I'd like to have a vote on my mark and on Hollings's mark. I don't see any sense in going through the budget function by function if we can't agree either on my proposal or Hollings's proposal. Frankly, I don't think either one can pass. I can't hold my guys together on my proposal; and none of them will vote for Hollings's. . . . If neither proposal passes, which I expect will happen, then we'll see what we can do about saving the process.

He was right. He did not win in committee. The Domenici Plan (or "mark") failed by a 10-12 vote. Party lines held except for two defecting Republicans who followed the president's wishes and not their chairman's. "That was an exciting exercise," he said afterward. "I predicted the way it came out. But there was always a chance."

Two Republicans had deserted him. When he moved, three days later, to "save the process" by reporting out the pro forma second budget resolution, the two defectors were back in camp. But now, two different Republicans broke ranks. And they did so, again, when the pro forma resolution eventually squeaked past the whole Senate. Two other Republicans decided not to vote at all on the second resolution. In this last act, therefore, Domenici did need bipartisan support. Five Democrats joined in passing out the resolution; each one arguing that he did so to help the chairman save the budget process.

Considering these last two committee votes plus the early setback on the first budget resolution, six different committee Republicans (William Armstrong, Charles Grassley, Orrin Hatch, Nancy Kassebaum, Steve Symms, Dan Quayle) had voted against Chairman Domenici on key votes in 1981. Only five (Mark Andrews, Rudy Boschwitz, Slade Gorton, Robert Kasten, John Tower) of the twelve were reliable supporters on key votes. And one of those five (Andrews) was his least-frequent committee supporter overall. (See Table 3-3, Chapter 3.) The chairman was indeed trying to lead a very shaky majority of policy individualists. That fact both magnified his past accomplishments in leading them to agreement and rendered any future success precariously unpredictable.

The events of the second budget resolution showed the chairman to be a gentle, somewhat aloof coalition builder. He did not, for example, talk beforehand to the two defecting Republicans who cost him his victory on the Domenici Plan. One of them commented afterward, "I haven't got him figured out yet. He'll bend. But I don't know what he really wants. He never called me and said he had to have me on that vote. Some of the others tried to convince me I was wrong." A Republican committee member's budget adviser painted a sharper picture of the chairman's style.

> He doesn't consult enough with the guys on his side. He consults mostly with his staff. There's more to being a chairman than proposing a plan. You have to talk to members and see what they want.... Some senators like to do the intellectual work of drafting legislation. Others like to get to know the other members and build support for the legislation.

Domenici, by clear implication, was one of the former. He had met with his committee members, but some of them, at least, had been given no sense of involvement. It may be that the very intensity of his close staff relationships made other people feel left out. And that feeling may have cost him support.

His gentle reaction afterward was stylistically similar to this picture of detachment beforehand. Said one defector,

> The next day we were kidding around and Domenici said to me, "Well, I guess you're going to resign from the committee now." I said, "I'll offer my resignation like Stockman did; you can kick me around for a while; and then you can refuse to accept it like the president did." Slade Gorton spoke up and said, "No, we're going to praise you for the great job you did and accept it." They were letting me know how they felt.

One of the chairman's own staffers described his similar refusal to engage in reprisals against the second defector.

> Right after Senator X turned on him in that committee vote, Domenici allowed him to hold hearings—and on a subject Domenici was interested in. If he had voted against my plan, I'd have taken the hearing away from him. Domenici is not like that.... Sometimes I'm amazed at how uncompetitive he is.

He was determined to succeed. But he did not seem to relish the inside politics of coalition building. He did not talk much about it—publicly or privately. And clearly, he was reluctant to engage in political hardball.

In the aftermath of the defeat, a Domenici staffer described his coalition-building style:

> There's a Lyndon Johnson school that says you go after each vote as hard as you can, that says you can twist an arm and people will forget it so you can go back and pressure them the next time. Domenici is not like that. He does not believe in operating that way. He wants to keep his bridges for the next time. When he takes a position, he has a conceptualization underneath it; and when he tries to persuade others, he has that conceptualization to fall back on. He does not persuade people by giving them something or taking away something. He persuades them because his ideas make sense.

A budget committee chairman does not control tangible rewards. So he is largely constrained to lead by argument. That condition dovetails with Domenici's own longstanding predispositions, as "a policy guy, not a political guy." It also magnifies the importance of the Budget Committee staff. And that dovetails with Domenici's longstanding predisposition to lean very heavily on his staff.

John Ellwood has argued that the relative success of the Senate Budget Committee has rested on the fit between the institutional propensity of senators to be generalists (as opposed to House member's institutional propensity to specialization) and the macro-argumentation forced upon participants in the budget process.[86] Pete Domenici's reluctance to play hardball was, therefore, complementary to his primary reliance on macro-argumentation as the driving force of his leadership. His preference was to lead by economic argument and then to bargain incrementally, at the margins, over the budget numbers needed to attract majority support.

In this second budgetary season, Domenici based his committee leadership, once again, on partisan support. Once again, he nodded in the direction of bipartisanship. "While my goal was to try to achieve a bipartisan agreement on such an approach," he said when introducing his mark in committee, "I am sad to say that I do not believe that kind of coalition can be reached at this time." [87] He kept communication lines open to two or three of the centrist Democrats; but he never negotiated seriously with them.[88] It was as if he honored the bipartisan tradition of the committee, but still felt compelled—by the strong president-Senate linkage, by the policy mandate interpretation of the election, and by its strategic corollary—to abandon that tradition. Looking back, at the end of the year, Domenici still contemplated bipartisan possibilities. "You have to realize that the committee wasn't always as partisan as it was this year." [Fenno: "What made it partisan?"]

> Taxes—the Democrats didn't approve of the tax cuts. Nor the economic assumptions. Then the events of August and September widened the breach and it became polarized. If I had known that the president was going to oppose them, I would not have presented my figures for the second budget resolution. I would have tried for a bipartisan plan.

These comments—together with his reluctance to engage in strenuous coalition building—disclose a general hesitancy about how he wanted to govern.

He was a partisan chairman who was not yet totally comfortable with his partisanship. He never totally abandoned the idea of bipartisanship. "I don't have a theory about it," he continued,

> I don't know yet just what I can do. I haven't really been tested yet. I didn't have to run a bipartisan committee this year. So I don't know whether I could or not. I think I know all the personalities involved. I know who I could get on the Democratic side, but I'm not sure how

far I'd have to go to get them. But I'd start the other way. I'd see how many Republicans I could hold and make that my baseline. I'm not sure how far I would have to go to hold all of them. Maybe I couldn't. But I'd still make the Republicans my baseline. I'd make sure before I jumped to the Democrats that I knew exactly where I stood with all the Republicans.

That, indeed, is what he did on the final, substantively meaningless, committee vote. "I guess I'm confessing that the vaunted success of my chairmanship has operated within a very narrow gauge," he concluded. "I don't know how well I'll do next time."

He was still learning how to lead his committee. Looking at the committee's second budget resolution, it could hardly be said that the budget process was "working." It was only alive. The resolution was totally out of touch with the real world it purported to deal with. Committee members described it mildly as "a blow to the budget process" and strongly as "a sham." It squeaked through on the Senate floor 49-48, without so much as a single mention on the three evening newscasts.[89] Journalists dusted off their judgments of 1980 in language like: "The Year the Budget Process Nearly Crumbled," "The Breakdown of the Budget Process," "the virtual collapse of the Congressional budget process," "Budget process founders."[90] In point of fact, the pro forma action was the death knell for a serious second budget resolution. It was never heard from again. Those who supported the resolution did so, they said, to preserve the budget process.

That was Pete Domenici's view, too. "I think, in exercising my responsibility here," he told the committee, "I have what I perceive to be a responsibility to the process.... I believe the budget process is going to play a very vital role in the next three years. We will get things done that have to be done."[91] A Domenici staffer took the same long view.

> When you think of the high point of the year when we got reconciliation out and made it stick, it's ironic that we have come down to this—nothing, or next to nothing. [But] this is just a skirmish in a long war.

The chairman had kept the process alive. He would fight, according to its rules, another day. The budget process was designed to structure conflict. The conflict continued. And Domenici remained at the center of it.

The events of the second budget resolution had altered the relationship between Domenici and the president, less than the press pronounced, but more than Domenici would admit publicly. When he presented his plan to the committee, the national press interpreted the move as anti-Reagan: "Reagan Defied by GOP," "Republican Senators on Budget Unit Defy Reagan." [92] The New Mexico press escalated the language even further, by personalizing the conflict, such as, "Domenici Leads Budget Rebellion." [93] Domenici was most anxious to see what the local headlines would say, and he was dismayed by their interpretation. He interpreted his action not as antipresident, but as pro-Congress—as the assertion of a congressional responsibility, the following of an institutional imperative.

The media played up the idea of conflict; but the chairman played it down. In the final committee report, he wrote, "Giving the Administration the benefit of Congressional thinking on matters of this import has great merit. My proposal, rather than coopting Administration action, would have been a reenforcing influence." [94] In an interview for a Las Cruces TV station the day after his defeat, he was asked, "The administration says a balanced budget is less important now. What do you say?"

> I happened to have been present [when the president said that]. . . . It was an off-the-cuff remark. It was triggered when the media came in to photograph a White House meeting. Someone asked about the balanced budget in 1984 and he said it was only a goal. It's not so that he's not concerned about deficits. I hope it's not so. He's just saying it may not be exactly in balance. That's what I'm saying, too.

He struck a similar stance on "Face the Nation" in late November.

> I look for the president in January, when he sends us this new budget, to set the fiscal policy of this country on a path that dramatically cuts deficits in '83 and '84. . . . Those who want to see where the government is going . . . can indeed rely upon the fact that we're moving dramatically toward a balanced budget.[95]

He was going out of his way to play up his area of agreement with the president.

Team play was instinctive with Domenici. It had proven its value in the first budget season. And it had proven its necessity in the second season. In that season, Domenici had lost. And the enduring lesson of that loss was this: with the president, he had triumphed, but without the president, he could not prevail. "This has been quite a year, hasn't it?" he said. "The old prez is going to come out looking strong again on this one." Several forces were at work, therefore, to keep Domenici working with the president.

On the other hand, Domenici had taken a position different from that of the president. For the first time, he had moved without the support of either the president or the majority leader. It was a hesitant step; but it was a step that finally put some public distance between himself and Ronald Reagan. He was no longer just the loyal lieutenant. One of his staffers commented:

> We've been wondering all year how long it would be before
> Domenici disagreed with the president. He almost disagreed with
> him on the economic assumptions of the first budget resolution. It
> appears that Stockman agreed with that position all the time, but he
> didn't tell us. The question is: How long are you going to stay down
> in the engine room while the ship is sinking?

At the very least, his action put him in a position of independence from
which, as a proven Republican team player, he could put pressure on the
president. At the most it could be the first in a sequence of moves that
led to greater distance between them. His decision to "move ahead"
with his own plan was a significant step in combining independence
and influence in the governing process.

At year's end, he was content with his personal accomplishments.

> I think I've grown in the job. I'm getting a lot of my ideas into policy
> now instead of sputtering the way I used to. I like what I'm doing and
> I feel fully utilized. I have the resources and I know how to use them.
> It's much better than it used to be.

And journalists' judgments—across the political spectrum—provided
supportive testimony. Late in 1981, in a column headlined "Domenici
Provides Solid Leadership," David Broder wrote that "If there is an
award for exemplary consistency in the face of massive confusion, the
1981 winner would have to be Senator Pete Domenici of New Mexico." [96] Early in 1982, James Kilpatrick wrote that "When he addresses
himself to the budget, it's like advice from E. F. Hutton. When Domenici
speaks, everybody listens." [97] Clearly, he had attained a new level of
accomplishment in the business of governing.

But in terms of the context in which he would be governing, he was
less content. Near the end of 1981 Domenici and the Senate leadership
team prepared for their meeting with the president to give him their
views on his new budget—on its substance and on its political feasibility. On the matter of feasibility, Domenici believed that the Republican
senators had a valuable sense of what was doable in Congress and had
earned the right to be heard on the subject. "Who does he think is
getting these things for him up here?" he asked. "If it weren't for Baker,
Dole, Hatfield, and Domenici, he wouldn't have gotten anything
through Congress." But he was not optimistic that the president would
listen.

On the substance of the matter, he was even more pessimistic. "I
don't think he believes those deficit figures yet," he said, "I'm so
depressed, I may just stay home." And, looking ahead to the president's
new budget, he commented, "I don't know how well I'll do next time. If
the president goes with these huge deficits, it may be impossible to sell
them to anyone in Congress." He was ending 1981 on a decidedly

downbeat note. The night before his meeting with Reagan, his top aide captured the mood. "Good luck tomorrow, boss." he said. "Really good luck. But what you need most is the intervention of divine providence."

Pete Domenici's first two budgetary seasons had sharpened the three central problems of the chairmanship: the degree of dependence and independence in relations with the president, the degree of partisanship and bipartisanship in relation to the committee, and the degree of policy assertion and process protection in relations with the institution as a whole. Domenici's actions in his first year demonstrated a sense of loyalty together with movement toward independence in relations with the president, a reliance on partisanship together with a readiness to pursue bipartisanship in relations with the committee, and an emphasis on policy goals coupled with a bottom-line determination to protect the budget process in his relations with senators as a whole.

Each of these relationships demonstrated, too, existing constraints on leadership—especially the reliance on others. In his second budget season the limits of the chairmanship became even more apparent. For it had been a time of defeat. It was also a time of transition from a posture of "follow the president" to a posture of independent legislative leadership. It showed that, even in adversity, a chairman could set goals or targets, could rally support, and could accumulate influence. The third season would be marked by the completion of the transition and by the reversal of the defeat. It would be marked, too, by a more impressive achievement of his governing-related goals.

NOTES

1. *Albuquerque Tribune*, December 10, 1980.
2. It should be noted that this study takes place before passage of the Gramm-Rudman-Hollings legislation and the procedures and targets it prescribed. A brief discussion of Domenici's relation to that legislation will be found in Chapter 6. The generalizations in this book about the process, the Budget Committee, and the chairmanship would not have to be revised much even after that change. Support for that assumption can be found in: Alan Murray, "The Budget Process Isn't the Problem," *Wall Street Journal*, May 23, 1988; David Wessel, "Gramm-Rudman Fails to Shrink Deficit Much, Causing Pressure to Use Gimmicks to Meet Targets," *Wall Street Journal*, December 29, 1988; John Yang, "Ever-Growing Deficits Establish the Failure Of Gramm-Rudman," *Wall Street Journal*, October 3, 1989; and Jackie Calmes, "Gramm-Rudman-Hollings: Has Its Time Passed?" *Congressional Quarterly Weekly*

Report, October 14, 1989.

3. Jack Walker, "Setting the Agenda in the United States Senate," *British Journal of Political Science* 7 (October 1977): 423-445.
4. Allen Schick, *Congress and Money* (Washington, D.C.: The Urban Institute, 1980), 7-8.
5. Ibid., 353.
6. Ibid., 128.
7. "The only reason I ran last time was because of this budget process, because I had been given a role in it and I wanted to make it work." Breakfast talk to Maine Bankers Association, U.S. Capitol, March 1979.
8. Paul Wieck, "Budget Cut Reviews Will Be Test of Domenici's Clout," *Albuquerque Journal*, March 3, 1981.
9. John Ellwood, "House-Senate Relations and the Budget Process," unpublished, 3.
10. Senate Budget Committee, "Transcript of Proceedings, Markup Session on First Budget Resolution for Fiscal Year 1983," April 29, 1982, 188.
11. William Safire, "The Great Follower," *New York Times*, March 17, 1980.
12. "Calling a Charade a Charade," *Wall Street Journal*, May 28, 1980.
13. Timothy Clark, "A Forum for Debate," *National Journal*, June 6, 1980.
14. In addition to the above, see *Congressional Quarterly Weekly Report*, June 7, 1980; *Newsweek*, March 31, 1980 and June 23, 1980; and *Congressional Record*, June 4, 1980, E2739, and June 5, 1980, E2757.
15. Richard Cohen, "Promise Unfulfilled," *National Journal*, September 9, 1980.
16. An excellent general discussion of electoral mandates is Kay L. Schlozman and Sidney Verba, "Sending Them a Message—Getting a Reply: Presidential Elections and Democratic Responsibility," in Kay L. Schlozman (editor), *The Election as a Democratic Institution* (Winchester, Mass.: Allen and Unwin, 1987), 3-25.
17. *Washington Post*, March 11, 1981.
18. Curtis Wilkie, "President Attacks O'Neill, Democrats," *Boston Globe*, June 17, 1981.
19. Richard Cohen, "Senate Republicans Are Riding High Even if They Don't Take Control," *National Journal*, September 20, 1980.
20. Richard Cohen, "The Senator from Tennessee May Hold the Key to Reagan's Economic Plans," *National Journal*, April 4, 1981.
21. Richard Cohen, "For the Congressional Budget Process, 1981 Could Be the Make or Break Year," *National Journal*, January 10, 1981.
22. Gail Gregg, "Beleaguered Budget Process Faces New Pressures in 1981," *Congressional Quarterly Weekly Report*, January 10, 1981.
23. Richard Cohen, "For the Congressional Budget."
24. Richard Cohen, "The Senator from Tennessee."
25. Gail Gregg, "Beleaguered Budget."
26. Richard Cohen, "For the Congressional Budget."
27. Gail Gregg, "Beleaguered Budget."
28. For an early jurisdictional joust, in private, see David Stockman, *The Triumph of Politics* (New York: Harper and Row, 1986), 165-166. The early revelation of Stockman's doubts about Reagan administration policy came in William Greider, "The Education of David Stockman," *Atlantic*, December 1986.
29. *Albuquerque Journal*, January 11, 1981.
30. *Albuquerque Journal*, February 12, 1981.
31. *Albuquerque Tribune*, January 11, 1981.

32. *Albuquerque Journal,* January 4, 1981.
33. *Albuquerque Journal,* February 16, 1981.
34. Two excellent discussions and commentaries—one early and one recent—are Allen Schick, *Reconciliation and the Congressional Budget Process* (Washington, D.C.: The American Enterprise Institute for Public Policy Research, 1981); and John B. Gilmour, *Reconcilable Differences?* (Berkeley: University of California Press, 1990). See also Stockman, *Triumph of Politics,* 159-160.
35. Ellwood, "House-Senate Relations," 19-20.
36. Schick, *Reconciliation,* 36-37.
37. Senate Budget Committee, "Transcript of Proceedings on First Concurrent Budget Resolution for Fiscal Year 1982," April 8, 1981, 219.
38. David Broder, "Hill, Reagan Aides Eye Painful Cuts," *Washington Post,* January 2, 1981. See also Helen Dewar, "Senate Budget Panel Balks at Social Security Benefit Cuts," *Washington Post,* March 19, 1981.
39. Helen Dewar, "Reagan Rips 'Phony' Hill Budget Data," *Washington Post,* March 18, 1981.
40. Stockman, *Triumph of Politics,* 168.
41. Ibid., 162-163.
42. Hedrick Smith, *The Power Game* (New York: Random House, 1988), 469.
43. Ibid., 31.
44. Steven Weisman, "Reaganomics and the President's Men," *New York Times Magazine,* October 24, 1982; and Jonathan Rauch, "Pete Domenici Stands at Center of Storm as Budget Deficit Crisis Comes to Head," *National Journal,* February 1, 1986.
45. Smith, *Power Game,* 469.
46. Helen Dewar, "Senate Budget Panel Rejection Called 'Bump' to Reagan Drive," *Washington Post,* April 11, 1981; *Albuquerque Journal,* April 11, 1981; and Helen Dewar, "Deficit Shoe Is Now on the Republicans' Foot," *Washington Post,* April 15, 1981.
47. Richard Beer, "Republicans Still Acting Like Minority: Domenici," *Albuquerque Journal,* April 15, 1981.
48. *Albuquerque Tribune,* April 10, 1981.
49. *Albuquerque Tribune,* April 10, 1981.
50. *Wall Street Journal,* April 20, 1981.
51. Rowland Evans and Robert Novak, "Averting Republican Retreat," *Washington Post,* April 22, 1981; and *New York Times,* April 11, 1981.
52. John Gilmour depicts this change nicely in terms of the sharp decline in the success of Democratic amendments inside the committee. Gilmour, *Reconcilable Differences?,* 135.
53. Stockman, *Triumph of Politics,* 225. See also Robert Fulton, "Federal Budget Making in 1981," *New England Journal of Human Services* (Fall 1981): 28-29; Evans and Novak, "Business as Usual," *Boston Globe,* July 15, 1981; Helen Dewar, "Rebuffing Reagan, Senate GOP Insists on Budget Parley," *Washington Post,* July 11, 1981; Thomas Edsall, "GOP Leaders Rebuff Reagan on House Version of Budget," *Baltimore Sun,* July 11, 1981; and Roberta Hornig, "Senate Republicans Ignore Reagan Plea on Budget Strategy," *Washington Star,* July 11, 1981.
54. A sampling: Meg Greenfield, "The Democrats' Vanishing Act," *Washington Post,* July 8, 1981; David Nyhan, "The Can-do President," *Boston Globe,* August 26, 1981; Thomas Edsall, "Reagan Wins May Be Far Reaching," *Washington Post,* August 13, 1981; David Rogers, "A Lesson in Civics,

Reagan's March Through Congress," *Boston Globe,* August 14, 1981; Martin Schram, "Reagan the Tax Lobbyist: An Artist at Work," *Washington Post,* August 13, 1981; David Broder, "Don't Mess with Reagan," *Boston Globe,* August 9, 1981; Mary McGrory, "Going West with an Easy Heart," *Boston Globe,* August 7, 1981; Steven Weisman, "Reagan's Style: Focusing on 'The Big Picture,'" *New York Times,* August 7, 1981; and Evans and Novak, "The Revolution Rolls On," *Washington Post,* June 6, 1981.

55. Dale Tate, "Reconciliation's Long-Term Consequences in Question as Reagan Signs Massive Bill," *Congressional Quarterly Weekly Report,* August 15, 1981, 1463.

56. *Washington Post,* July 7, 1981.

57. *Congressional Record,* April 2, 1981, S3327.

58. Martin Tolchin, "Leader in Record Spending Cut," *New York Times,* March 27, 1981. See also Eileen Shanahan, "The Fat Gets Hard to Find," *Washington Star,* April 20, 1981.

59. Helen Dewar, "With Budget, Immigrant's Son Becomes Senate Star," *Washington Post,* September 9, 1981.

60. See note 38.

61. *Washington Post,* October 26, 1981; *Washington Post,* September 20, 1981; *New York Times,* October 15, 1981; and *Washington Post,* October 26, 1981.

62. Helen Dewar, "On New Menu for Congress, Spending Is Still the Main Course," *Washington Post,* September 9, 1981. For more on the change in mood, see also David Broder, "On Budget, Washington Witnessing a Return of Politics as Usual," *Washington Post,* September 25, 1981; Fred Barnes, "On Eve of Speech, Reagan's Worst Problem Is GOP Division on Economy," *Baltimore Sun,* September 24, 1981; Haynes Johnson, "After Reagan's Honeymoon Begin the Days of Polarization," *Washington Post,* October 4, 1981; "Reagan's Confidence Gap," *Newsweek,* September 21, 1981; and Robert Kaiser, "A Nervous Time for Reagan Backers," *Washington Post,* November 11, 1981.

63. Martin Tolchin, "Honeymoon Nears End for Reagan and Congress," *New York Times,* October 15, 1981.

64. Lance LeLoup, *The Fiscal Congress* (Westport, Conn.: Greenwood Press, 1980), 86-88.

65. *Washington Post,* November 6, 1981, October 19, 1981, November 7, 1981; and *Newsweek,* November 16, 1981.

66. John Berry, "Reaganomics or Credibility Gap," *Washington Post,* September 20, 1981.

67. Gilbert Lewthwaite, "Domenici Wants $30 Billion Cut from Pentagon," *Baltimore Sun,* September 14, 1981. See also Thomas W. Lippman, "Regan, Domenici Urge Curtailing of Entitlements," *Washington Post,* November 30, 1981.

68. Stockman, *Triumph of Politics,* 306.

69. Martin Tolchin, "Domenici Finds He's Man in Middle," *New York Times,* September 23, 1981; *Albuquerque Journal,* September 23, 1981; and Martin Schram, "If Reagan Clings to Military Buildup, GOP's Dreams Could Come Unglued," *Washington Post,* September 20, 1981.

70. Stockman, *Triumph of Politics,* 312-17.

71. The story from inside the administration is told in ibid., 304-326.

72. *Congressional Quarterly Weekly Report,* September 26, 1981. On Reagan "offensive," see Martin Schram, "Reagan 'Fall Offensive': Casualties, Not Vic-

tories," *Washington Post,* October 26, 1981; and Robert Kaiser, "Probably Good Politics, But Budget Problems Remain Unsolved," *Washington Post,* November 24, 1981.

73. Helen Dewar, "Senate Republicans Weigh Heavier Defense Cuts, Higher Taxes," *Washington Post,* October 8, 1981.
74. Martin Tolchin, "Senate Republicans in Rift with Reagan over Spending Cuts," *New York Times,* October 8, 1981.
75. *Washington Post Weekly Edition,* October 18, 1981.
76. *Washington Post,* October 27, November 4, November 10, November 11, 1981; *Baltimore Sun,* November 10, 1981; and *Congressional Record,* December 8, 1981, 14745.
77. Helen Dewar, "GOP Is Balking at Delay on Reagan Budget Cuts," *Washington Post,* November 12, 1981.
78. Stockman, *Triumph of Politics,* 350-351.
79. *Washington Post,* November 7, 1981.
80. Senate Budget Committee, "Transcript of Proceedings, Markup Session on Second Budget Resolution for Fiscal Year 1982," November 13, 1981, 84.
81. Jerelyn Eddings, "GOP Makes Pitch for Support," *Las Cruces Sun-News,* November 10, 1981.
82. United Press International, "Reagan Asks Senators to End Balanced Budget Push," *Albuquerque Tribune,* November 12, 1981.
83. Associated Press, "New Tax Boosts; Benefit Cuts Get Two-Month Reprieve," *El Paso Times,* November 11, 1981.
84. Robert Timberg, "GOP Panelists Seek Balanced Budget," *Baltimore Sun,* November 13, 1981.
85. Schick, *Congress and Money,* 258-264.
86. Ellwood, "House-Senate Relations," 12.
87. Senate Budget Committee, "Transcript of Proceedings," November 13, 1981, 153.
88. Ibid., November 13, 1981, 199; and November 16, 1981, 282.
89. American Enterprise Institute, *News Digest,* December 10, 1981, 9-10.
90. *New York Times,* December 27, 1981; *Wall Street Journal,* November 24, 1981; *Newsweek,* December 7, 1981; and *New York Times,* January 14, 1981.
91. Senate Budget Committee, "Transcript of Proceedings," November 19, 1981, 386.
92. *Washington Post,* November 13, 1981; and *New York Times,* November 13, 1981.
93. *Albuquerque Journal,* November 13, 1981.
94. Senate Budget Committee, "Report on the Second Concurrent Resolution on the Budget, Fiscal Year 1982," 1981, 13.
95. Transcript, "Face the Nation," November 23, 1981, 6.
96. *El Paso Times,* December 21, 1981.
97. *New Mexican,* March 7, 1982.

The Chairman as Leader

CONTEXT: JANUARY—AUGUST 1982

In January 1982 Pete Domenici began a new "season" as chairman of the Senate Budget Committee. By our reckoning it was his third. In his first season, under the influence of a perceived electoral mandate, he loyally supported a Republican president and his budget policies. And he shared in a legislative triumph. In his second season, influenced by a spent mandate and by economic warnings, he moved to stake out a position of modest independence from the president. This time, however, his cautious initiative failed. In the long-term perspective, this second budget season, from September to December 1981, would prove to be a watershed time for him. As he put it years later, "The big difference was between the first budget and all the rest." The difference was that "all the rest" would be far more difficult and far less triumphal. For the rest of his years as chairman, Pete Domenici found himself in the uncomfortable position of trying to persuade President Reagan to do things the president was fundamentally opposed to doing.

The headlines of a *Wall Street Journal* profile captured the chairman's problem as his third season began: "Budget Chairman: Sen. Domenici, Earnest and Frugal, Poses Test for Reagan Fiscal Plan; Cutting Deficit is Top Goal of Senate Budget Chief; Will He Fight the President?" [1] By passing a pro forma second budget resolution in December, Congress had acceded to the president's request for time to rework his budget. The legislators had decided to wait. But the chairman had used the second season to experiment with policy leadership by planting a policy standard—the so-called Domenici Plan. He awaited the president's 1982 budget submission, therefore, in a more aggressive posture. "I'm not going to be hiding behind a tree," he said in January. "If I don't like it and I think it's wrong, I'll say so."[2]

Domenici's second budget season can be considered "transitional" because it moved him to assert a measure of independence. As he did so, a related change took place. He became fully committed to his chairmanship. Shortly before the transitional season began, a top staffer commented that,

> Every senator wants to make his mark, wants to be remembered for something he did. Pete is not likely to make his mark by engineering budget cuts. I think—and this goes back to his days on the Albuquerque City Council—he has always had a desire to make his mark by bringing economic development to New Mexico.

Throughout the transition season, staffers still talked of his less-than-total commitment to his new job, and the need to pump him up to take charge. "Pete says he doesn't want to take national leadership on the budget, but [we] say, 'Oh, yes you do.'" Or, "Pete says, 'I'm hiding under my desk.' When he says that [we] say to him, 'A leader is a person who stands in the scorching sun so other people can stand in his shadow.'"

By March 1982, however, a staffer could say,

> Domenici is acting a lot more statesmanlike now. . . . Last year he said he was staying on the Environment and Public Works Committee so, if [Chairman Robert] Stafford retired, he could move over to that committee as chairman. He thought the Budget Committee might become too hot for him politically. I heard him say that. But he doesn't talk like that now.

A chairmanship, it seems, takes some getting used to, a time of adjustment, of trying the job on for size. A successful chairmanship requires a conscious commitment to making one's mark in the job. Between July 1981 and March 1982, Pete Domenici came to that commitment, and it fixed the course of his career for the next five years.

Keeping in mind the lesson of the second season—that he could not pass a budget resolution without the acquiescence of the president—Domenici would have to work out a new and different relationship with Ronald Reagan in the new season. And he would have to do so within a new configuration of constraints. Externally, the economy continued to worsen—interest rates stayed high and unemployment grew. Projected deficits—the bottom line of the Domenici Plan—continued to soar. Political conditions worsened, too, with the onset of the election year, which promised to change the atmosphere of budget making from construction to recrimination—a sea change from a politics of taking credit to a politics of avoiding blame.

Internally, the lines of political conflict were not immediately clear. But the effect of these external conditions seemed to augur less unity for the Republicans and more unity for the Democrats. With the electoral mandate interpretation spent, congressional Republicans were having increasing difficulty retaining their extraordinary unity of the first season. And the possibility was that electoral pressures might cause them to scatter further in a burst of every-man-for-himself policy activity. This possibility was strengthened by the president's rapidly falling popularity—to a new low for one-year presidents.[3]

The Democrats, on the other hand, had found sufficient unity—around the theme of "fairness" in terms of discretionary nondefense spending—to reinvigorate their majority in the House. That unity, in turn, was bringing the Democratic House back to parity with the Republican Senate in the budgetary equation, and turning Speaker Tip O'Neill from a bystander into a player in budget politics. The sum of these changes left open the possibilities for increased partisanship and the possibilities for renewed bipartisanship. A lot would depend, of course, on the disposition of the president and the provisions of his budget.

EARLY SEQUENCES: INSTITUTIONAL AND PARTISAN

Pete Domenici began the third season hoping that the new budget would move in the direction of his own plan, a mix that would bring budget deficits down so that they approached a balance two or three years down the road. Meeting with the president in January, he and the other Senate Republican leaders stressed the tax element of the mix and the need to increase taxes to help bring about deficit reduction.[4] Sensing the president's reluctance to do that, Domenici began to contemplate the need for bipartisanship. Unless the president could start deficits "moving dramatically downward" or could "muster popular support" for ever-larger deficits, he said later in January, "then a truly bipartisan approach to the first budget resolution, even if it differs substantially from the president's plan, is absolutely imperative."[5] Prospects were not bright. A leading journalist said in February, "The obstacles to a serious congressional initiative on the budget are formidable and the odds against its success are high."[6]

When the president's budget was presented to Congress in early February, it projected a $92 billion deficit, declining to $72 billion two years later. It also proposed a defense spending increase of $33 billion and a discretionary nondefense spending reduction of approximately the same amount. And it called for $12.4 billion in various revenue increases. (See Tables 3-1 and 3-2.) The long-awaited budget mix attracted no legislative support. Indeed, it was the first of five consecutive presidential budgets that could not pass Congress. But President Reagan dug in behind it. "The budget we have proposed is a line drawn in the dirt," he said. "We have faith in our program and we are sticking with it. To the paid political complainers, let me say as politely as I can, 'Put up or shut up.' " [7] For Pete Domenici and the other Republicans who would have to steer a budget through Congress, the president's initial presentation was both a disappointment and a challenge.

When the president proposes his budget, there typically follows a period of posturing and maneuvering before the Budget committees swing into serious action. Legislature and administration try to measure their differences and assess the possibilities for agreement. For Chairman Domenici, the testing time entailed a series of assessments involving the likelihood of agreements and disagreements with the president and, simultaneously, the possibilities of bipartisanship and partisanship within his committee. After hearing the president's proposal, Domenici entered into a period of stop-and-go action. Partly the pattern was dictated by the action of others; partly, it resulted from his own internal conflict between impulsiveness and caution. In time, the strong desire to act overcame the desire to go slow. But his immediate reaction was two weeks of silence.

Two Domenici staffers described his dilemma.

> A friend of mine on the House Budget Committee asked me, "When is Domenici going to get out front with the Domenici Plan?" I told him that the plan was put forth in a set of circumstances where the president presented no program—trying to create the basis for a second budget resolution. But now we have a new situation where the president has a program. Domenici is loyal. If only the president would stay neutral . . . and let us work it out. But he isn't neutral now; and he didn't stay neutral on the second budget resolution. He has sent down a program that is unacceptable to Congress. But we can't do anything without his support or neutrality. [So] Domenici is keeping a low profile.
>
> The next few weeks are a crucial period of decision for Domenici. Last year at this time, we had a resolution ready and we had [Fritz] Hollings locked in. We had done all the preliminary work between the election and January. And we had made our contribution to it. This year, the president announced his program; but Domenici did not have a part in producing that program. The things he suggested were not accepted. When the budget came down, everybody went into shock. . . . Domenici is just waiting.

Privately, the chairman went to New York to talk with some of Wall Street's top economists. He quietly updated his plan and waited for the propitious moment to present his views.

TABLE 3-1 1982 Budget Resolution for Fiscal Years 1983, 1984, 1985
(in billions of dollars)

	President	Domenici (May 3)	Domenici (May 5)	Budget Committee (May 6)	Senate passed
		Fiscal 1983			
Defense	263.0 (+13%)	238.6 (+5%)	249.8 (+10%)	251.7	251.7
Social Security	—	freeze	freeze	-6.0	—
Other pension program COLA/Pay	—	freeze	freeze	freeze	—
Total revenues	666.1	663.0	676.0	667.0	668.4
Total outlays	757.6	752.0	782.1	773.1	784.3
Deficit	91.5	89.0	106.1	106.1	115.9
		Fiscal 1984			
Defense	291.2 (+3%)	267.0 (+5%)	273.8 (+3%)	278.3	278.3
Social Security	—	—	—	-17.0	—
Total revenues	723.0	751.0	749.0	739.0	741.4
Total outlays	805.9	787.5	818.0	808.0	833.3
Deficit	82.9	36.5	69.0	69.0	91.9
		Fiscal 1985			
Defense	338.4 (+9%)	298.8 (+5%)	309.9 (+6%)	316.5	316.5
Social Security	—	—	—	-17.0	—
Total revenues	796.6	835.0	832.0	822.0	825.5
Total outlays	868.5	828.8	871.5	861.5	890.7
Deficit	71.9	6.2 [a]	39.5	39.5	65.2

Sources: For column one, *Congressional Quarterly Weekly Report*, February 13, 1982; for column two, chairman's mark, May 3; for column three, chairman's mark, May 5; for column four, Senate Budget Committee Report; for column five, Conference Report.
[a] Surplus

TABLE 3-2 1982 Revenue Proposals: Fiscal 1983 Budget Resolution
(percent)

	President	Domenici (May 3)	Domenici (May 5)	Budget Committee (May 6)	Senate passed
		Fiscal 1983			
Increase in revenues	+12.0	+18.0	+30.0	+20.0	+23.4
		Fiscal 1984			
Increase in revenues	+18.3	+49.0	+45.0	+35.0	+39.4
		Fiscal 1985			
Increase in revenues	+18.5	+55.0	+50.0	+40.0	+45.5

Sources: For columns one and two, chairman's mark, May 3; for column three, chairman's mark, May 5; for column four, Senate Budget Committee Report; for column five, Conference Report.

The top-ranking committee Democrat, however, decided not to wait. Fritz Hollings seized the occasion to kick off his 1984 presidential campaign and to establish what was to be its theme. He attacked the president's program, "put up" an alternative plan of his own, and asked for bipartisan support for it. It featured freezes on spending and reversals of the 1981 three-year tax cut.[8] By thus taking the lead, Hollings was of enormous help to the Republicans in general and to Domenici in particular. He allowed the Republicans to profess interest in his plan, thereby communicating their dissatisfaction with the president's budget in an oblique way and softening up the president for dialogue.

For Domenici, Hollings—by going first with his proposal—took some of the sting out of Domenici's later alternative, making it appear mild by comparison. One staffer put it this way. "Let him get out front. It will make our job much easier. The president has a plan; Hollings has a plan. We'll be in the middle.... To have Hollings, a super hawk, attacking the defense budget is helpful." Another aide put the Hollings effect differently. "Hollings came out of the backfield first and went through the line. Domenici followed him and made a lot more yardage than he could have made otherwise." A third staffer combined both points. "Domenici swam in Hollings's wake. Hollings performed a great service to Domenici by going first. It made Domenici seem moderate."

The episode highlights the crucial importance of *sequence* in explaining policy outcomes. Alongside the familiar language of left-right-middle to describe policy making, political scientists also need the less familiar language of first-second-third. Who goes first can be as important as who stands where. Sequencing (policy making in time) as well as positioning (policy making in space) needs to be analyzed to understand political phenomena. In both respects, Hollings helped Domenici; and Domenici happily helped Hollings to center stage.

Domenici's strategic decision was not whether he would state his position on the president's budget, but when and how strongly. He decided to use a February speech to a major business group, the Conference Board, as the forum. On the matter of timing, he said, "If I weren't the chairman, I wouldn't have had the opportunity to give that speech in the first place. But if I had not been chairman, I would have given the same speech three weeks earlier. I wouldn't have waited three weeks." In terms of its forcefulness, the speech was to be Pete Domenici's second, and most important, declaration of independence from the president.

He did not want to rupture relations with the president. He did not see himself as opposed to the president. He saw himself, rather, as exercising influence in a way that would in the long run help the president or, as his staffers put it, "pull Reagan's chestnuts out of the fire" and "get Reagan's ass out of the ditch." He felt compelled, however, to state certain political and economic realities as he saw them. A few days before his speech, he told the president in a White House meeting: "I hate to be the bearer of bad tidings, but I don't think it's going to work with these deficits." [9] He saw himself—and his committee—as gatekeepers, telling the president what would and would not "go" in Congress.

Domenici staffers described the chairman-president relationship in the manner of a fisherman measuring a fish—hands outstretched, with palms facing inward. They wanted to maintain some "distance" between the two, but they measured that distance more carefully than any fisherman—just so much and no more. The chairman knew he would need the cooperation of the president at some point in the budget process. And he intended to keep that course open.

Domenici's Conference Board speech was calibrated in that spirit. He stressed his agreement with the president's long-term economic values, goals, and strategy. But he stated flatly that "The president's budget will not pass Congress in its present form. It fails to do enough to cut spending and accepts almost benignly what are malignant deficits." Nor was the budget sufficiently comprehensive. Again, the Domenici alternative called for a five-part package: greater defense cuts, greater entitlement cuts, smaller nondefense discretionary cuts, higher revenue increases, and bigger deficit reductions than the president asked for. Some of the proposed cuts came in the form of spending freezes, like Hollings's; but unlike Hollings's, Domenici's tax increases came from loophole closings rather than cutbacks in the three-year program of income tax cuts.

In a change of emphasis, Domenici stressed as the first in a list of budget "weaknesses" the fact that "The 1983 budget, like the 1982 budget, fails to respond to the perception that it is inequitable." His growing sensitivity to the issue of "fairness" had been keeping pace with Democratic criticism, and had now become a basic part of his discontent with the presidential policy mix. "I think," he said in January, "we're getting very close to a perception—and perhaps a reality—that it's not fair." [10]

This concern for fairness provided him with an opening to the Democrats. As he reoffered his plan, Domenici was, again, thinking bipartisanship. Or, at least he was talking and offering bipartisanship. "I believe that the Senate can develop a bipartisan consensus and I intend to work toward that, starting with Senator Hollings and others on my committee." The concluding remarks of his speech praised the president as "more on target on what needs to be done to the federal budget and the economy than any president in this century." "I hope I can persuade him," he said, "to eventually support a plan not dissimilar to what I have outlined today...." [11]

The Conference Board speech drew a good deal of media attention and landed Domenici on "Meet the Press" two weeks later. But it did not move the president. A week after the speech, Reagan journeyed to Domenici's backyard in Albuquerque—without Domenici—and exclaimed, "You've been hearing a lot about so-called alternatives. Many of these are not alternatives at all, but political documents designed for saving certain legislators' political hides rather than saving the economy." [12] When Senate Majority Leader Howard Baker remonstrated with him, the president said he did not mean Republicans. Media interpreters said, as one column expressed it, that "Domenici has been slapped down by the president." [13]

Domenici's response was to do nothing to alter the existing "distance" between himself and the president. So, on "Meet the Press," he predicted compromise and supported his own budget mix in a manner that emphasized—to the president's own taste—spending cuts more than tax increases. "I believe the most important thing ... is to forget about taxes for a minute . . . and build a package of restraint that we say we will do. If that's no better than the president, then forget it. If it's significantly better than the president, then I think you begin to have some negotiating room."[14] The president phoned Domenici afterward to congratulate him for his words and thank him for his conciliatory tack.

A couple of days after the program, Domenici said, "I've been behaving myself. . . . It was pretty pro-Reagan, didn't you think? They can't get mad at me for what I said, can they. . . ? We can't do it without taxes, but first we've got to convince him we've got a little restraint in our blood." "Domenici is on a wholly new plane now," commented a staffer. The relationship between president and chairman had re-stabilized at a new level of independence and mutual regard.

That did not mean, however, that either one was yielding much ground. Domenici was "flexible on the numbers" but was concerned about keeping "balance among the parts, so that it will be perceived as fair." "He thinks that will make it easier for the president," said a staffer. "It will be a more saleable package when 'old Dutch' decides he's going to have to run with it." Domenici worked as part of the Senate's "fiscal five" (Baker, Domenici, Dole, Hatfield, Laxalt) to construct "a package of constraint" within a comprehensive leadership plan to propose to the president. Reagan's attitude was that they could formulate an alternative if they wished; but he would indicate no policy "give" or willingness to compromise in advance.[15] For want of a more positive signal, the efforts of the fiscal five stalled in mid-March.[16]

In late March, I asked Domenici, "Have you ever persuaded Ronald Reagan of anything?" "No." "Do you know how to persuade him?" "No. Reagan doesn't believe in numbers anymore. It's futile. It's a futile exercise." The words "stalemate," "impasse," and "dead center" began to acquire a vogue among media scorekeepers.[17] Chairman Domenici decided that the budget process had been delayed long enough, and he wanted to meet his own responsibilities through Budget Committee action. He shifted his attention to his committee, caucusing with the Republicans and talking individually with centrist Democrats (Hollings, Lawton Chiles, Bennett Johnston, James Exon) to see what might be worked out on that front. (See Table 3-3.)

As Domenici followed his line of responsibility inward to his committee, leaders with a broader responsibility than his were turning toward the House Democrats to see what they might accept and under what conditions they would join a bipartisan budget-making effort. Speaker O'Neill had greeted the Reagan budget with, "It's going to be a more interesting year this year. We're going to have a lot of victories this year."[18] White House chief of staff James Baker opened talks with House budget leaders, with the knowledge, acquiescence, and consultation of Senate leader Howard Baker. For a couple of weeks in late March, Domenici was left out in the cold. He wanted to start committee markup, but he was asked by Howard Baker not to do so until negotiations with the House developed. "Baker is carrying the ball and the burden," said a staffer. "He should. These things cut across everyone's turf. Domenici has done all he can."

But Domenici, for all his devotion to Baker—who was again allied with Domenici, as he had not been in the second season—was not so content. He was in a "let's roll" mood and was impatient and frustrated at being held back. He was frustrated in terms of his own participation.

> When I gave my [Conference Board] speech, things went pretty well for a while. It was liberating for me. I got my two bits in. At least people started talking about the deficits and they started coming around to our position. Now it's getting frustrating again. There's no dialogue and no mechanism for the kind of dialogue we ought to be having. I'm out of it. Nobody's talking to me. [Howard] Baker wants to delay the budget resolution and let it all pan out.

He was impatient in terms of his committee's responsibility.

> We're completely screwed up the way things are going around here. I'm mad. I think we'll have a disaster. We might not have a budget. The leaders of a lot of the committees are starting to come in with their own plans for the budget—taking positions on this cut or that COLA [cost-of-living adjustment]. If the committees get out ahead of the budget process, if they get out front, we'll never produce a budget resolution. . . . The leader is afraid that if we move on the budget, the House Democrats will screw us. I think he's wrong. . . . We could have a budget resolution by next Friday. I probably won't do it; but I think we should. We wouldn't have to bring it to the floor. We could just let it simmer. At least it might start a dialogue. We could let the Budget Committee take the brunt of the criticism over the Easter recess. That might help Baker if things started to move.

Other people—the administration, the House, other committees, party leaders—seemed now to be dictating his course for him. The chairman did not like the sharpened sense of constraint.

So, four days later, Domenici took action. He convened the committee for three days of markup sessions before the Easter recess. "We're sending a signal," he told the media, "that we've got to move." [19] And he told the committee, "it is absolutely urgent that we move and move with dispatch. . . . I do not think the economy is going to get any better until those in the marketplace have a clear idea that we intend to dramatically reduce the out-year deficits. . . ." [20] At this point, the president's $92 billion deficit projection for fiscal 1983 had already ballooned to \$124 billion.[21] Domenici had no intention of framing a budget in those sessions. In fact, he had no idea as to what would happen if he tried. He believed that any resolution "would have to be" bipartisan and that "it's better if it is." But he could not count twelve votes for any solution.

The spirit of these early markups was strongly bipartisan—especially on the part of ranking Democrat Fritz Hollings.[22] And the one concrete decision taken was a warrant of that bipartisanship, as the committee, by 16-1, agreed to use the economic assumptions of the Congressional Budget Office in producing the committee's budget numbers.[23] The decision reversed its decision of the previous year, a decision that had launched the committee on its partisan course. As for the president, Domenici could only say that "my hope springs eternal that we will make some headway with the White House before we move too far along here, but I do not know that yet." [24] The sessions meandered through speeches and staff presentations to no effect. The chairman fixed a specific time for the next meeting immediately after the recess.

The same day Domenici convened the first markup, however, he and other senators were drawn into the James Baker talks. And a day later, Domenici became one of seventeen people—five administration, five Senate, seven House—who met thirteen times during the next month to see whether a budget resolution satisfactory to the three parties might be negotiated. The Senate Budget Committee, at Howard Baker's request, did not meet as long as these "Gang of Seventeen" negotiations continued. In these meetings, the full-blown, election-year politics of blame emerged. The principals, in absentia, were the president and the Speaker. Neither one would come forward with a comprehensive proposal, because neither trusted the other one not to take political advantage of it. The president wanted the Speaker to throw in with him on reducing cost-of-living adjustments for entitlement programs; the Speaker wanted the president to throw in with him on the repeal of tax cuts. But each wanted the other to "go first" so that the blame for any unpopular outcome would fall on the initial proposer.

Again, the sequencing of political positions is seen as extremely important, especially if one thinks of interpretation or credit or blame as the desired outcome. Media scorekeepers adopted the Alphonse-Gaston metaphor. In Howard Baker's terms, "It really has gotten down to the Gaston and Alphonse stage. I think it's a question of who goes first." [25] The ultimate in blame avoidance occurred when, after the negotiations had broken down irrevocably, no one would get up from the table until Baker suggested, "Let's all stand up together." Which they did. Then they dispersed to play the blame game in other arenas—each side blaming the other for the failure to agree.[26]

The negotiations of the so-called Gang of Seventeen moved the Senate Republicans—including Domenici—from the epicenter of the budget action to the periphery. Baker continued to be the Senate spokesman. Mostly, he wielded the Senate Budget Committee as a weapon to keep the negotiations moving—threatening one day to have the committee begin its own markup when things lagged and "rescinding" the threat when progress occurred.[27] Domenici waited impatiently at the end of Baker's tether as the May 15 statutory deadline for the resolution approached. Media accounts reported him as saying, "Hey, we aren't getting anywhere, let's quit." [28] His staff advisers were pushing him to exercise his own responsibility to protect the budget process by restarting markup sessions. "What a mess," exclaimed one Domenici adviser three weeks into the negotiations. "These people have been meeting and there are wide divergences of opinion. . . . Domenici has hemmed himself in by his decision to be constructive and not to go off on his own half cocked on something that won't get anywhere. But he may have to decide to do something on his own next week. I think we've got a very serious, dangerous problem."

Whether one views the Gang of Seventeen meetings as circumventing or as lubricating the budget process, the normal mechanism was not being used. And therein lay a larger danger. "I'm advising him to go to markup," continued the adviser.

> If we go out, we should go with a bang not a whimper. . . . The way to keep the process alive is to use it vigorously. We could lose it in one of two ways. One way is to have people reject it. The other is to go slow, saying—"Wait a while,"—such that by the time you do anything, you are superfluous. Nobody needs you and nobody cares about you. You just get left behind.

Again, one side of him wanted to move; the other side held back. He waited—as Baker wished—for the negotiations to exhaust themselves. Which they did.

When the Budget Committee reconvened six days after the end of the Gang of Seventeen negotiations, the question of bipartisan/partisan support for a committee decision remained open. Domenici's attitude, described by a staffer two weeks before, had been that,

> He thinks he can get twelve Republican votes to vote out a budget resolution very close to his. We could take it to the floor, have a very tough battle, and, perhaps, carry it on the floor. He would much prefer to do something on a bipartisan basis.

The next day, he had spoken of his desire for bipartisanship on the Senate floor.[29] The theme of his opening remarks when the committee reconvened was one of collective responsibility.

I have voted for every budget resolution to be reported out of this committee to the floor, to give the Senate a chance to adopt a resolution, ever since I have been on this committee. I have voted for some that I had serious objections to and had lodged the objections as we moved along. But I really felt compelled to deliver a budget resolution to the Senate to work its will.... Our very basic responsibility is to send the Senate a resolution, debate it, and let the full membership dispose of it.[30]

This time, reconciliation instructions would be included in the budget resolution. "I hope," he said, "that most of you will share the attitude that the institution and process are important enough to preserve, and that things will not be better, but are apt to be worse if we do not produce a budget resolution, even if it is not exactly what we want." [31]

He did not explicitly call for bipartisanship, but his tone was conducive to it. And so was the personal standing he had achieved in the world of budget making. During the week that the committee was meeting, one national reporter said to his colleagues,

I did a profile on Domenici recently, and my editor told me to go find somebody to say something bad about him. I said, "Nobody will say anything bad about him—maybe last year, but not this year." He said, "There must be somebody who will say something bad about him." I said, "You go find somebody to say something bad about him."

One cannot know, for certain, what his committee members thought of him. They paid him numerous public compliments; but those represent routine political grease. Observation suggests that the reporter's story is accurate, in that no one—just as in the case of his constituents—disliked Pete Domenici.

More than that, his members respected his knowledge and hard work, credited his earnest desire to be constructive and responsible, and appreciated the difficulty of his task. They even seemed to be protective of his leadership, blaming any problems on someone else, not him. Only once did I observe any committee member, Republican or Democrat, go out of his way to make things unpleasant for the chairman. For what it was worth, therefore, Domenici could count on the personal goodwill of his members as he approached the task of majority building.

Beyond the committee, however, a great deal of partisan "recrimination" was in the air.[32] The Gang of Seventeen had broken up amid bitter charges by Speaker O'Neill and the president. And partisanship emerged in the committee on the first day back, in a speech by Hollings. He rehashed the Gang of Seventeen negotiations (in which he participated) at great length, blamed the president for their failure, and moved that the committee vote immediately, up or down, on the president's original budget. Hollings called for "a bipartisan solution," but his tone was not conducive to it. By forcing the Republicans to vote against their president, as they surely would, he wanted to embarrass them and him and disrupt their ties.

Two weeks before, Hollings had formally announced his candidacy for the Democratic presidential nomination.[33] And he had had by far the poorest attendance record of the seventeen negotiators—missing five of their thirteen meetings. So Domenici might have been prepared for Hollings's partisan outburst. But he was not. He and Hollings tangled briefly over the veracity of Hollings's account of what happened; and they tangled again when Domenici peremptorily denied Hollings an immediate vote on the president's budget. As Hollings and several other Democrats protested his decision, Domenici abruptly gaveled the mark-up to a close.[34] "Senate Panel, in Partisan Mood, Begins Drafting Budget for 1983," read a headline.[35] Though it was not totally apparent at that point, the changed atmosphere signaled the end of hope for committee bipartisanship.

Domenici interpreted the Hollings episode as meaning that he had lost his ranking minority member and that, without Hollings, a bipartisan strategy would not work. "He has violated the covenant," Domenici said after the meeting. And, as it turned out, Hollings's 1982 support for his chairman would show a greater dropoff from 1981 than that of any other committee Democrat.

A Domenici staffer described Hollings's defection as "an example of how little things can change big things." The staffer continued,

> After the Gang of Seventeen negotiations broke down. . . , Domenici said, "What do you think our first move ought to be?" "Call Fritz Hollings," we said. We thought the Gang of Seventeen had made a great deal of progress and that the committee could build on that record in a bipartisan way. He called Hollings and Hollings came over with a staffer. He and Domenici agreed to try to cooperate to see what could be worked out along bipartisan lines.
>
> As important, they agreed not to hash over the past and start handing out blame for what had gone wrong. They agreed that if they, as leaders, did not engage in that sort of partisan rhetoric, the others on both sides would probably not do so either. They made a deal. When we wrote Domenici's opening speech, we did it in that spirit.
>
> Talking with Hollings's staff the next morning, we knew things weren't going right. When we got to markup, there was a speech by Hollings that was so strong and so partisan that Don Riegle wouldn't even read it. . . . Then Hollings shows up and delivers it. He could not restrain himself. He couldn't hold back. He couldn't resist the opportunity to get attention.
>
> Domenici was mad as hell. When Hollings finished, Domenici gaveled the meeting to a close—which was very uncharacteristic of him. He regarded it as a betrayal of an agreement. When we got back

to his office, he said, "We've been betrayed. What do we do now?" We said, "You need twelve votes. They will have to be Republican votes." And from that day we set about getting twelve Republican votes.

More accurately, Chairman Domenici needed thirteen Republican votes—twelve senators plus one president.

MAJORITY BUILDING IN COMMITTEE

As Domenici set out to build an all-Republican majority, there were grounds for pessimism and optimism. In the larger context, there were pessimistic signs of policy differences among Republicans and between Republicans and the business community. In the committee context, a related source of pessimism was the emergence of the policy individualism that had been built into the group. Howard Baker had already predicted that "If the Senate proceeds to write its own budget, I think we will then enter an absolute jungle of conflict." [36] There was, also, the stark fact that in his most recent attempt to get twelve votes for his second budget resolution, the chairman had failed.

One staffer summed up the pessimistic view in late March.

The Republicans have held a lot of meetings. They say "Go to it, Pete. We're all behind you. You're doing a great job." But when it comes time to vote, we'll have nine votes. A and B want it all done with entitlements. C doesn't want one drop of red ink. We lost three last April till we finally got them back; in November we lost two others. We'll end up with nine or ten votes. Then what?

Another staffer laid some of the blame for committee disunity on the chairman's governing style.

Domenici takes too much of it onto himself. The problem is that the members do not feel they have a stake in the committee anyway. That's for starters. It's not anybody's first choice. And the chairman has no goodies. He has to give them a stake in it somehow. The way to give them a stake is to let them participate in shaping the draft budget. As it is now, Domenici brings in his mark. All the other guys have to go separately to CBO and get numbers for their own plan. They don't immediately accept Domenici's plan because they had no part in drawing it up.

Republican disagreements in general and policy individualism in the committee, the argument went, were not offset by any strong attachment to the budget process or by any binding ties of loyalty to the chairman.

The grounds for optimism did not depend on any special allegiances either. They rested, instead, on the ability of the chairman to find a package that would, under the right circumstances, win the approval of twelve Republicans. And that was Chairman Domenici's strength—leadership by policy argument. He had taken the lead in conceptualizing a macro-economic plan in the fall. He had essentially reargued it before the Conference Board in February. With the budgetary situation now "dead in the water," he was prepared to further update the Domenici Plan and present it as the most viable rallying point for committee Republicans.

Pete Domenici is an educator; and he operates from a wealth of knowledge about his subject. As chairman, it was his style to design the best public policy he could, explain it to whomever would listen, wait patiently for the right time to push it and, only then, reach out to make accommodations to build a majority. One of his staffers used the gardening metaphor to capture his springtime educational activity. "You prepare the soil, prepare the soil, prepare the soil. That's what he's doing. . . . He's a gardener. He plants the seeds and watches them come up. . . . He looks at things in the long run. . . . He won't harvest till the sun is in the right position and the soil is just right." For most of the spring, Domenici cultivated two gardens. Publicly he talked in terms of bipartisanship; but privately he kept his eye on the possibilities of partisanship.

In late March he expressed cautious optimism about the partisan option.

> I'm feeling better about the Republicans all the time. We had a good meeting yesterday. I think we can get a resolution out that takes a good chunk out of entitlements, a chunk out of defense, a freeze on discretionary spending, and some increase, but not too much, in taxes. If we can get the budget to within $40 billion of being balanced by 1985, I think I can get the Republicans to vote for parts of it they don't like.

From the beginning of the committee's spring markup sessions, the Domenici theme of committee responsibility was being articulated by various Republican members. They called upon the committee: to "provide some leadership in this field . . . do our duty" (Nancy Kassebaum, March 30), "to carry the flag and move forward" (Rudy Boschwitz, March 30), "to take the bull by the horns . . . and get on with it" (William Armstrong, March 30), to "[follow] our responsibilities under the law and the Constitution to do this job ourselves" (Slade Gorton, April 1), to "make tough decisions . . . to bite the bullet" (Charles Grassley, May 4), and "to get this thing moving . . . [because] for us to do nothing is a mistake" (Steve Symms, May 4).[37] These public expressions were couched in the language of committee responsibility. But the same attitude could also provide the underpinning for a sense of partisan responsibility. And, in private, that response was taking shape.

As Table 3-3 makes clear, the committee's Republicans, despite their occasional defections, had been the chairman's strong supporters in 1981. Their high support levels had enabled him to secure his leadership with a partisan majority. As Table 3-3 also makes clear, the committee Republicans were about to give the chairman even stronger partisan support in 1982. With the bipartisan Gang of Seventeen having failed and, then, with committee bipartisanship also having failed, the strategic premise of 1981—that the Republicans had to prove they could govern—was being rekindled. The idea was taking shape privately among the members, as it had already taken shape for the chairman, that this year they would have to lead the president. "In our caucuses," a committee aide recalled,

> they would say things like, "we don't need the president." When Social Security came up, they would say, "We're not worried about Social Security." We've got some pretty feisty guys on that committee. And they had gotten the feeling that "if no one else here is going to do anything, we'll have to."

As the committee reconvened for its first session following the Hollings speech, a staff aide described the twelve Republicans as "a hockey team suited up and ready to take the ice. Open the gate and out they'll come. Put the spotlight on them, drop the puck, and they'll skate. They are ready to play." That optimistic view of a team "ready to play" was what Chairman Domenici was counting on. For he was about to "open the gate."

Domenici was not so optimistic about the president. On May 3, the day before they reconvened, the Budget Committee Republicans met with the president. During the meeting, Domenici described his revised plan—a freeze on most spending programs, a one-year freeze on all entitlements, a defense increase, an offsetting $122 billion three-year increase in taxes, and a deficit projection for 1983 of $89 billion. When he did so, there was, he said, "complete silence," broken finally by Howard Baker's, "Yes, but. . . ." Then, as Domenici described it, "Much froth and concern and consternation was expressed by everyone. Nobody said, 'Do not present it, senator.' Nobody said, 'It is bad public policy, Mr. Chairman.' We just left saying we surely have to get together and get a budget, do we not, and that is how we left." [38] The president "refused to signal what he would accept." [39] As for the president's attitude toward Domenici's plan specifically, the chairman said, "I think it is fair to say . . . that he does not favor it." [40] Nonetheless, the next day, Domenici presented it formally to his committee. It was his boldest, most independent leadership move yet.

TABLE 3-3 Budget Committee Support for Chairman Domenici: Committee Votes, Ninety-Seventh Congress

Senator	% Votes with Domenici 1981 (N=87)		% Votes with Domenici 1982 (N=26)		% Totals 97th Congress (N=113)	
	a	b	a	b	a	b
Gorton [c]	94	(94)	100	(100)	96	(96)
Quayle	80	(92)	100	(100)	85	(94)
Symms	83	(88)	88	(96)	84	(90)
Kasten	83	(87)	88	(92)	84	(88)
Kassebaum	79	(79)	92	(96)	82	(83)
Grassley	80	(93)	88	(96)	82	(94)
Armstrong	79	(87)	81	(100)	80	(90)
Boschwitz	75	(93)	96	(96)	80	(94)
Hatch	70	(91)	81	(95)	73	(92)
Hollings	54	(54)	27	(29)	48	(49)
Andrews	46	(78)	46	(86)	46	(80)
Chiles	48	(51)	35	(38)	45	(48)
Johnston	41	(50)	35	(35)	40	(46)
Tower	38	(92)	35	(100)	37	(93)
Exon	38	(39)	27	(39)	35	(39)
Sasser	37	(43)	23	(46)	34	(44)
Hart	34	(45)	15	(21)	30	(40)
Moynihan	24	(29)	23	(33)	24	(30)
Metzenbaum	24	(28)	15	(33)	22	(28)
Riegle	21	(25)	19	(26)	20	(25)
Biden	7	(19)	19	(22)	10	(20)

[a] Percentage of times member voted with Domenici—all votes on which Domenici voted. Member may have been absent, and member absence lowers score.

[b] Percentage of times member voted with Domenici—all votes on which Domenici and member both voted. This calculation controls for absences. (Column "a" emphasized, on the assumption that the chairman would want his supporters to be present and voting.)

[c] Names in italic type = Republicans; names in roman type = Democrats.

When the committee members assembled, on May 4, the chairman's "mark" awaited them on the blackboard. "[It] represents," he said, "what I think our fiscal policy should be. It varies somewhat from the September plan that I offered but not by very much." [41] For fiscal 1983 his proposal called for 10 percent growth in defense; a one-year freeze on all cost-of-living adjustments and federal pay raises; zero increase in nondefense discretionary spending; $18 billion in tax increases; and a deficit of $89 billion. (See Tables 3-1 and 3-2.) "I want to make it clear," he said in opening the meeting,

> This is strictly my mark. I have cleared it with no one and consulted with no one about its content.... The White House has not blessed this plan. It is not a Republican plan. It is not the results of any caucus

of all Republicans in the Senate nor of those on this committee. . . . I do not know whether I have one single vote for it or whether I have five. . . . I have not sought, as of this moment, to get a majority of senators, my side or both, to support it yet.[42]

Domenici was not all that innocent. He had just caucused with committee Republicans and, of course, he had been picking up information on their positions for some time.

His private calculation, at that moment on May 4, was that he had seven votes and that he could probably get four more in subsequent negotiations and maneuverings. His hope was that if he got twelve committee votes, he might be in a position to win over the president. He further believed that whatever was done would have to be done that week. His strategy was to hold the committee in session until the Domenici Plan was passed—or defeated.

The chairman's most pressing problem was with three conservative Republican freshmen (Grassley, Symms, and Bob Kasten) who objected to the three-year tax increase proposed by Domenici. The chairman's strategy was to help the most dedicated supply sider, Kasten, to secure an early vote on his preferred revenue figure, to vote it down, and then to negotiate his own revenue figure down to a level acceptable to Kasten. The hope was that he could attract the other two antitax-increase senators along the way. So, when the committee met on the morning of May 5, the chairman used his procedural authority to direct that Kasten's alternative revenue motion be the first order of business, thus bypassing the pending request by Hollings for a vote on the president's budget. The substitute revenue motion, calling for $73 billion—instead of Domenici's revenue figure of $125 billion—in new revenue, drew only four Republican votes.

But at midday Domenici was not sure the strategy had succeeded. "He's had his shot. But I still don't know about Kasten." He decided to move toward one of the other, less adamant, doubters. "I'll try to get a new revenue line. I'll call Grassley and tell him that I'll compromise at $102 billion and he can spread it out over the three years however he wishes." He learned, however, that Kasten's threshold number was $95 billion. Kasten wanted revenue projections below that figure to make certain that the third year of the tax cut and indexation would be preserved. After receiving assurances directly from the president on both counts, Kasten—along with Grassley and Symms—agreed to a "new revenue line" of $95 billion in tax increases over three years.[43] The deficit projections for the three fiscal years (Table 3-1) thus became $106 billion (1983), $69 billion (1984), and $40 billion (1985)—double what Domenici had originally thought necessary to hold his Republicans together.

That left the two most powerful senators on the committee uncommitted—John Tower and Orrin Hatch. Each was chairman of an important and busy Senate committee. Both were less likely to attend Republican caucuses or formal committee activities than the others. Their views were not so well known to the chairman. Hatch had voted against the pro forma second resolution on the Senate floor in the fall; and he was one of the four votes for the Kasten revenue figures. He was quoted as saying, "I haven't voted for a deficit yet, and I don't know why I should start now." [44] Tower had not been present for the latter vote. A committee staffer reflected Domenici's uncertainty about these two.

> Hatch is afraid he'll be unelected and he is totally unpredictable. Tower is potentially the most dangerous threat to the entire budget process. He has only one thing that interests him in life, to get a bigger defense budget. . . . When he was left out of the [Gang of Seventeen] negotiations he threatened to bring the whole thing down.

While the Budget Committee deliberated, Tower was marching his Armed Services Committee through the defense authorization bill, disregarding the sequence prescribed by the budget law.[45] He had already forced the Budget Committee's computations for defense to be done differently from the rest of the budget so as to give him a more favorable baseline to work from. Committee Democrats kept calling attention to these anomalies throughout the proceedings—and even forced a vote on the propriety of the defense "numbers"—but to no avail.

In the crunch, Tower went along with Domenici—probably because he was left such a wide berth within his defense bailiwick and probably out of loyalty to the party leadership.[46] Hatch was "another story. He said he had to have the president. We thought maybe the pressure of the other eleven might bring him in. But we couldn't be sure." In fact, they never were sure. Orrin Hatch, the swing man in this case, was the only Budget Committee Republican who was facing reelection in 1982.

Committee sessions in the morning and afternoon of "fateful Wednesday," May 5, were devoted to much speechmaking, some wrangling, and a few votes. The Democrats presented no concerted alternative to the Domenici Plan. They were committed only to forcing a vote on the president's budget—as a political embarrassment. Otherwise, they harassed Domenici with procedural arguments and motions. Hollings presented a full-blown alternative—following the proposals of his speech—but it was never treated as *the* Democratic alternative. Indeed, his pivotal revenue proposals did not command even a majority vote from his fellow Democrats. It was the Democrats' intention—insofar as they had one—to let the Republicans stew in their own juice and to do whatever they could to divide the committee Republicans from the president. The vote on the president's budget was, as expected, 0-20. It was the only "victory" the Democrats could manage in the committee. The scorekeepers duly recorded it as a "repudiation" and an "embarrassment" to the administration's fiscal plan.[47] But, as the unanimous vote indicated, the real action had long since moved to the Domenici Plan.

While the Democrats consumed most of the public time, Domenici was working feverishly on his majority. At the noon lunch break, he said,

> We're gonna get it done. They made us vote on all these things we had already decided on. That's all right with me. I don't have a budget yet. I'm close but I don't have it. So I don't care if they screw around all day with their votes. I'm pretending I'm mad at them. But I'm faking it.

He had secured a commitment from Tower; but he had yet to reach agreement on the revenue figures with the three antitax senators. And, of course, he did not yet know whether that negotiation would cost him the support of those committee members who wanted a larger tax increase. As it turned out, that did not happen.

When he had secured agreement on the revenue number, in midafternoon, he decided to move to win over the president. But he did not plan to win him over with macro-economic argument—which he now regarded as "a futile exercise." He planned to win him over by the sheer political force of a unanimous Republican phalanx. He would present the president with a train about to leave the station and ask if he wished to be aboard or left behind. He hoped that the president's involvement in the failed bipartisan enterprise, the Gang of Seventeen, had softened him up for a partisan approach.

When Domenici made this crucial decision, he had eleven committee votes. But his strategy for securing the "thirteenth," presidential, vote depended on having twelve committee votes. So he *assumed* he had the twelve Republican votes, and he called Howard Baker to tell him that his committee was about to vote out the budget.

Two days later, in his office, an exuberant, grinning chairman recounted the events surrounding this bold—uncharacteristically bold—move.

> I called the leader and I said to him, "I've got twelve votes and I'm going to pass my budget out of the committee." He said, "Well, don't you think we ought to check with the administration? We can't pass a budget without the administration." I said, "Mr. Leader, you told me to move ahead on the budget. I've got twelve votes and we're going to pass it." He said, "Well, you know I'm with you. Anything you say." About ten minutes later I get a call from Jim Baker. "Don't you

think we ought to talk about this?" I knew that would happen. As soon as I got off the phone with [Howard] Baker, he called the White House and told them, "Domenici's got twelve votes for the budget and he's going to pass out his budget."

So [Jim] Baker and Stockman come up to Leader Baker's office. [Steve] Bell [committee staff director] and I go over. Jim Baker pulls out a sheet of paper and says, "Here's a budget." I take the sheet of paper, look at it, and I toss it aside. [Here, he takes a piece of paper from his desk and dramatically tosses it aside, reenacting the scene.] "I can't get twelve votes for that budget." Jim Baker said, "Don't you think you ought to look at it?" Howard Baker said, "Maybe you ought to think it over."

Now, you know I've never been in that situation before in my life. I thought I had twelve votes; but I couldn't be sure I had twelve votes. But I said to them, "I can't pass that budget." And I turned to Bell and asked him, "Can we pass that budget?" "No, sir." Leader Baker said, "Whatever you say, Pete. You know I'll support you."

"Well," said Jim Baker, "let's take your budget and see if we can't make a few adjustments." We negotiated for a while . . . and they agreed to support it.

That agreement would bring the twelfth vote—*and* the thirteenth.

But the Domenici-Baker-Stockman agreement did not end the day's dramatic events. The budget, as agreed upon, still had to be voted out of committee. Domenici could not be certain that the Republicans (or Democrats) would not seek amendments nor was he certain about when to move for a vote. He began—characteristically—to worry about these matters of unity and timing. And he turned, as always, to "Leader Baker" for help. At a couple of points during the day, said Baker's staffers, "Domenici came scurrying through the back door saying he wasn't sure he could get it through." It was a familiar pattern—from decisiveness to caution.

"When Domenici is under pressure he is in here all the time or calling Baker," said a leadership aide. "He calls him at night. He's in constant contact. He's the extreme case." On May 5, on the brink of success, Domenici was characteristically worried—this time about the fragility of his majority. One of his aides described the problem. "We could get twelve votes, but could we get them all at the same time? These votes were like electrons moving in a field. They were in a certain configuration which kept changing. . . . We figured we had thirty-six hours in which all twelve . . . would be in the right place."

Howard Baker agreed with his calculation; and he intervened to push for immediate committee action. "He was the one who decided when the budget would come out of committee. . . ," said a top staffer.

He wanted the budget out that night and he wanted it out at that time. If it had come three days later, it would have been shot down. If it had come three weeks earlier, it would have been torn to shreds. I don't think anyone in this body would argue with him on that.

He asked Domenici to get the committee Republicans together for a meeting in his office around dinner time. And, there, Baker took the lead in heading off any incipient disunity.

There were several Republicans who wanted to offer amendments at that point—to load up the train as it was about to leave the station. Baker intervened again. An observer said,

> There was a lot of yelling and screaming. But the small man with the big ears is pretty good when there's yelling and screaming. He doesn't get mad very often. But when he does, they sit up and listen. And they did. . . . He said, "This is it. We will offer no amendments on our side and we will vote down all amendments from the Democratic side."

When that meeting adjourned, the committee members caucused in Domenici's office and agreed to follow Baker's judgment on timing and on unity.

Chairman Domenici spoke afterward about his friendship and his working relationship with Majority Leader Baker. It dated at least from Domenici's role, in 1976, as one of Baker's two so-called campaign managers in his hairline 19-18 victory in the contest for party leadership.[48] Clearly, their close relationship was a vital part of the chairman's success—as the preceding episode makes clear. In Domenici's words,

> We are real good buddies. If the two of us didn't work together, you wouldn't get a budget. If he worked alone, you wouldn't get a budget. If I worked alone, you wouldn't get a budget. . . . We have complete confidence in one another. We sit down and talk things out; we come to an agreement and we do it. We never second guess each other. I have absolute confidence in his judgment. If he says we ought to do it, we'll do it. When we get to the floor, we divide up the work. If I get worried and go off and make a few deals, I'll tell him what I've done and he never second guesses me.

That exemplary teamwork would be soon tested again on the Senate floor.

The Budget Committee had been in recess since 5:00 p.m. when they reconvened at 7:15. The chairman proposed "a modified mark" to incorporate his negotiations, explained each change, and concluded by saying,

> I want to announce that the president of this United States will endorse and support this proposal. I submit it tonight after negotiations with the White House as a budget that the president will, indeed, support and will take to the people.[49]

It was a moment of high drama. Crowds had been in the corridor all day waiting in vain to get in. So many television networks had wanted access that only one pool camera was allowed in; but the hallway was packed with TV monitors and technicians with various affiliations. Domenici's top office staffers had come over to witness the denouement. As he recapitulated the day's events, Domenici savored the moment of accomplishment.

> Did you see the look on their faces when I said, "By the way, the president of the United States supports this budget"? They told me Hollings turned pale. None of them thought I could pull it off. They didn't know what to say. All they did was keep asking me whether I was sure I had an agreement.

The Democrats, by turns, huddled and groped for relevant comments or questions. They succeeded in badgering Domenici to get reassurance, first from James Baker and then from the president himself. Twice, therefore, the chairman left the committee room to make the necessary phone calls. Finally he was able to say, "I just spoke to the President. . . ." He said, " 'I hope you can pass it. I am for it. I will do everything I can to see that it is passed and becomes law.' " [50]

A short while later the committee voted on "the modified Domenici proposal, as supported by the president." The vote, with one absentee on each side, was a partisan 11-9. It was the chairman's second major victory of the day. To reporters afterward, he said, "The president felt the time was ripe for a midcourse correction. He's a negotiator. He felt now was the time to help his friends up on the Hill."

The next morning, Domenici was in the White House Rose Garden being congratulated by President Reagan.[51] Later that day, the Republicans voted down every Democratic proposal—with the Democrats' frustration building to petulance by evening. At 10:20 p.m. the modified Domenici budget was reported out of committee by a partisan majority of 12-10. The *Wall Street Journal* account of the proceedings was headlined, "In High Stakes Fight over Budget, Domenici Just Outmaneuvered Democrats." [52] This article, framed, hangs on the wall beside the entrance to his private office, a prized account of his landmark success in achieving his career-long goal of internal influence inside the Senate.

The chairman had done a lot more than outmaneuver the Democrats. He had persuaded the president to do something he was fundamentally opposed to doing and in the area of the president's greatest interest. He had found a way to move the president. He emphasized his broad philosophical agreement with Reagan; he established the legitimacy of his own institutional responsibilities; he avoided direct confrontation; and he presented himself as a team player. Above all, he developed solid partisan political support for his position. "We learned a lot about the president," said Domenici's closest adviser.

> When he goes to buy a house, he doesn't want to talk to the real estate
> agent or the county sheriff or the neighbors or anyone else. He wants
> to talk to the person who owns it. "Do you own the house?" That's
> what he wants to know. "If you own the house, I'll talk to you." We
> owned the house. And he bought it.

It was typical of Ronald Reagan to state his position strongly and inflexibly. It was typical of him to stand firm behind that position until the very last possible moment. It was typical of him that, while he stood firm, he would not take in a lot of information or pay attention to others. But in the end, he did take in information, he did pay attention, and he did compromise. So, while he looked for long periods as though he was inattentive and ideological, he was at bottom a compromiser. The question always was: how do you get his attention? That, it seems, took some length of association. In his third budget season, Pete Domenici had found one way to do it. He "owned the house."

May 5 was a day of supreme triumph for the chairman. For the first time, someone outside the Reagan administration had called the shots on the nation's budget. On May 6 the lead editorial in the *New York Times* was entitled "President Domenici?" [53] The idea was that the president was not acting like a president, but the senator was. It was as good an indicator as one could find that a man who once was afraid to step forward in the Senate, but who had always wanted to be recognized as a national policy maker, had achieved that goal. He was being credited, in the nation's most prestigious paper, with having a coherent vision of national policy worthy of the presidency itself.

MAJORITY BUILDING ON THE FLOOR

The chairman had a budget. But the Senate chamber and the conference committee lay ahead. The basic problem was the thin 54-46 Republican majority and the need to keep defections to the barest minimum. "I feel good," said Domenici after his committee victory. "But I'm worried. Of course it wouldn't be me if I weren't worried." His worries quickly took on a special focus because implanted within the committee budget by the Pete Domenici-James Baker negotiations was a political time bomb— a three-year $6 billion plus $17 billion plus $17 billion ($40 billion) proposal for "Social Security solvency." (See Table 3-1.) The idea was a compromise between Domenici's insistence on a one-year freeze of Social Security cost of living adjustments and the White House's categorical rejection of any such concrete plan. The compromise called for inserting a dollar amount of "Social Security savings," which the negotiators estimated would be necessary to keep the fund solvent for each of the next three years but *without* specifying how such savings would be achieved.

These "plug" numbers were an inspired effort to change the terms of political argument from "Social Security cuts" to "Social Security solvency." But in the context of previous administration missteps on Social Security and a Democratic party desperately casting about for an issue in the upcoming election, the reinterpretation of the argument failed to gain political credibility. It was the very open-endedness of the "plug" number that made it vulnerable to Social Security recipient fears and to political attack—for it could be interpreted as meaning not fund solvency but "benefit cuts."

Democrats immediately made this single line in the committee-passed budget the point of their attack. On the day the president congratulated the chairman in the Rose Garden, the *Washington Post* headlined: "Democrats Blast New Budget Plan: Reagan Defends $40 Billion Cut in Social Security." [54] For two weeks Washington rang with thrust and counterthrust. On the Senate floor May 12, Domenici gave an extemporaneous defense of his actions as "responsible" and voiced his interpretations of the argument.

> I take full credit for being responsible. I take full responsibility for producing a truthful budget. I take responsibility for putting in this budget the truth about Social Security. I take full responsibility for truth in budgeting. The truth is that Social Security will most probably be insolvent next year. The further truth is that it most probably needs the amounts of $6 billion, $17 billion, and $17 billion, respectively, for the fiscal years 1983, 1984, and 1985. . . . So let us just face the issue: A truthful budget that tells the Senate precisely the facts and then says to the Senate, "Quit playing around with 36 million Social Security recipients. Make the system solvent." [55]

On that same day, the House Republican leadership pronounced a death sentence on the idea. Minority Leader Robert Michel said, "You've got to take that off the table, before you even start. . . . I cannot accept it as it is." [56] And Minority Whip Trent Lott echoed, "Social Security is out. Period. No plug. No honorable mention." [57] Their refusal had a crucial bicameral component. "I've told them all along, don't expect the same game they played over there to be played over here," said Michel. He knew that every House Republican faced the prospect of an electoral barrage on the issue. "You've got to give guys who have to run every two years some running room." [58]

The group of moderate Senate Republicans who were up for reelection were not far behind. On May 14 seven of them cosponsored an amendment to delete the $40 billion.[59] That same day, Domenici once again defended it on the Senate floor. "I consider it truth in budgeting." [60] On May 13 the president had declared a willingness to compromise on the Social Security item. "I don't think his comments were terribly helpful," said Domenici.[61] On May 18, at the regular Tuesday Republican caucus, Domenici agreed to drop the number altogether from the budget, leaving a reconciliation instruction to the Finance Committee to keep the fund solvent. In effect, the field was left to the Presidential Commission on Social Security. Domenici had been forced to beat a political retreat from his preferred policy position. It was a replay of the sequence surrounding the president's aborted "September offensive" in the fall of 1981—Domenici pushes; president accedes; House Republicans protest; president recedes.

The Social Security episode revealed a limitation of Pete Domenici's governing style. Recall the comment of a top aide long before he became chairman that "He's not a political guy. He's the least political senator around. He's a policy senator." As chairman, the New Mexican became more political, but he still governed in pursuit of a policy vision, not a political vision. His idea was that good policy is good politics. He wanted to pass a responsible budget; and he defended it in those terms. But in his concentration on making good budget policy he could lose sight of its political consequences. This difficulty became evident in his defense of the Social Security budget item as "truth-in-budgeting."

On the day after the budget was reported out of committee, the president called to wish the chairman a happy birthday. The segment of the conversation, from Domenici's side, went like this:

> We're going to get some of our people together over the weekend and strategize. We're going to win this one because it's right.... Yes.... Exactly.... Right.... Let me give you one thought on that—truth-in-budgeting. Social Security has always been part of the budget. What do they expect the Budget Committee to do, ignore it?

He turned to the group in his office and said, "He's going to do tomorrow's radio broadcast on Social Security. He's going to take it to 'em." A little later, he put in a call to a pivotal committee supporter. "You put your good head to work on how we can sell the Social Security package," he said. "I think we ought to talk about truth-in-budgeting. What else do they expect a budget committee to do, ignore it?"

Truth-in-budgeting was the line of argument Domenici himself used on the Senate floor. But it was a line of argument inappropriate and inadequate for the huge task of salesmanship he faced on one of the nation's most sensitive, volatile political issues. The question was whether the policy could be sold to the recipients. And it could not be sold by reference to the Budget Committee's responsibility. The argument "What do you expect a budget committee to do, ignore it?" reflects a gimlet-eyed view of the political problem that loomed beyond the confines of the Budget Committee. But it is a view of the world that grew out of Domenici's strenuous devotion to the production of good public policy and his focus on the political problems within his committee. If the Social Security proposal was to be sold, the idea that benefits were about to be cut would have to be countered with the idea that the checks might not be delivered at all. The question of "any benefits" had to be superimposed somehow on the question of "benefit levels." But that could not be done by stressing truth-in-budgeting or by stressing Budget Committee responsibility. They were narrow arguments, small arguments. They were arguments that only a Budget Committee could love.

There is, of course, nothing unusual about what we might call a chairman's "committee vision." It helps to explain the need for party leadership—for someone to take a broader political view. Howard Baker contributed that broader view for his Budget chairman. A Baker aide noted,

> Domenici wanted to come with a hard budget, a budget that was right. Howard Baker agreed with him that it was right. But he has to think beyond what is right.... He told Pete, "You may be able to get that budget through the committee. You may even be able to get it past the Senate. But if you do, it will lie over there on the floor of the rotunda and it will never reach the House and we may never get a budget through Congress."

Baker did not believe that a numerical Social Security provision would pass the Senate. But he was certain that it would not pass in the House.

Chairman Domenici was less sensitive than Baker to these consequences beyond the Senate. As his comment to Budget Director Stockman in the fall of 1981 indicated, he was apt to see House-member reelection problems as irresponsibility—as "spineless," "cut-and-run" behavior. A politically shrewd Republican House member of the Gang of Seventeen described Domenici's perspective in that bicameral negotiation.

> He is a very serious, very bright, very hard-charging guy. He wants to be responsible. So, he'll go back over there and produce something that will cause us horrible trouble over here. His attitude is, "OK, we'll fix it up over there in the Senate." He doesn't know anything about the House. He doesn't care about the House. He isn't the least bit interested in the House. He doesn't understand the political sensitivities involved. He's prepared to cap entitlements without any regard to the constituency problems over here.... He is very bright. He knows the figures. He is a good guy. But he's absolutely nonpolitical and he's only interested in the Senate.

Domenici admitted, afterward, that "We could have had a deal with [Representative Richard] Bolling if I had understood how they negotiate over there."

"Senate vision" comes as naturally to a senator as "committee vision" comes to a chairman. It is a basic but critical truth that for senators, the Senate is the measure of all things—not the House. But Senate vision comes with special impetus to the Budget Committee chairman. For he carries, as we have said, an authority that has become increasingly important for the Senate as an institution. The Budget Committee chairman is forced, by dint of his position, to become a distinctively Senate-oriented man, the protector of a new-found Senate power within the bicameral system. Whether or not he consciously sets out to be an institutional senator, he is constrained to become one. His institutional maintenance goals may make negotiations within the bicameral system more difficult. But it must be understood as an institutional as well as a stylistic matter where Pete Domenici was concerned.

By relying on a partisan majority to report out his budget, Domenici committed himself to a similar reliance on a partisan majority to see the budget through the Senate. But, as his Social Security retreat indicated, the two majorities were not identical. Committee Republicans were more wedded to their product than were noncommittee Republicans. Committee Republicans were slightly more conservative than noncommittee Republicans. And committee Republicans were freer from electoral jeopardy than their party colleagues. Of the nineteen Republicans facing reelection in the fall, only one was a member of the Budget Committee; and he had been the most reluctant twelfth vote. These three differences combined to highlight the restlessness of a group of noncommittee moderates already running for reelection.

It was they who spearheaded the revolt against the Social Security numbers. And they became Domenici's major worry as the floor context came into view. "We have a lot of moderate Republicans up for reelection this year...," said a committee staffer.

> Social Security is a difficult issue for them. When they complained, the first thing we did was make them show us they could beat us. Which they did.... So Domenici said, "OK, we'll take out the Social Security numbers. They're only estimates anyway. But we'll keep the reconciliation instruction in along with a reporting date."

Baker and Domenici took that change to the regular Tuesday Republican luncheon. "We thought," said another committee staffer, "that taking out the $40 billion would be enough to keep the party together. We were prepared for an assault from the conservatives. But it came from everywhere else. We didn't know what hit us."

The moderates wanted increases in discretionary and entitlement spending, such as student loans, veterans, Medicare, housing, and "add backs" to cover 1982 deferrals.[62] Having tailored the budget in his committee to win conservative votes—squeezing entitlements and revenue increases to minimize the deficit—Domenici now had to win moderate votes, by increasing nondefense spending and allowing the deficit to rise. If the budget were to survive Democratic assaults on the floor, he would need to get the support of Republican moderates without losing the support of Republican conservatives.

Domenici described his majority-building efforts at the luncheon of May 18.

> I got up and said I was very unhappy. I said I was afraid we would be eating lunch all week, losing three or four amendments every day until we wouldn't have a budget left. I said I thought we ought to find out who was going to do what. It was decided we needed another meeting later that afternoon.
>
> About thirty-five Republicans came. They meandered in. My staff and I knew where the sticking points were. So we ticked 'em off and I said, "If we do this, will that take care of you two guys; if we do this will that take care of you six guys?" We did that for several groups and then we asked them, "If we do all these things, will you agree to no more amendments. . . ?"
>
> Some grumbled that "You can't put a budget together here in this room." I told them we knew what we were doing and that if they didn't hold the line, we would not get a budget. I told them they would have to go out on the floor and cast some tough votes—against veterans. That's tough. . . .
>
> Well, three or four said they couldn't agree. It was humiliating. But the rest of the guys put their hands in the air and agreed not to vote for any amendments. Baker spoke; and I said a few words about party loyalty. We went out of there with our fingers crossed. We did not have full support.

Baker's staff was satisfied that the meeting had produced, if not unanimity, then consensus.

> When they left, there was a consensus. "You'll get your budget. We'll stick together." Everyone knew how small a margin we had to work with—five votes. On matters of great importance to particular individuals, it was understood that people might vote against us. But they would do it through the majority leader. He keeps the tally in his head.

At this point, the process of coalition building had brought the final, out-year (fiscal 1985) deficit figure in the Domenici Plan from a projected surplus of $6 billion on May 3, to a projected deficit of $20 billion *early* on May 5, to a deficit of $40 billion as passed by the committee on May 6, to a deficit of $65 billion as presented to the Senate on May 19. (See Table 3-1.) The chairman had been forced to give away much of the store to preserve the budget process and the notion that the Republicans were capable of governing.

The three conservatives with whom he conducted his final negotiations inside the committee were now extremely restless. "I'm working through a very tough decision right now," said one of them,

> whether or not to support this budget resolution. It doesn't treat taxes the way I want. It doesn't treat Social Security the way I want. I agreed to compromise in the committee. I told Pete Domenici I'd go along with $95 million even though I was afraid it would threaten the third-year tax cut. I thought it was the responsible thing to keep the budget process going. But with the new changes, I don't know what to do. Should I vote for the resolution and keep the orderly process going or should I just stop it and let chaos result? My supply-side staffers are telling me, "To hell with it. Let it go." My inclination is in favor of order. I want to support Howard Baker and Pete Domenici. . . . But I can't tell you how much I hate that budget I see. It's a difficult decision.

He voted for "order." But the bargaining process presaged a long-run difficulty for the chairman—that the preservation of the budget process might come only at the cost of steadily escalating deficits and steadily eroding support. At some point, of course, the preservation of the process might not be a sufficient excuse for budgetary decisions. But that time was not yet.

The budget staff stayed up all night preparing the necessary package for the Senate floor and consulting with the Senate parliamentarian on procedural protection for the package. They wanted to withdraw the $40 billion for Social Security solvency on their own before the Democrats could propose an amendment to do so—thus preventing the Democrats from claiming additional credit in the Social Security contest. On the morning of May 19, Majority Leader Baker exercised his prerogative of first recognition by the chair to replace the committee budget with the negotiated "modification." [63] At this point the modification became the committee bill and subject to amendment.

Among committee staffers, the mood was one of great anxiety. Watching from the gallery, one of them commented,

> Did you see the movie *Search for Fire*? If you think how long and how hard they worked to find fire, that's what it's been like trying to get a budget resolution. . . . We have to huddle together and buck each other up all the time. There's such a big, bad, terrible world out there. . . . Now, there's a piranha psychology down there. Once an amendment carries, the whole thing may be torn apart.

Republican uncertainty was reflected by the rare presence of the vice president in the chair when the first amendment—an increase in

Medicare, was debated. He was both a symbol of the administration's position and a potential tie breaker. The amendment was defeated 39-60. The vice president was not present when a jobs program amendment was blown away. But he returned for the third amendment, which proposed a cut in the defense budget. It posed the first serious threat to the committee, in part because its author was Budget Committee member Nancy Kassebaum. Thirteen Republicans voted with her. The vote was 53-44 to table. The committee staffers in the gallery were visibly relieved. "That's as close as they'll ever get," exclaimed one of them as the group left.

For the next eight amendments, on May 19 and 20, his prediction held true. The Republican lines held against increases for education (two defections), environment (four defections), handicapped (seven defections), veterans (one defection), and against several revenue changes. On only one of them (handicapped) was the vice president called back to preside. But on the ninth amendment the optimistic staff prophecy failed. Late on the evening of May 20, the vice president returned to the chair to preside over the first proposal to undo a COLA freeze. It involved the pension program for retired railroad employees—to which the government is a contributor. He was there for good reason. At about midnight, the amendment was indirectly supported when a tabling motion failed 58-41, with thirteen Republicans defecting from the Budget Committee position. But before the succeeding up-or-down vote on the amendment itself could be called for, Baker and Domenici decided to recess the Senate—which they did, by the only straight party-line vote of the entire proceedings.

Overnight, the committee tried to regroup the Republican forces. The staff drafted a modest COLA increase for railroad retirees, hoping to win back the Republican defectors by giving ground in their direction. The vote, in the morning, to table this Domenici substitute was to be the test of their success. With the vice president ready to break a tie, the committee needed to win back eight of the defectors.

But Domenici could change only four votes; and his substitute was tabled 53-44. A committee staffer came into the gallery. "We didn't have the votes. We were short by two." The chairman spoke later about the railroad retirement amendment.

> There were two ingredients. People were hurt and they wrote in. I got about 700 letters—741 letters. There was heavy lobbying by their unions. They lobbied all over the corridors and in the offices— ordinary working folks. This was their one big issue.

On the final up-or-down vote, the original amendment was passed 57-40. All thirteen Republican defectors reverted to their previous evening's position. And one more joined them. The Budget Committee had suffered its first floor defeat.

The committee worry was that, having now been breached, the Republican line would not hold and "the piranha psychology" would prevail. "We tried to stop it," recounted Domenici. "We delayed it; we tried everything. But we couldn't stop it. I was afraid I would lose them all and not get a budget." And a committee aide echoed,

> We may lose the whole resolution. The conservatives . . . say every-thing has already been given to the liberals and, if all these pension amendments start going through, they'll vote against the whole thing. The White House has gone to lunch, leaving Pete out there all by himself. They're no help at all.

The gloom proved to be unwarranted. On the next amendment, by Minority Leader Robert Byrd, to increase unemployment compensation, ten of the defectors rejoined the Republican ranks in support of a successful tabling motion. And twelve more amendments were either tabled or voted down—including pension increases for military retirees and increased veterans' benefits. The final deficit figure for fiscal 1983 was $116 billion. (See Table 3-1.) When his amendment failed, Byrd's frustration spilled out into an attack on "lockstep" Republican "partisan-ship" that was, in effect, a tribute to the ability of the majority to maintain its cohesion.[64]

Republican support for the Budget Committee had slipped a little from its high point in 1981, but not much. With committee members leading the way, party support for Domenici remained notably strong. (See Table 3-4.) Of the fifty-three Republicans, twelve supported the committee every time they voted in 1982. Among them were Majority Leader Baker and Finance Committee Chairman Dole, who gave Chair-man Domenici strong support at every critical juncture during the debates. Twenty-four other Republicans voted with the committee on 90 percent or more of their votes. Nine more supported the committee at least 75 percent of the time. The other eight were problematical. When the budget resolution passed 49-43, only two Republicans voted no. They were the party's extremists—liberal Lowell Weicker and conserva-tive Jesse Helms.

There remained, in the majority party, a strong collective desire to govern, and to be perceived as governing. Media scorekeepers began to write that the Senate Republicans were, in fact, running the country. That desire was the glue that held the partisan majority together. It was a kind of glue exemplified by the responsibility themes of Pete Domenici and Howard Baker.

TABLE 3-4   Floor Support for Chairman Domenici: Budget Votes, Ninety-Seventh Congress

Senators	Number	*Domenici support scores* [a]					
		1981 (58 votes)		1982 (40 votes)		Total (98 votes)	
		Mean [b]	*Range* [c]	*Mean* [b]	*Range* [c]	*Mean* [b]	*Range* [c]
Budget Committee Republicans	(10)	94%	(98-89%)	88%	(97-68%)	92%	(98-81%)
Non-committee Republicans	(41)	90	(100-57)	82	(97-41)	86	(100-50)
All Republicans	(53)	91	(100-57)	83	(97-41)	88	(100-50)
Budget Committee Democrats	(10)	45	(88-21)	28	(36-18)	39	(67-18)
Non-committee Democrats	(35)	42	(75-16)	31	(84-15)	38	(79-17)
All Democrats	(45) [d]	43	(88-16)	31	(84-15)	38	(79-17)

[a] Percentage of votes with Domenici when both vote.
[b] Average of individual support scores.
[c] Highest and lowest individual support scores.
[d] Henry Jackson, Harrison Williams, and their successors omitted. All served partial terms.

In the majority leader's suite the next week, there were post-mortems on the behavior of the troops. "We got the budget with style. There were some very brave senators. . . ," said one aide, "and some real chickenshit senators, who showed ass instead of being medal-of-honor team players." For two of the moderates facing difficult reelections there was praise. For one who had a 96 percent committee support record on the twenty-eight floor votes:

He's a good senator. He's a consolation to the guys who are scared. He says, "I'm going to run and tell the folks the checkbook is dry. If they don't believe me or don't want to hear me, I'll be ambassador to New Zealand." He made that speech.

For one whose "committee support score" stood at 71 percent: "He runs in the most Democratic state in the union. He was up front about his opposition. But he stood with us on most issues and he voted for the budget." On Senator Nancy Kassebaum, whose defense-cut amendment posed the first serious threat to the budget: "She performed with style. She felt so strongly about defense that she had to offer her amendment. She put everyone on notice that she would do it. She said so in the Budget Committee. She showed just how much the defense increase threw everything else in the budget off, given the bottom line we were dealing with."

In the Budget Committee offices, the instant replay focused on the railroad retirement defeat. There was a general sense of relief that it had not broken the dam, coupled with some recrimination for the loss. "Our mistake was in not compromising that out in caucus," said one staffer.

> I don't know whether Senator X screamed on that one or not. But what he did was go over to the Democrats, tell them to offer it, and he would get them some votes. The night before we knew it was probably lost.... Our position the next day ... should have been enough to satisfy the people who wanted something done. But we didn't get the message out. Most of the votes that went against us in the end would have stayed with the committee if we had needed them. But we fell just one or two votes short. We lost X, Y, and Z. Y was the most crucial. He had stood by us in every other situation. But he felt he had given a flat-out commitment to support the program. Z was the biggest disappointment. He had supported the budget in committee, and he went against us. We were afraid of losing some more votes after that, but we didn't.

Another staffer echoed the unhappiness with Republican senators X and Z. "We have the feeling that some of those guys who voted against us violated their oath. X was the worst—advocating the railroad retirement increase.... Senator Z doesn't have to run for four years, and he'll never be beaten." Senators X and Z had committee support scores during floor voting of 67 percent and 68 percent respectively.

These staff-level post-mortems—which cumulate to shape senatorial reputations—display a considerable sympathy for people who are under a difficult electoral gun and very little sympathy for those who are not. They also display a strong belief in the sanctity of commitments made both in and out of Washington. They show a strong belief that in opposing your "team" you should not blindside them or give off false signals. Rather, you should signal your true intentions well in advance. These beliefs will bend under mitigating circumstances; but they are basic to the business of establishing reputations as "medal-of-honor team players."

It is graphic evidence of the cumulative impact of sequential action on outcomes that, at the very end of the floor debate, Pete Domenici was forced to argue against his own long-held budgetary preferences. Senator Bennett Johnston, a moderate Budget Committee Democrat, proposed a "balanced budget amendment" that rewrote the budget and its accompanying reconciliation instructions. It proposed an increase in taxes and proposed a balanced budget in 1985. It pegged all COLAs to gross national product growth, and it cut defense and discretionary spending. Altogether it produced a set of numbers very close to "the Domenici mark" of the fall of 1981 and of the spring of 1982. It represented Domenici's preferences before he began the task of majority building in committee and on the floor. Despite the lateness of the hour and the shortness of time—ten minutes were allowed on each side of the amendment—there was a rush of committee anxiety. "Our fear was that the administration might even embrace it on the floor. . . . There was a moment when you thought something really big might happen," recalled a committee staffer.

Some of Domenici's most valued committee members and colleagues rose to support the amendment. But Domenici, Dole, and Baker stood firm in defense of their product. Domenici admitted it would be hard for him to vote against the amendment. He noted that Social Security would be cut under the COLA formula and wished aloud that he had had the understanding of committee Democrats for that problem "on the evening that we reported out our budget" and "over the last six, eight, nine months." Dole praised the amendment as a warrant of future bipartisanship. For the present, he stressed how hard it had been to get the agreement among Republicans that finally existed. And Baker summed up the cumulative impact of sequence.

> The major difficulty it has is that it comes at a time when we are at the very end of this process, when the committee system has operated, when we have gone through dozens of amendments and hours upon hours of debate. Mr. President, this is not the time to write a budget resolution in the last few minutes of this debate.[65]

The amendment was tabled 70-21. But among the twenty-one opposing votes were twelve Republicans; and among the twelve Republicans were six members of the Budget Committee. For a brief moment, it was possible to glimpse the policy individualism that had been suppressed just below the surface of party unity on the committee. Among the nine conservative Democratic supporters were four members of the committee—the very same four with whom Domenici had kept up communication and on whom Domenici had pinned his hopes for bipartisanship earlier in the year. Their votes were another reminder of what might have been. One of Howard Baker's top aides exclaimed,

> That's the thing that bothers me about the whole process—the bipartisanship. They drag us through the entire process and then at the last minute they came up on the floor with a substitute that is very close to what Domenici wanted in the first place. . . . The substitute shows you just about where a majority of the Senate

wanted to be. If we had had a bipartisan budget from the beginning, we would have had about fifteen Democrats. Then the moderate Republicans could have voted their conscience and their constituencies—against the budget. I think Baker and Domenici would both have preferred it that way.

The legislative sequence had its own accumulated, irreversible momentum. And the preferences of many individuals had been submerged by bargaining and commitment along the way. They could not be cut loose and reformulated at the last minute, however appealing the vehicle might be. It was another instructive lesson in the sequential politics of early, later, late, and too late. It was also another measure of Chairman Domenici's signal accomplishment in moving to secure a committee majority at the time he did.

MAJORITY BUILDING IN CONFERENCE

The difficulties the Senate Committee had to overcome to produce and pass a budget paled by comparison with the entanglements that plagued its counterpart in the House. The minimum task in either chamber, of course, was to find a majority to support a budget. In the Senate, from the time Pete Domenici decided to take an independent lead as chairman it was clear what kind of majority would be supporting what kind of budget. The majority would be partisan; the budget would be the Domenici Plan. Domenici's path was made possible, in the final analysis, by the binding ties of party. Leadership was a necessary ingredient. But the chairman could work closely with his committee members, with the majority leader, with the administration, with other committee chairmen, and with fellow senators precisely because they were all Republicans. As a group, they had come to the conclusion that their ability to agree on a budget was the crucial test of their ability to govern the country. And they had come to the further conclusion that proving their collective ability to govern the country took priority, at that point in time, over proving their individual devotion to policy particulars.

In the House, none of these cohesive ingredients were present—not the glue of party, not the stimulus of leadership, and not the incentive to govern. Consequently, it was not clear until the very moment a budget passed what kind of majority would support what kind of budget.

The House Budget Committee chairman never had the total support of his committee members or his party's leadership or his fellow committee chairmen or his fellow House Democrats—and certainly not of the administration.[66] But neither did any other Democrat. Once

Speaker O'Neill's influence on the Gang of Seventeen negotiations ended, he was powerless to prevent all the natural Democratic factionalisms from asserting themselves. The minority party Republicans worked to build agreement among themselves while waiting for enough conservative Democrats to spin off from the intra-Democratic warfare to make a majority. The White House gave low-key support to the Republican budget, taking the position that "we'll let the Congress work its will." [67]

In late May, eight different budget plans (plus eight amendments) were presented to the House, and every one of the plans was voted down. The Republican leadership proposal lost 235-192. The Budget Committee proposal was given the strategic advantage of going last— the argument being that, faced with that budget or no budget, a majority would vote for it. But it, too, lost—265-159. This week-long inability to find a majority willing to govern the country was, as in 1980, a low point for the budget process. And it served to highlight the accomplishment of the Senate Republicans.

A House Budget Committee leader described the House situation as "paralysis, fear, confusion, and polarization." [68] "There's so much anger and frustration out there, you couldn't even offer the Lord's Prayer," said the author of one proposal.[69] Fifty-five members voted no on all eight budgets. It was commonly said that "Voting no is the best political vote." [70] Speaker O'Neill threw up his hands. "I say to my liberal and conservative friends, I don't know how you get together." [71] The president called the budget process "the most irresponsible, Mickey Mouse arrangement that any governmental body ever practiced." [72]

News headlines read: "Shellshocked House Sifts Through Wreckage of the Budget"; "The Budget: An Impasse, Without a Consensus, It's a Punt, Not a Pass"; "The Budget: Capitol's Ongoing Horror Show, Process Disintegrating as Congress Fights On." [73] Key House members commented that "our budget procedure is coming apart at the seams," [74] and "there is real concern whether the budget process can survive." [75] It was 1980 all over again. As both parties set about to try again, there was speculation that a majority could not be found.[76] Once again, the essential fragility of the process—in the absence of implementing majorities—was put on public display.

Ten days later, the two parties presented reworked budgets to the House. No amendments were allowed; and the Republican proposal was given the strategic advantage of last vote. The Democratic proposal was what the Speaker called "a true Democratic budget," one that would represent "the true philosophy of our party." [77] It was designed more to win "principles" and to help maintain a majority in the November elections than to build a majority in June.[78] The Democratic leaders did not make the votes matters of party loyalty.[79] By contrast, Republican leader Michel said that "We're playing the margin game out there to get 218 votes." [80] And the votes were made a matter of party loyalty for Republicans. "We started bearing down on some of our members in a more militant fashion," said Michel.[81] The Republican proposal passed 216-206, with fifteen Republican defections and forty-six Democratic supporters. It was the same coalition that passed the 1981 Reagan budget—but this time in a mood of exhaustion rather than euphoria. "There is," said Michel, "a damp and dreary atmosphere in this House; there is no drive, there is no enthusiasm and there is no resolve." [82] But there was a budget. There remained a budget process. There would be a conference with the Senate.

Chairman Domenici did very little during House deliberations except wait. "I talked to a few guys. There was a lot of staff-to-staff explaining. But as far as getting involved in a big way, no. They made their own budget decisions." In the fall, in Hobbs, New Mexico, he had called the House "that glob of humanity" and "that monstrous institution." It was not a sympathetic view. The day after the House's budget decision, his reaction went from criticism to analysis to sympathy. All reflected elements of his "Senate vision."

"Well, the House passed a budget," he began. "And most of them don't have the slightest idea what's in the bill. They showed themselves to be absolutely gutless when they voted against eight budgets. I think they realized the public was looking at them, that the public didn't care which budget they passed just so long as they passed a budget." He went on to explain the outcome.

> I take my hat off to Bob Michel. He's quite some player, isn't he? Not to take anything away from him, but I think the Democrats were kinda played out. Once they went through the self-flagellation exercise and lost the [committee] budget, they didn't have the fire anymore. The press did a good job on that. They showed the whole thing to be a screw-up—which it was. The country wanted a budget.

Then he stopped himself and became reflective.

> I suppose it's easy for me to say all this and take the positions I've taken because I'm not up for reelection, not now. I've come to the conclusion that it's not worth running—or winning—if you can't go ahead and do some of the things you really believe in. But I don't know how I would feel if I had to run for reelection this year and deal with Social Security and veterans and Medicare. Those are tough issues. It must be a bitch to run every two years. I couldn't stand it.

This sensitivity to bicameralism was not his first reaction; but it was a necessary one if he was to have a successful conference with the House.

Almost immediately, he was on the phone with his staffers ascertaining which of his committee members wanted to be conferees and what—within a negotiated party ratio—the Senate group would look like.

> You mean A wants to stay on my wonderful committee. . . ? B wants to go too. . . ? I can't take C with me. . . . So [the Democrats] will have D, yeah; and they will stop before they get to E? Good. I don't want E or F or any of those wild guys. Last time, they brought them in, they said, "to represent the full range of our policy views." Well, if they do that, I'll have to represent the full range on my side. . . . So we will have A, B, etc. . . . That means I'll have to call G and tell him it won't work. He'll be mad. But it won't work.

Both party groups offered conference membership in order of seniority, until their quotas were filled. It was not a process over which the chairman had much control. In the end, he got some colleagues that he wanted and some he didn't.

When Senate and House conferees met four days later, James Jones, the Democratic chairman of the House Budget Committee, set the tone. "As I see it. . . ," he said, "it is going to be essentially a difference of opinion between two budgets which the president has endorsed, and this is almost a family matter within the Republican party to mediate."[83] A majority of House conferees—the Democrats—did not approve of the budget they had to defend. But they had no intention of obstructing the process. They planned to step aside, let the two groups of Republicans negotiate, and report out the result. Domenici acknowledged that on the Senate side the partisanship that had propelled the budget to that point would have to continue. "I am aware," he said, "that in the Senate, only three members of the minority party voted for it. I don't think we are going to change much of that here."[84]

Since each chamber's conferees would vote as a group—with majorities of each group having to be in agreement—Domenici had to hold his six-member Republican majority together against his four-member Democratic minority. He thanked the House Democrats for their passive posture. "There will have to be," he said, "an inordinate amount of good will on your side, and flexibility, as being the conduit or the referee to get a resolution that you can take to the House and pass."[85] With the exception of one moment of near disaster, the conference proceeded for three days in that spirit. As Domenici put it, "[Our] goal and objective and purpose here . . . is to try desperately and as quickly as possible to get a budget."[86] The ability to pass a budget was the ability to govern. "No matter what we come out with," said House Budget Chairman Jones, "this is just another step in the budget process in rebuilding the confidence that we have the ability to get a hold of fiscal policy."[87]

For a couple of days the conference committee met sporadically and talked desultorily, while House and Senate Republicans negotiated out their differences. "It was all done in private," said one Senate staffer.

> We only had three public sessions. We cut two of them short because there were so many deals being made in private. We weren't negotiating with the Budget Committee Democrats. We were negotiating with all these other principalities in the House—like Representative X on the veterans. He had twenty votes that wouldn't vote for the budget unless we put that money back.

On the third and final day, the Republican conferees put their negotiated budget resolution on the table. "I think the Republicans have solved their squabble," said Domenici when, on behalf of the Senate, he formally proposed it as the agenda for the conference.[88]

The House Democrats ceded to the Republicans the strategic advantage of the status quo by agreeing to it. Any changes proposed by House Democrats (or Senate Democrats) would come as an amendment to the Republican budget. So long, therefore, as the Senate Republicans stuck together the negotiated budget could not be changed. That, in fact, is what they did, voting down nine Democratic amendments to the various functions and accepting one. Several matters of reconciliation language were settled without a vote. The bottom-line deficit figure of $103.9 billion that Domenici had presented to the conference remained intact when it was over. Four Democrats joined four Republicans to vote the budget out on the House side. On the Senate side, the conference report was signed only by the Republicans.

Chairman Domenici did not, however, survive without one last, nerve-wracking threat to his partisan majority. On the day the conference opened, he received a letter from the president asking that the chairman stand by the Senate numbers, higher by $900 million than the House numbers, for "Function 150: International Affairs." The president argued that the lower House figure would "cripple" American interests abroad—especially in the Middle East. It was an argument Domenici had no difficulty agreeing with personally. He had protected the Senate numbers against more than one proposed cut on the Senate floor. He believed, however, that strong antagonism to foreign assistance among House members would threaten budget passage in that chamber if he acceded. And he soon learned not only that House Democrats were prepared to agree to the president's request but that at least one of his Republican Senate conferees had agreed also.

His problem surfaced in a private negotiating session between House and Senate Republican conferees in Howard Baker's office. As one observer described it,

> We had worked out most of our problems and were about to end the meeting when, all of a sudden, [Senator] Rudy Boschwitz said, "There isn't enough money in the 150 Function. Foreign aid is too low. The

president wants more money than we have in the bill." We had started $900 million apart, and the House group had already agreed to go $286 million above their figure, in outlays. As soon as Boschwitz started to speak, [Representative] Dick Cheney, who is a very reasonable guy, said, "No. The House cannot accept one penny more than we have. If we add one more penny, the House will not accept the conference report." He stood up. Bob Michel stood up and said flatly, "That's nonnegotiable." They turned their backs—even while Boschwitz was talking. And they all—all the House conferees—left.

By the time of the Republican conferees' next meeting, the president had told both Baker and Domenici that he needed the full $900 million and State Department officials had begun to lobby for it.[89] "We knew," said a participant,

that Boschwitz would propose adding the $600 million and that if it passed it would blow up the whole conference. . . . Domenici went to Jones and said, "You can't vote for another $600 million. Won't you vote to kill it and save the conference?" Jones said, "No, I've got to vote for it. I can't cut all my ties in the House. You guys will have to kill it." So we went to work and developed a compromise—increase budget authority but keep outlays where we had them. Domenici called the president and told him about it. The president said he wanted the original Domenici figures, but that he didn't want to jeopardize the whole budget. He would accept it.

But the outcome, in the conference, was filled with uncertainty.

Domenici knew that the House Democrats would propose the $600 million increase and that the Senate Democrats would probably support it. He knew that at least one Senate Republican would support it. ("We knew Boschwitz wouldn't budge," said an aide, "He's the most persistent person in the Senate when it comes to aid for Israel.") And he could not be sure he could hold the others. So he moved to hedge against the adverse effects of a tie vote among the Senate conferees, by planning to word the motion in such a way that a tie vote meant rejection of the increase. This required, once again, the use of the chairman's procedural prerogatives.

To make a change in the proposal as brought to conference, a majority vote by the Senate conferees was necessary. On each of the eight previous Democratic motions, Chairman Domenici had asked the question: "Does the Senate reject the proposal?" Assuming unanimity among the four Democrats, a unanimous vote among the six Republicans would be needed to reject the proposal. If one Republican defected, there would be a tie 5-5 vote, the motion to reject would not carry, and the Democrats would win. But on the foreign aid vote, Domenici planned to put the motion: "Does the Senate *accept* the proposal?" In this case, a tie 5-5 vote—assuming one Republican defection—would mean that the vote to accept would not carry, and Domenici would win. He could be defeated, in other words, only if he lost two Republican votes—only, that is, if the motion to accept won a majority of six votes. And, when the issue was joined in the conference, he believed that was exactly what might happen.

"Just five minutes before the vote we learned that Hatch was going to vote against us," recalled a staffer. "Domenici went white when we heard that. That's why you saw all that scurrying around the table." The uncertainty grew when Senator Tower spoke strongly in favor of the increase and said, "I am sorry for having this. I may vote with my chairman. But I do so, *if* I do, with enormous reluctance." [90] Senator Hatch, spoke very emotionally in associating himself with Senator Tower and then in saying, "I also believe we have got to have a budget. I think that may be the most paramount thing here today . . . [and] I will support it." [91] When Democratic Senator Howard Metzenbaum requested a call of the roll (the first and only one of the conference) it seemed clear that a major hitch in the long process could be imminent. During Domenici's plea "that my conferees help me" so as not "to put the whole budget at risk," [92] the room grew completely silent for the first time in three days.

The transcript of the proceedings conveys something of the uncertainty and maneuvering that accompanied the roll call.

> SENATOR DOMENICI: Will the Clerk call the roll?
> SENATOR METZENBAUM: What is the vote on?
> SENATOR DOMENICI: The motion is do we accept the House's [Representative Stephen] Solarz amendment.
> SENATOR METZENBAUM: Is it not the question—it is my understanding that—
> SENATOR DOMENICI: We are going to vote right now. It is whether we accept it.
> THE CLERK: Senator Metzenbaum?
> SENATOR METZENBAUM: Aye.
> THE CLERK: Senator Armstrong?
> SENATOR DOMENICI: No by proxy.
> THE CLERK: Senator Kassebaum?
> SENATOR KASSEBAUM: No.
> THE CLERK: Senator Hollings.
> SENATOR METZENBAUM: Aye by proxy.
> SENATOR DOMENICI: Do you have his proxy?
> SENATOR METZENBAUM: I am authorized to speak.
> SENATOR DOMENICI: We have written proxies as a rule here.
> SENATOR METZENBAUM: I can get it.

CONFERENCE CHAIRMAN JONES: Let's continue to vote.

SENATOR DOMENICI: He knows that.

THE CLERK: Senator Johnston?

SENATOR METZENBAUM: Aye by proxy.

SENATOR DOMENICI: I do not believe the Senator has the proxy of Senator Hollings.

SENATOR METZENBAUM: Ms. Tankersley [a Senate staffer] told me that I did.

THE CLERK: Senator Boschwitz?

SENATOR BOSCHWITZ: Aye.

THE CLERK: Senator Hatch?

SENATOR HATCH: No.

THE CLERK: Senator Tower?

SENATOR TOWER: No.

THE CLERK: Mr. Chairman?

THE CHAIRMAN: No.

THE CLERK: Five ayes and five nays, if you accept the—

SENATOR DOMENICI: We accept the proxies.

SENATOR METZENBAUM: It is my understanding that the motion was more appropriate as to whether we reject, that nobody on this side made a motion to accept, and I believe it was the Chair's motion to reject.

SENATOR DOMENICI: We have to, one way or another, accept that for it to be added to. And the vote is five to five. We did not accept it. Do you want to repeat the roll again?[93]

The moment did not have the high, drawn-out drama of the chairman's May 5 announcement that he had secured the president's approval for his budget plan. But it was the most tense and the most emotional public moment of the entire year. Partisan hardball had broken through the veneer of courtesy—as Republicans could taste final victory and Democrats could taste final defeat.

The comment of a top Senate Committee staff member evokes both the emotion and the stakes.

> When Metzenbaum jumped in and said he had their proxies; I couldn't believe it. I couldn't believe he had Hollings's proxy. Domenici said he did not believe him—called him a liar. There were more hard words after the meeting and Domenici never apologized. When we polled the Republicans, Hatch went with us; and it all hinged on Tower's vote. He gave us a tie. Ouwwwwch, was that close! It was the whole ballgame. If we had lost that, we would have blown the conference. We would have had no bill, no budget. We

never thought Hollings would give Metzenbaum his proxy on foreign aid. We never thought he'd give him his proxy on anything! They had saved the proxies for just that one vote. They had not used them at all up to that vote. They were trying to wreck the conference. And they almost did.

That is, of course, the partisan view from over the chairman's shoulder. But it is he who had the responsibility for moving the budget forward; and he had chosen to do it the partisan way. Senate committee Democrats were never helpful in the conference. When Chairman Jones recessed the meeting immediately after the foreign aid vote—to cool the situation— the two remaining Democrats left and none of them ever returned.

It is some justification for the detailed explication of the 1982 budget season to note, once again, how fragile the process is, and therefore, how fateful each small hurdle can seem to be. When the conference report went back to the two chambers, it was accepted, thus giving Congress a budget resolution. The resolution provided that it would automatically become the second budget resolution if no other budget action was taken. And no one expected any. In the House, the conference report carried by the slimmest of margins, 210-208. In the Senate, the vote was 54-45, with three Republican defectors balanced by three Democratic defectors. Committee Democrats again attacked the partisan "stonewalling" manner in which the majority had been constructed; but they blamed the president rather than the Budget Committee chairman.[94]

Domenici defended the budget and the process. "It is most significant that this resolution moves us off a path of rapidly rising deficits and onto a path of declining ones, not declining as fast as I would like; but I think it is the best we can produce under the circumstances." [95] "I am sorry there was no other way to get a budget.... [But] when you are in the majority you need to govern.... Governing is a lot more difficult than that simple approach that some in this body take of being against everything and for nothing unless what they are for is something they know will not pass." [96] In the final analysis, governing, for the Budget Committee chairman, meant getting a budget as close to what he wanted and, at the same time, one that would pass. In 1982, he came as close to balancing good public policy and institutional maintenance as he would ever come.

As the third budget season came to a close in the summer of 1982, Domenici was at the peak of his Senate career. He was an integral part of the Republican Senate team that had taken budgetary leadership away from the administration and was, indeed, governing the country. He ended 1982 with the same focus on the partisan team that he had begun with two years earlier. Said Domenici,

> People in Washington say that the Republican leaders as a group are much better than they ever thought we would be. Baker, great; Dole, great; Hatfield, very sophisticated; Domenici, surprised as hell about Domenici. I think the party will get some momentum because we've done good work and we've looked good doing it. Dole is great on TV; Baker, great; I do OK. The Democrats got momentum out of their chairmanships. We ought to be able to get some [now].

Opinion polls showed that already, most people thought that the Republican party was better able to run the country than the Democrats—an edge they retained through 1984.[97] This was mainly the accomplishment of Ronald Reagan and the Republican Senate—the direct derivative of the policy mandate interpretation and its strategic corollary about governing.

The centrality of budget making to governance had given Pete Domenici a very large role in that accomplishment. Looking back, at the end of 1982, he said,

> I never thought I would ever have the potential for influence that I've had over the last two years. I honestly think I've had as much or more influence on the procedure and the substance of policy than anyone else up here. Bob Dole has been an implementer in high style. But the direction of public policy and how you get there, those ideas have been mine. Of course, mine within certain limits. I would have frozen everything last September—frozen all the entitlement programs—if I had my way.

Budget making had dominated the congressional agenda; and Pete Domenici had orchestrated congressional budget making.

Our detailed examination of his behavior conveys some sense of Domenici's developing skill at governing. A chairman's leadership must be viewed as a contextual and a sequential activity. If he is to take the policy lead, he must gather support. And the gathering of support depends heavily on calculations of time and situation, of when and where to act. Domenici's success depended upon several such decisions about timing—to wait first on the administration and then on his Senate colleagues before presenting his package, to wait while the Gang of Seventeen tested the possibilities of bipartisanship, to wait for presidential initiatives to give legitimacy to a tax increase, to pause to allow bipartisanship to be tested in committee, to work slowly to solidify partisan support in the committee, to move boldly to gain presidential support, and to jump in with a procedural ploy when the conference was threatened. Leadership involves both waiting on events and seizing the day. Domenici demonstrated skill in both respects. And that added to his influence, his reputation, and his independence.

Domenici believed that his main job as chairman was to preserve the budget process. He had done that, in his own fashion, with a partisan majority. Was he worried about that? "No, I don't worry about it," he said.

> It only worries me that it won't last. We will have to go back to bipartisanship eventually. But I am very comfortable with my eleven Republicans. I have gained confidence in them and they have gained confidence in me. Even though it's mostly my budget, it's nice to have some loyalists who are willing to stand up and defend it. . . . I know that this partisan pattern does not conform to normal practice in the Senate. It isn't the way Senate business is conducted. Mostly things are done in a bipartisan manner in this institution. I don't know whether your political historians will say our pattern is wrong or right or better or worse. But I'm perfectly comfortable with it.

Two years as chairman under a Republican president had rendered him much more ready to promote partisanship than he had been as a minority senator. He had adapted to it as the necessary concomitant of the majority's responsibility to govern. For the moment, at least, Chairman Domenici was implementing party government in a system without strong parties.

As for Domenici and the president, they remained at the third season's end cooperative but not close. "Right now," he said in August, "relations with the administration are good. They fluctuate. They don't watch what you say on a daily basis. They know that you're a team player and that you're trying to help them." Domenici's new-found independence had brought some stability to the situation. But he was, as usual, worried. "Man, I'm beat all the time now," he said. "I'm so uptight about whether we're doing the right thing. Even when I sleep, I don't sleep. You know what I mean." The problem was that, despite all he had accomplished, the country faced runaway deficits. The 1982 deficit, originally projected at $45 billion, was on its way to a record $128 billion. The Domenici Plan budget, passed by Congress with a projection for 1983 of $115 billion, was on its way to $200 billion. And there was no end in sight.

"The president doesn't understand any of this," Domenici said. "He really doesn't. The numbers we see are terrible. And the boss man is completely oblivious to them. I don't know how much longer I can stay with him."

That was a problem that would not go away. The two men had been thrown together by the elections of 1980. They had been thrown together by the task of governing the country. They had been thrown together because budget making is so central to governing the country. That set of forces is too strong to allow for any lengthy separation. So whatever his many worries, Domenici would have to "stay with him." Besides, his association with Reagan—whether dependence or transition or independence—had made Domenici's career rise possible. So they would continue to work out the relationship begun in 1981. By 1982 the main lines of that relationship had been established—around which there would be future fluctuations in other budget seasons. After all, Domenici's 1982 triumph did not make him budget leader for life. And future seasons might well be less rewarding. These were the satisfactions, frustrations, patterns, and prospects he carried with him into the Ninety-eighth Congress.

NOTES

1. *Wall Street Journal*, January 25, 1982.
2. "The Hard Times of Ronald Reagan," *Newsweek*, February 1, 1982.
3. Ibid.
4. *Washington Post*, January 10, 1982.
5. Owen Ullman, "Bipartisan Budget Plan May Solve U.S. Financial Woes," *Gallup* [New Mexico] *Independent*, January 13, 1982; and Dale Tate, "Budget Experts Warn Process Could Fall Under 1982 Strains," *Congressional Quarterly Weekly Report*, January 23, 1982.
6. David Broder, "A Case of Self-Entrapment," *Washington Post*, February 14, 1982.
7. Lou Cannon, "President Defends Budget as Only Hope for Recovery," *Washington Post*, January 10, 1982.
8. *Congressional Record*, February 10, 1982, S688; and "The Deficit Rebellion," *Newsweek*, February 22, 1982.
9. *Newsweek*, March 8, 1982.
10. Helen Dewar, "Hill Chiefs Mull Budget Control," *Washington Post*, January 3, 1982.
11. All excerpts from the speech are from: "Speech Before the Conference Board by U.S. Senator Pete V. Domenici, February 23, 1982," (press copy).
12. *Washington Post*, March 2, 1982.
13. Joseph Kraft, "Brokering a Budget Deal," *Washington Post*, March 23, 1982.
14. Transcript, "Meet the Press," March 7, 1982, 7. See also, Paul Wieck, "Budget Alternative Sanctioned," *Albuquerque Journal*, March 10, 1982; and "Reagan Applauds Domenici Proposal," *Albuquerque Tribune*, March 8, 1982.
15. Helen Dewar and Lou Cannon, "Reagan Gives No Ground in Budget Talk on Hill," *Washington Post*, March 10, 1982; and *Newsweek*, March 22, 1982.
16. *Washington Post*, March 17, 1982.
17. Helen Dewar, "Dead Center: Where the Budget Battle Sits," *Washington Post*, March 21, 1982; and "Stalemate Over the Budget," *Newsweek*, March 29, 1982.
18. *Washington Post*, February 2, 1982.
19. *Washington Post*, March 31, 1982.

20. Senate Budget Committee, "Transcript of Proceedings, Markup Session on First Budget Resolution for Fiscal Year 1983," March 30, 1982, 3.
21. "Unemployment Hits a New High," *Newsweek,* April 12, 1982.
22. Senate Budget Committee, "Transcript of Proceedings," March 30, 1982, 5-10.
23. Ibid., 9. Vote will be found on page 111. See also *Washington Post,* March 31, 1982.
24. Ibid., 17.
25. Helen Dewar and Lou Cannon, "Budget Impasse Persists Amid Talk of Compromise," *Washington Post,* April 21, 1982. See also *New York Times,* April 20, 22, 1982.
26. Martin Tolchin, "A Month's Budget Talks Finally Came to Naught," *New York Times,* April 30, 1982. For Pete Domenici's reaction to the end of the talks, see transcript, "Budget Impasse," MacNeil/Lehrer Newshour, April 29, 1982.
27. Steven Roberts, "Budget Compromise: Push and Pull in an Election Year," *New York Times,* April 22, 1982.
28. Tolchin, "A Month's Budget Talks."
29. *Congressional Record,* April 22, 1982, S3890.
30. Senate Budget Committee, "Transcript of Proceedings," April 29, 1982, 188-189.
31. Ibid., 189.
32. *Washington Post,* April 30, 1982.
33. Helen Dewar, "Jungle of Conflict," *Washington Post,* April 19, 1982.
34. Senate Budget Committee, "Transcript of Proceedings," April 29, 1982, 242-246.
35. Steven Roberts, "Senate Panel, in Partisan Mood, Begins Drafting Budget for 1983," *New York Times,* April 30, 1982.
36. Dewar, "Jungle of Conflict."
37. These comments will be found, in order, in Senate Budget Committee, "Transcript of Proceedings," March 30, 1982, 18, 34, 27, and 44; April 1, 1982, 174; and May 4, 1982, 282, 309.
38. Senate Budget Committee, "Transcript of Proceedings," May 4, 1982, 259.
39. Robert Merry, "In High Stakes Fight over Budget, Domenici Just Outmaneuvered Democrats," *Wall Street Journal,* May 11, 1982.
40. Senate Budget Committee, "Transcript of Proceedings," May 4, 1982, 259-260.
41. Ibid., 257.
42. Ibid., 249-250.
43. For the "Additional Views" in which each of the three explains his vote, see, Senate Budget Committee, Report on First Concurrent Resolution on the Budget, Fiscal Year 1983, 97th Cong., 2d sess., 1982, 153-158.
44. Martin Tolchin, "Test for Budget Process in Congress," *New York Times,* May 4, 1982.
45. George Wilson, "A Defense Spending Chip Put on Bargaining Table," *Washington Post,* April 21, 1982.
46. Merry, "In High Stakes Fight."
47. Helen Dewar, "White House, Hill GOP Leaders Find Budget Agreement," *Washington Post,* May 6, 1982; and Martin Tolchin, "White House and GOP Leaders Reach Agreement on 1983 Budget," *New York Times,* May 6, 1982.
48. *Congressional Record,* October 11, 1984, S14374.
49. Senate Budget Committee, "Transcript of Proceedings," May 5, 1982, 465.

50. Ibid., 521.
51. The view of these events from the Reagan administration's perspective is reported by Steven Weisman in "Acting the Part of Leader," *New York Times*, May 7, 1982.
52. Merry, "In High Stakes Fight."
53. *New York Times*, May 6, 1982.
54. *Washington Post*, May 7, 1982.
55. *Congressional Record*, May 12, 1982, S4933.
56. *Washington Post*, May 12, 1982.
57. *New York Times*, May 12, 1982.
58. Ibid.
59. Helen Dewar, "GOP Leaders on Hill Vow to Push Squeeze on Social Security," *Washington Post*, May 15, 1982.
60. Ibid.
61. Ibid.
62. See *Congressional Record*, May 19, 1982, S5476.
63. *Congressional Record*, May 17-19, 1982, S5353-5356, S5406-5409, S5464-5470.
64. *Congressional Record*, May 21, 1982, S5788-5791.
65. Ibid., S5831-5838.
66. *New York Times*, May 14, 29, 1982; and *Washington Post*, May 27, 29, 1982.
67. *Washington Post*, May 27, 1982; and *New York Times*, May 30, 1982.
68. Steven Roberts, "Budget Chairman Urges Lawmakers to Meet Halfway," *New York Times*, May 29, 1982.
69. Helen Dewar, "House Rejects Cuts in Medicare, Shatters Strategies on Budget," *Washington Post*, May 28, 1982.
70. *Washington Post*, June 11, 1982.
71. *Washington Post*, May 29, 1982.
72. Roberts, "Budget Chairman Urges."
73. *Washington Post*, May 29, 1982; *New York Times*, May 29, 1982; and *Boston Globe*, June 6, 1982.
74. *New York Times*, June 2, 1982.
75. Martin Tolchin, "Value and Loss to Congress of Adopting No Budget," *New York Times*, June 4, 1982.
76. *Washington Post*, June 3, 10, 1982; and *New York Times*, June 4, 6, 8, 10, 1982.
77. *New York Times*, June 3, 1982.
78. *Washington Post*, June 9, 1982.
79. Martin Tolchin, "GOP Budget Wins Approval in House by Vote of 219- 206," *New York Times*, June 11, 1982.
80. Helen Dewar, "House Panel Calling Reagan's Bluff, Sends Budget to Floor," *Washington Post*, June 4, 1982. See also comments of Rep. Trent Lott, *New York Times*, June 4, 1982.
81. *New York Times*, June 6, 1982.
82. *Congressional Record*, June 22, 1982, H3739.
83. House Budget Committee, Senate Budget Committee, "Transcript of Proceedings on First Concurrent Budget Resolution, Fiscal Year 1983," June 15, 1982, 3.
84. Ibid., 7.
85. Ibid.
86. Senate Budget Committee, "Transcript of Proceedings," June 17, 1982, 157.
87. Senate Budget Committee, "Transcript of Proceedings," June 15, 1982, 10.
88. Senate Budget Committee, "Transcript of Proceedings," June 17, 1982, 49.

89. William Chapman and Herbert Denton, "State Skirted White House to Push for Foreign Aid," *Washington Post*, June 19, 1982; and *Washington Post*, June 24, 1982.
90. Senate Budget Committee, "Transcript of Proceedings," June 17, 1982, 197.
91. Ibid., 198.
92. Ibid., 195.
93. Ibid., 199-201.
94. *Congressional Record*, June 22, 1982, S7273ff.
95. Ibid., S7268.
96. Ibid., S7321, S7335.
97. See Paul Blustein, "Democratic Economists Agree: Reaganomics Is a Bust," *Washington Post Weekly Edition*, July 25-31, 1988.

4

Changing Contexts,
Changing Leadership

LEADERSHIP IN CONTEXT

After two years as Budget Committee chairman, Pete Domenici had become one of the three or four acknowledged leaders of the U.S. Senate. In January 1983, when Majority Leader Howard Baker announced his intention to retire two years hence, Domenici's name quickly surfaced among a handful of potential successors. On the basis of his governing performance, the suggestion was logical. And it was taken seriously.[1] But two years remained before the new leader would be chosen. And also in two years, the senator would have to run for reelection in New Mexico. What he did in those two years might well affect his future career. But in late 1982 and early 1983 he had little time to anticipate any future career junctures. Nor did he have time to enjoy his recent accomplishments. The budget process had become nothing if not, as one who watched it daily said in the spring of 1983, "a time-consuming, mind-numbing, numbers-crunching monster."[2] Almost immediately after his 1982 victory, the chairman plunged back into the grueling grind. This chapter traces the fourth and fifth seasons of his budget-making activity.

We are tempted to say that Domenici could look forward to "more of the same." Yet his first three efforts at budget making had taken place in quite different contexts and had produced quite different patterns of leadership. They were anything but "the same." On the other hand, his three seasons of activity had identified for him, and for us, most of "the same" variables that would continue to shape the Senate's budgetary enterprise. It would be helpful to review these variables briefly.

Since our view of budget politics is a chairman-centered one, we should begin by reemphasizing the basic importance of the chairman's

133

goals. From the beginning of his Washington career, Pete Domenici's most transparent goal was to become a policy-making "player" inside the Senate. The chairmanship had brought him that influence. His first two years in that position, he said later, "made me a senator." He wanted to keep or expand the policy influence he had gained. A second goal—institutional maintenance—had been imposed on him by his chairmanship. And Domenici adopted that one, too—to protect and to preserve the budget process itself. The two goals did not always lead to the same decision. In his first season, he explained his decisions on policy grounds; in his second season, process explanations gained prominence. In the two years ahead, he would often be forced to choose between his desire for inside policy influence and his desire to keep the budget process alive.

While taking into account the chairman's personal goals, we have also laid heavy emphasis on the effects of the larger context in which he worked. These contextual features presented him with both opportunities and constraints. In the last chapter, we watched him take advantage of his opportunities at various points in the budget process to provide leadership—to his committee, to his party, to his institution, and to his president. He could set an agenda, set a tone and a direction, bring people together, keep things from falling apart, and act as a spokesman. But we also came to understand that he operated within a set of constraints that rendered him subject to events and reliant on people over whom he had no control. "I'm confessing to you," he said in late 1981, "that my vaunted committee chairmanship has operated within a very "narrow gauge." And while the directions in which he leaned remained clear, his impact on bottom-line budget outcomes—on spending patterns and deficits, for example—remained severely circumscribed and nearly impossible to trace.

Most constraining, we have found, are the grand parameters of budget making—*economic conditions* and *electoral proximity.* These broad contextual variables operate both retrospectively and prospectively. Is the economy getting better or worse? What do people think about it? Changing answers to these questions forced changes in budget making between the summer and fall of 1981. Has an election just passed or is one in the offing? What interpretation or expectations do the public and the politicians hold concerning these elections? Domenici's first-season activity was sharply limited by the answers to these questions. Politics and economics combined to shape varying patterns of activity in each of Domenici's first three seasons.

Subject to these broad contextual variables but separable from them are the political relationships among the participants in majority building. Of paramount importance is the attitude and the behavior of the *president.* In each of the first three seasons the chairman needed the support of the president. In the first two seasons, the president dictated the outcome. In the third season, he acquiesced in it. In all three cases, the president's political strength helped to persuade the chairman to build a partisan majority in his committee. He was encouraged in his partisanship, too, by the remarkable party cohesion of the Republican senators—which was itself a derivative of presidential leadership. There was, of course, no guarantee that the same degree of presidential policy activism or partisan unity would prevail in the two years ahead. If they should not, then, the chairman would have an incentive to entertain a strategy of bipartisanship to pass a budget out of his committee.

The attitudes and actions of *other Republican leaders* were also of predictable importance in the chairman's world. In 1982 the support and assistance of Majority Leader Baker had been a critical factor in Domenici's leadership success. So, too, had been the cooperation and the forbearance of those committee barons who were his natural rivals in the budgetary realm—Finance Committee Chairman Robert Dole and Appropriations Committee Chairman Mark Hatfield. The proadministration team of which Domenici considered himself a part may have been the derivative of a temporary set of political conditions. And as the budget-related behavior of both moderate and supply-side Republicans demonstrated, the interests of other party factions would always have to be taken into account.

We cannot confine these generalizations to the president's party alone. The predispositions, preferences, cohesion, and leadership among interested and influential Democrats represent another significant variable. Sometimes Domenici received help from them; often he absorbed their harmless rhetoric; sometimes he endured genuine attempts at disruption. The state of the Democrats would predictably have some effect on the makeup of committee majorities. But like the other elements of context, the exact nature of the effect will vary.

It makes a difference, also, to budgetary outcomes, what the major *issues* are and how they get framed. Entitlements, for example, did not become a budget-making issue until 1982. And when they did the chairman failed to win acceptance for his version of the issue—as Social Security solvency instead of Social Security cuts. In his second season, on the other hand, his success in framing the major issue as saving the budget process won him some support from the Democrats.

Which brings us finally to the budget process itself. If we think of the process as a set of governing *rules* that are subject to change and to manipulation, then the rules that exist at any point in time are another variable to examine in each budget season. In 1981 we encountered a significant reinterpretation of the rules providing for reconciliation. The two budget seasons that lie ahead in our examination will provide us with other examples of the effect of budget-making rules on budget making.

In the next two budget seasons, we will, again, find these several variables helpful in explaining Chairman Domenici's budget-making behavior. But we will find them assuming different patterns. In 1983 a recovering economy, an electorally revived Democratic party, and an immovable president on the issues of defense spending and taxes encouraged the chairman to employ a protracted bipartisan strategy, which produced a process-dominated outcome. In 1984 a deficit-ridden economy, an upcoming presidential election, and a flexible president encouraged the chairman to stretch the rules, employ a speeded-up partisan strategy, and produce a policy-dominated outcome.

THE CHAIRMAN AS MAINTAINER: 1983

The chairman's leadership prospects for 1983 were complicated by new economic and electoral circumstances. The year began with the economy in recession but with signs of an emerging recovery. Deficit reduction remained Domenici's overriding economic concern. And that concern called for fairly drastic action. But some of his supporters of the previous •year—including President Reagan—were opposed to any change in policy that might harm the recovery. As the *Washington Post* saw it, "With the economy headed up rather than down, last year's sense of urgency has dissipated." [3] The 1982 elections had decreased the Republican majority by two, making partisan majority building on the Senate floor more difficult than the year before. The elections had also produced twenty-six more Democrats in the House, a partisan resurgence that promised to make majority building in all parts of the system more precarious, regardless of the policy involved. It promised a new intensity of credit/blame calculation, which, in turn, would be exacerbated by the upcoming struggle for control of the presidency and the Senate in 1984.

Domenici's leadership posture in 1983 was vastly different from what it had been in 1982—precisely because of what had happened from late 1981 through 1982. Step by step, he had established his independence from the president. He had established himself as a protector of legislative budgetary prerogatives, and as the legislative gatekeeper for the Reagan budget. A key observer described him in early 1983 as "a central, outspoken figure in the efforts of Senate Republicans to reshape Reagan's budget to make it palatable to Congress." [4] A *National Journal* analysis, in February, carried the headline, "Domenici Walks a Fiscal and

Political Tightrope as Budget Committee Chairman." And the author wrote,

> While trying to maintain his stripes as a party loyalist and tight-spending conservative, Domenici has become more outspoken in leading the fight against President Reagan's proposed defense increases.[5]

It was, by now, a familiar story line.

Domenici's proximate policy goal—deficit reduction—was well established. Even as the Reagan budget was being formulated in late 1982, the chairman began to express his concern for the rising deficit (the past year's deficit was now projected at $208 billion) and to stipulate certain requirements for congressional acceptance of a budget. In December, for example, he asserted that "There's no way in the world to put together a budget package without reductions in the military."[6] With the Social Security issue now subject to settlement by a presidential commission, the remaining areas of special sensitivity were the size of the defense budget and the desirability of a tax increase. Domenici believed that some tax increase was an integral part of any balanced package. But the president, who had been persuaded in 1982 to swallow a $98 billion tax increase, was adamantly opposed to another round. So Domenici steered attention away from this most sensitive area (taxes) and sought common ground with the president in what he felt might be a negotiable subject (defense). It was the same crabwise bargaining tactic he had devised in 1982, when he had first advocated spending restraint while postponing a confrontation on taxes. He would give the president more of what he most preferred in the hope of moving him toward that which he least preferred.

When it was announced, the president's budget proposal called for a 10 percent increase for defense, a freeze on discretionary domestic programs, regulatory increases in revenues, standby or contingency tax proposals, and a $189 billion deficit. (See Appendix, Table A-3.) Domenici focused on the defense item. In "a very, very tough meeting" [with the president], the chairman told the president that the best they could hope to get out of the Senate Committee was a 5 percent defense increase.[7] As if to confirm that message, the newly energized Democratic House moved quickly to pass its budget resolution—calling for a 4 percent increase in defense—along with a $30 billion increase in domestic spending and a $35 billion tax increase. Republican House members protested this "partisan steamroller."[8] The president's reaction was to dig in behind his own budget. He made a nationally televised address defending it—with special emphasis on the 10 percent defense increase. This presidential attitude meant trouble for the chairman. In reference to it, he said in March, "I don't see how we're going to get a budget under the present circumstances."[9]

But Domenici was equally embattled on another front because the president's attitude had its reflections inside his own committee. The latent policy individualism of the Republicans resurfaced. Three or four stood solidly with the president in opposition to any tax increase; one stood solidly for a larger tax increase than Domenici could accept. Others were solidly against the president on defense. "There is a very big split among the Republicans," said Domenici in April. "If the Committee voted today ... we wouldn't get the 12 votes that are necessary. We couldn't get a consensus today."[10] In 1983, Chairman Domenici no longer "owned the house."

With his Republicans in wide disagreement, he began to toy with the bipartisan alternative. He was determined, as always, to carry out his institutional responsibility to get a budget by whatever means available. "If we can resolve the military issue in a bipartisan way acceptable to the White House," he said, "that would go a long way to getting together on some of the other issues." To signal his bipartisan intentions, he took now senior Committee Democrat Lawton Chiles with him to the White House to tell the president that if he did not compromise on defense, the two senators would move jointly to let the Budget Committee "work its will"—that it was their responsibility to do so.[11] But the chairman could not present a committee majority as a fait accompli. And he could not repeat his 1982 performance.

The president did not move; and, so, the committee did. The result was to unleash the committee's policy individualism and to bring the president's budget under heavy siege. On defense, the committee voted 19-2 against the president's 10 percent defense increase; and they voted 14-7 against an eleventh-hour White House proposal of 8 percent. At which point the president called Domenici personally to request that the committee delay further action.

The president's call precipitated the most directly independent move yet by the chairman. So much so that years later, it remained traumatic and vivid. Domenici described it as the "big confrontation" that followed when he got "on the telephone in the back room ... in the middle of the markup ... with the beads of sweat [coming] down my forehead."[12] The president said to him, "You can't finish today. You have to put if off." To which Domenici replied, "No, I will not. I'm sorry, Mr. President. I can't wait." The chairman continued:

> I have all the respect in the world for you, but I've been waiting for weeks. There is no give on your side. Cap Weinberger won't give an inch. I have a responsibility, too. I have twenty-two senators on this committee. It's an important part of the United States Senate and I

have a job. It wouldn't do any good to talk. What for? We could talk again. We can sit down, but there isn't any more room. You've had all the time you can get. There's just no more time. I'm sorry.[13]

Immediately thereafter, in a move described as "Reagan's sharpest rebuke yet from his own party and perhaps his biggest defeat on Capitol Hill," the committee voted 17-4 *for* the 5 percent increase the chairman had originally specified.[14]

In a continuation of bipartisanship, the committee then added $11 billion in increases for discretionary domestic programs. Following the lead of their fellow Democrats in the House, committee Democrats then proposed a $30 billion tax increase. Republicans feared that this would threaten the third year of the 1981 tax cut. On that matter, the committee deadlocked 11-11 along party lines. One pro-tax-increase member, Republican Mark Andrews, supported the Democratic proposal.[15]

But having blocked the Democrats' proposal, the Republican majority was totally unable to agree on an alternative. "Many of us support the president on taxes, others want much more in new taxes and some want to allow the deficits to continue to rise toward $200 billion," said Domenici.[16] He was described as "stymied by bitter divisions in the GOP ranks." [17] At that point the chairman confronted an unyielding president on defense and an unmanageable committee majority on taxes.

Table 4-1 provides a picture of committee member support for their chairman in 1983. Compared with the picture for 1981 and 1982 (see Table 3-3), Table 4-1 shows an erosion and a fragmentation of Republican support since the previous year. Nine Republicans gave their chairman stronger support in 1982 than any Republican did in 1983. And the level of support for Domenici *dropped* for eleven out of twelve Republicans. Conversely, the comparison shows that the level of support for Domenici *rose* for nine out of ten Democrats. Further, the scrambling of the rankings brought about by the increased support of centrist Democrats (Chiles, Exon, Johnston) and the decreased support of antitax Republicans (Armstrong, Hatch, Kasten, Symms) depicts the chairman's difficulty in building a partisan majority and, therefore, the appeal of a bipartisan one.

Absent, it seemed, was the binding sentiment of 1982 that the majority party needed to demonstrate its capacity to govern. As one committee member put it, "In the first two years, there was a great sense that we had to govern. Now, we've started to go beyond that." [18] A party leader echoed,

Prior to this year the Senate has been fairly predictable. Fifty-one senators could be found to agree. That group marched down the aisle

TABLE 4-1   Budget Committee Support for Chairman Domenici:
Committee Votes, Ninety-Eighth Congress

	% Votes with Domenici 1983 (N=35)		% Votes with Domenici 1984 (N=4)		% Totals 98th Congress (N=39)	
Senator	a	b	a	b	a	b
Gorton ᶜ	80	(80)	100	(100)	82	(82)
Kassebaum	71	(78)	75	(100)	72	(80)
Quayle	69	(80)	100	(100)	72	(82)
Exon	66	(70)	25	(25)	62	(65)
Boschwitz	54	(70)	100	(100)	59	(74)
Grassley	57	(57)	50	(50)	56	(56)
Andrews	57	(87)	0	(0)	51	(77)
Chiles	54	(54)	25	(25)	51	(51)
Johnston	54	(73)	25	(25)	51	(67)
Armstrong	37	(62)	100	(100)	44	(68)
Kasten	40	(78)	75	(100)	44	(81)
Hatch	34	(63)	73	(75)	38	(65)
Metzenbaum	37	(37)	25	(33)	36	(37)
Symms	31	(61)	75	(75)	36	(64)
Biden	31	(73)	50	(50)	33	(68)
Moynihan	29	(42)	50	(50)	31	(43)
Sasser	29	(48)	25	(25)	28	(44)
Riegle	26	(36)	25	(33)	26	(36)
Hart	26	(33)	0	(-)	23	(33)
Tower	11	(57)	100	(100)	21	(73)
Hollings	14	(31)	25	(33)	15	(32)

[a] Percentage of times member voted with Domenici—all votes on which Domenici voted. Member may have been absent, and member absence lowers score.
[b] Percentage of times member voted with Domenici—all votes on which Domenici and member both voted. This calculation controls for absences. (Column "a" emphasized, on the assumption that the chairman would want his supporters to be present and voting.)
[c] Names in italic type = Republicans; names in roman type = Democrats.

and did their duty. [Now] it's a new ballgame.... [Majority Leader Baker] is not able to guarantee to the White House 51 votes on any proposal they send over.[19]

The previous year's strategy, therefore, of working gradually to solidify the Republican majority and then using that majority to win presidential concessions, seemed unavailable. That was the chairman's conclusion. "I made a decision there was little chance of getting a solid Republican budget resolution."[20] And he also decided that "I wouldn't wait any longer ... [there was] too much risk in delay."[21] And so he grasped the bipartisan alternative.

Domenici called for another vote on the $30 billion tax increase and voted *with* the Democrats in support of it and in support of the budget resolution that contained it. He carried three Republicans with him on the tax vote (Andrews, Gorton, Kassebaum) and one more (Boschwitz) on the final vote. The resolution, with its reconciliation instructions, carried a deficit of $163 billion, $25 billion below the president's plan.[22]

It was, indeed, more of a Democratic budget resolution than a Republican one. Every major change in the president's proposal had been brought about with unanimous Democratic support, together with increments of nonunanimous Republican support. "I certainly will do everything I can to fight those tax numbers," said Domenici after his vote to include them in the resolution.[23] The Democrats won the chance to bring a budget to the floor. The chairman won the chance to fight another day. His staunchest committee ally, Slade Gorton, pronounced the most widely quoted judgment on the year's budget activity: "1981 was the year of the president; 1982 was the year of the Congress; 1983 is the year of living dangerously." [24]

The chairman's action represented a decision to give his goal of institutional maintenance priority over his goal of good public policy. And it was interpreted as such. A reporter explained, "Domenici worked closely with Chiles in trying to end the budget impasse that both feared would destroy the congressional budget control process." [25] Majority Leader Howard Baker concurred,

> Were it not for the understanding between the Chairman and the ranking minority member that they owed the obligation to the Senate to get something to the floor for consideration, there might have been no budget resolution, and had there been no budget resolution, I think there would have been a great threat to the budget process.[26]

Domenici explained his action in similar terms.

> That this resolution exists at all is a tribute to the persistence of the bipartisan tradition that has been the hallmark of the Budget Committee ... no legislative vehicle can resolve the basic ideological differences now splitting the committee [but] the committee was able nevertheless, to do its basic duty—present to the Senate a proposed blueprint for fiscal policy for the next 3 years.[27]

As the resolution left the Budget Committee, it was by no means clear how, and by whom, a supportive majority might be constructed on the floor. The Republicans were fragmented; but they still controlled the floor proceedings; and Chairman Domenici was scheduled to shepherd a budget resolution he did not favor. Even less so did the president.

Throughout the season, Domenici had been careful never to place himself in a posture of confrontation with the president. He cast himself as a team-playing, gatekeeping interpreter of congressional sentiment and congressional responsibilities to the president.

> I consider myself a helper of the president, but I feel that I have a role to tell him what we think and what I think and what the Budget Committee sees, and so I'm frequently a constructive in-house critic.[28]

In all his 1983 conversations with the president, he sought to outline the broad areas of difference between the branches, while seeking indications of presidential "give." He never emerged with any sense of presidential give; yet he never closed the door to future negotiations. But he was weakened because he did not "own the house"—and because the president knew it.

It had been the president's style, in 1982, to begin with a hard-line position and then, when presented with evidence of a united Republican-controlled committee, to compromise at the moment of showdown. In May 1983 Domenici operated (correctly or not) on the assumption that the moment of showdown had not yet come. Spurred on, now, by the possibility of a Democratic budget resolution, he decided to try again to build a partisan Republican majority for the floor. With solid Republican support in hand, he hoped, more presidential support might be forthcoming. After all, a budget resolution without presidential support is sufficient to keep the budget process "working." But only a budget resolution with presidential support is an instrument for governing the country.

So, when the resolution emerged from his committee, he took the position that "I will work with the White House and with the Republican leaders in the Senate to try to put together a package more to the liking of the President." [29] A budget "more to the president's liking" meant moving toward a lower-tax, higher-deficit, split-the-difference-on-defense alternative. With the help of Baker and some Republican committee members, the chairman put together this kind of compromise to take to the floor as a substitute for the committee resolution. The new "Domenici-Baker Plan" called for tax increases of $2.6 billion, domestic spending increases of $11 billion, a defense increase of 7.5 percent, and a deficit of $192 billion. (See Appendix, Table A-3.) It depended on a partisan Republican majority for support. It was defeated 52-48.

On the one hand, the proposal did not go far enough to win the support of the president. On the other hand, it ran into the fatal opposition of seven centrist, pro-tax-increase Republicans on the floor. Several of these defectors had been the "medal of honor" players of 1982. And several of them had barely survived the election of 1982. They were in a markedly independent mood. For two years, said party whip Alan Simpson, "The Republican majority was put to the test of supporting a president who had received an awesome degree of support, and we met it beautifully. We jumped off the cliff at least 43 times." In 1983, he went on, "I can already see the attitude that with senators in trouble for reelection, we won't ask them to jump off the cliff now and they are asking us not to put the heat on them." [30]

Defeated by Republican disunity on the floor, and faced with the passage of budget resolutions that would win more Democratic than Republican support, Majority Leader Baker moved to recommit the resolution to the Budget Committee. Unless the Senate resolution commanded presidential support, he argued, no budget resolution would be enforced. The Senate voted to recommit. The *Washington Post* called it the first great failure of the Republican president with its headline, "GOP Juggernaut Grinds to a Halt on Budget Issue." [31]

Chairman Domenici went back to the drawing board, enunciating the time-honored pattern of dealing with the president. "We are going to have to have some accommodation from the White House," he said.

> I have had my share of attempting to accommodate the White House on the defense issue and I did not get anywhere in three weeks. It looks like I am going to have three days this time but, nonetheless, frequently *when you are under the gun people accommodate.*[32]

He was hoping against hope for a repeat of his 1982 success. But the signals from the president were discouraging. Saying that "I have compromised for two years now," Reagan categorically refused to accept any new taxes. And more ominously still, he indicated a distinct lack of interest in the entire budgetary exercise unfolding in the Senate. "Well," he said, "the budget resolution is *meaningless* to them. They've *never* abided by that." [33]

These presidential remarks of May struck a note very similar to the widely circulated sentiments of his secretary of defense that the budget process was useless and that congressional failure to pass a budget was not only to be accepted but welcomed. That line of argument lay behind Caspar Weinberger's intransigence throughout the many negotiations on the defense budget. It lay behind Chairman Domenici's frequent and sharp criticism of Weinberger. And there was every reason to believe that it lay behind the president's unusually firm stand on defense and tax matters.[34] It was an argument that was drawing sustenance from current press commentary. In the words of one columnist,

> The only genuine concern about the process comes from Senate and House members whose status in Congress depends upon the process. Consequently, the attempted systematic congressional control over spending, begun with such high hopes in 1974, is bankrupt.[35]

Whenever Congress has trouble making the process "work," media scorekeepers move in to record its frailties and herald its demise. It happened in 1980 and in late 1981. In the wake of the defeat of the Domenici-Baker Plan on the Senate floor, it was beginning to happen again in 1983.

Chairman Domenici's view was, of course, dramatically opposed to that of Weinberger's. To him the "no-budget" option was unthinkable. "It's insanity for the U.S. Senate not to vote in a budget resolution," the New Mexican told his colleagues. "I warn you. You'll rue the day. . . . We're going to have chaos in Congress without a budget resolution." [36]

Because of the president's intransigence, the chairman decided that he had to return to bipartisan majority building in the committee. And he turned to Lawton Chiles to coauthor a compromise, with lower tax and defense numbers than the earlier bipartisan committee effort. It lost 12-8 in "a highly charged partisan atmosphere," with only four Republicans and four Democrats following their leaders in support of it.[37] In trial-and-error fashion, Domenici then disinterred the Domenici-Baker Plan, which had been defeated on the floor, and tried to pass it with a partisan majority. That worked, 11-9, only because two Democrats were absent.[38] But it provided a vehicle—the only vehicle he could devise in committee—to take the bill back to the floor. Once back on the floor it was again defeated, twice, 56-43 and 57-43. Again, pro-tax-increase Republicans defected. Again, the recommendations of the Republican chairman and the Republican leader were voted down.

At this point there was only one alternative majority that had not been tested on the floor, a bipartisan one. Republican Slade Gorton offered a compromise resolution designed to produce substantial bipartisan support. It did. But because it attracted more Democrats than Republicans, it was turned down 52-48. At least that is why Republican leaders Baker and Domenici voted against it. They still hoped, somehow, for a dominantly Republican resolution, one that would give them some backbone in dealing with the House. Nonetheless, with the vote that close, Baker decided to try the Gorton resolution again—"to save the process." Supported by Domenici, he moved to reconsider. And, upon reconsideration, the budget resolution passed.

The resolution passed by the slimmest of margins, 50-49. It nearly lost. When the tally stood at 49-50 *against* the resolution, Budget Chairman Domenici dramatically changed his vote from nay to aye. His last-second change gave the Senate a budget.[39] Only twenty-one Republicans (including but three committee members) voted with him. On the other hand, twenty-nine Democrats (including five committee members) voted with him. It was more theirs than his. He preferred, and had worked hard for, a tax policy that would command Republican majorities. But, in the end, he had voted contrary to these preferences to keep the budget process alive. And it was his hardest test ever.

Media scorekeepers interpreted the outcome as "the worst setback Reagan has suffered in the Senate since his presidency began 2-1/2 years ago" and "the most embarrassing defeat [Howard] Baker has suffered since he became leader." [40] And Pete Domenici had delivered the pivotal blow in those Republican defeats. "It was very difficult," he said, "as difficult as anything I've ever done." [41] But his vote once again demonstrated that the institutional goals thrust upon him by his chairmanship ultimately took precedence over his policy goals as a Republican senator.

The conference committee met, compromised, and won support in both chambers. The president's reaction was, "I simply must oppose it vigorously." And Domenici noted simply that "he has his views and we have ours." [42] To the chairman particularly, Reagan said, "I know you've done the best you can, but it's not acceptable in any category." [43] "I wish," said the chairman, "that we could have one that met his every desire. But what he sent up here was simply not achievable." [44] These differences persisted to the end of 1983. And, in November's reckoning, it was the president's position that prevailed.

The final Democratic-oriented congressional resolution prescribed tax increases of $73 billion ($12 billion plus $15 billion plus $46 billion) over three years. (See Appendix, Table A-4.) To which the president's response had always been, "I will not support a budget resolution that raises taxes.... I will veto any tax bill that does this." [45] And that determination effectively killed further action. When the chairman of the Senate's tax committee was asked if he was going to implement the reconciliation provision of the budget resolution, he declared the tax instructions "a dead cat." "I can't go anywhere," said Senator Dole, "unless the President puts gas in the vehicle." [46] It was striking proof of the need to have presidential support for congressional budget resolutions—or at least solid majority party support in Congress. Without either, the reconciliation provisions of the 1983 budget resolution were never enacted into law.

When the year ended, the media scorekeepers described the lack of forward motion in familiar language—impasse, deadlock, gridlock, paralysis, and stalemate.[47] The condition had been brought about in part by grand economic and political parameters—by a good deal of reluctance to tamper with economic recovery and a good deal of partisan conflict. More specifically, it had been brought about by the inability of the president and the Budget Committee leader to reach agreement on policy, the inability of the committee Republicans to forge a solid policy majority, and the inability of bipartisan floor majorities to take further action in support of their votes.

Domenici's trial-and-error marching and countermarching back and forth between partisanship and bipartisanship, in search of committee and Senate majorities, had succeeded in getting a budget resolution. At the same time, the outcome demonstrated that a budget resolution is only the first step in the congressional budgetary control sequence. A resolution is sufficient to preserve the process. But it is not self-enforcing. Only strong, stable, and persistent majorities can implement reconciliation instructions. The patchwork budget coalitions of 1983 were lacking in all these respects—in committee and on the floor. They were coalitions without commitment.

They did signify a willingness, however, to continue the conflict within the same framework at a later date. In that respect, November 1983 was a repeat of November 1981. The process "worked" in terms of its survival, but not in terms of its substantive influence. The determination to keep the process is easier to come by in Congress than the determination to use the process to make good policy. It is the committee chairman's task to implement both goals—when and if he can. In 1983 that did not prove possible. He was simply unable to find a way to govern. The best he could do was to guarantee himself another chance to try.

THE CHAIRMAN AS POLICY MAKER: 1984

The budget season of 1983 was a disappointment to Pete Domenici. It had produced neither effective leadership nor good public policy. No governing coalition could be found; and no action had been taken to enforce the budget resolution. His own role had been extremely awkward. "Because I think the system is a good system," he said later, "I have [even] voted for a budget resolution I did not favor. I have gone to conference on that budget resolution that I did not favor, and I brought back a budget conference report that I did not favor." [48] He had met the goal of institutional maintenance, but he had lost the policy leadership he had gained in 1982. In 1984 he would try to get it back.

It has been argued, persuasively, that the economy drives the budget. It can also be argued that each year's budget process drives the following year's budget process. At least, that seems true within any single Congress. The failure, in the first session of the Ninety-eighth Congress, to enact implementing legislation made that task the first priority for the second session. Pete Domenici's special contribution to budget politics in 1984 was to communicate this sense of unfinished business and to restructure the budget process in a way that would make binding budget legislation the top priority of 1984. It was a decision to give top priority to substantive policy achievement. And it put great strain on the process.

He began to act in late 1983. For three months after the passage of the conference report, Domenici "remained deliberately silent on this issue, waiting to see how Congress would handle the reconciliation instructions. . . ." [49] As the 1983 session drew to a close without action, he took the floor to reclaim a position of leadership with regard to "the projected huge deficits this year and in the years ahead and the apparent paralysis in Congress on the deficit issue . . ." "I have been persistent and perhaps tiresome . . . warning the country and my colleagues of the problems since the late spring of 1981," he said as he argued that "deficits are embedded in the structure of the Federal Budget. They will not simply go away." [50] He urged immediate passage of reconciliation legislation, and a couple of weeks later he joined with Lawton Chiles in bringing to a vote an eleventh-hour package of spending reductions and tax increases.[51] These efforts failed—predictably. But they were intended less to succeed than to "prepare the soil" for his deficit reduction efforts in 1984. On the last day of the session, Domenici reminded the Senate that "the reconciliation bill is not dead. It is alive. When we come back, it will still be alive." [52] He planned to use it—to use the failure of one year's budget process to stimulate success in the next.

The deficit picture Chairman Domenici faced at the end of 1983, and which had been confronting and worrying him for more than two years, is portrayed in Figure 4-1. It shows the sharp rise of the deficit during the first three years of Domenici's chairmanship. It shows also, for each of the first three years, the planned decline of the deficit as contained in the final budget resolution—for the upcoming fiscal year and for the two succeeding out-years. It shows, for the second and third years, that the deficit far outran the previous year's budget projection. And for each of the three years the out-year projections proved to be even wider off their mark. For example, the fiscal 1982 budget resolution, the first of Domenici's chairmanship as passed in May 1981, missed its 1982 deficit target by $73 billion; it missed its 1984 projection of a balanced budget by $185 billion.

For three years, congressional budget making had remained behind the curve. Domenici knew that the budgets he took to the floor would not get him ahead of the curve. He knew that to pass budgets and preserve the process, he would have to make overly optimistic budget projections for the coming year. And he knew, also, that to pass budgets he would have to back-load most of his three-year savings on the out-years—thus making the out-year targets even less realistic. So each budget purported, as Figure 4-1 shows, to be placing the deficit on a downward glide path but was insufficient to do so. Hence, the endless

FIGURE 4-1   Federal Budget Deficit: Actual 1980-1986; As Planned by Congress 1981-1983

$ Billions

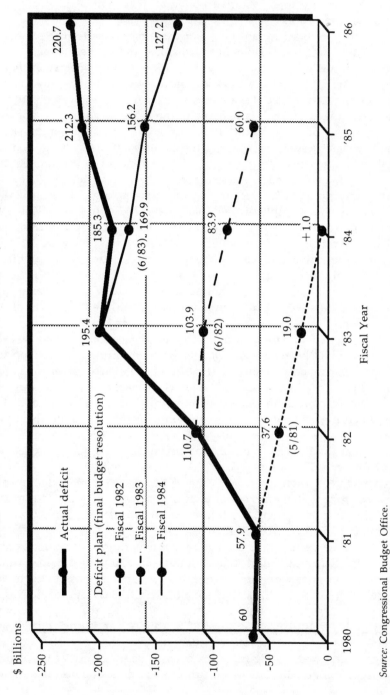

Source: Congressional Budget Office.
Note: Dates in parentheses indicate the month and calendar year that the final budget resolution was adopted for the ensuing fiscal year.

battles over discretionary domestic spending cuts, defense cuts, and tax increases tempered by political realities. Domenici could win the battles, but not the war. No committee chairman is ever given that much power. He never stopped fighting. But as the chart shows, rising deficits accompanied "old gloom-and-doom Domenici" to the end of his tenure as chairman.

As Domenici began work on the new budget in 1984, the economic and political parameters were much more conducive to action than they had been the year before. In Washington, a fairly solid consensus was forming that the health of the economy—now in strong recovery—required that "something must be done" by way of deficit reduction. The fiscal 1983 deficit, projected at $104 billion when the budget resolution passed in June 1982, had turned out to be $195 billion. (See Figure 4-1.) David Stockman's prediction of the previous April, that in the absence of action the nation would have deficits of $200 billion "as far as the eye can see," was widely accepted as true.[53] "Deficits, DEFICITS, *DEFICITS*," began one prominent December account. "Political rhetoric on the federal government's red ink flow and how to fix it has been spewing from the lips of Washington officials the way inflation had the city mesmerized three years ago." [54]

A related political consensus was also taking hold in Washington that success in the 1984 elections might well turn on who would be blamed if nothing were done. So everyone had an incentive to act. A key Senate participant soon observed, "We've become engaged in a bidding war to see who can reduce the budget the most." And he added, "It shows how far we've come in a year." [55] In April, *Newsweek* headlined its story on the bidding war, "Deficit Politics: Election Year Frenzy." [56] Those who agreed that "something must be done" also agreed on the matter of timing. Action would have to be taken early on, before the harsh credit/blame accusations of the campaign season made legislative cooperation impossible. The timing factor imparted a new sense of urgency to budget action.

From Chairman Domenici's standpoint these conditions were fairly propitious. But this time he could not wait if he were to take advantage of the opportunity. And so he proposed a strategy different from anything he had yet tried. He would use the existing, leftover reconciliation provisions of the 1983 resolution as the vehicle for moving a deficit reduction package through Congress early in 1984. As a vehicle, it had two advantages over the regular budget resolution. It was already at hand. And it would produce binding results.

He would urge the relevant committees to follow their existing reconciliation instructions, and he would also encourage them to make additional spending reductions, or tax increases, on their own. He would do all this *before* the Senate passed the regular budget resolution, setting new spending and tax targets. He would not convene the Budget Committee until later. He believed that the upcoming election would effectively truncate the budget season and would not allow for prolonged wrangling over the budget resolution prior to the enactment of actual deficit reduction. With the memory of the wrangling of 1983 fresh in view, one of his staffers called Domenici's plan "an up-front punch at the deficit instead of being dragged out as in the past." [57] The plan was to manipulate the normal budget sequence to achieve certain policy goals.

Domenici's sequential strategy was concocted with Senator Dole, whose Finance Committee would have to handle a very large part of the reconciliation package. Dole had been pushing for tax increases ever since his $98 billion increase in 1982. And in 1983 and 1984 he was every bit as aggressive as Domenici in decrying budget deficits. Said one scorekeeper at the end of 1983, "since late fall, Dole has assumed the mantle of Mr. Fixit on the deficit issue." Scorekeepers frequently lumped Domenici and Dole together as the twin leaders in deficit-reduction activities.[58] In 1984 the two continued what had been, since 1981, a highly supportive partnership. But they also began to engage in a rivalry, in a miniature bidding war of their own. With Majority Leader Baker's announced retirement, Dole and Domenici had begun to eye the vacancy. For political, policy, and personal reasons, then, the Senate's Republican leaders were itching to take action. The president remained a question mark.

The new season opened with the now familiar stylized routine. The Senate's Republican leaders trooped to the White House to discuss budget matters. They argued the need for drastic action and emerged in obvious disagreement with the president. The president, for his part, kept his counsel and asked for time. In 1984 the disputed carry-over items were military spending, discretionary domestic spending, and taxes. As always, the president focused his attack on the domestic item, while the senators pushed for action on the other two.

Domenici, again, acted as gatekeeper, telling the president that his projected budget could not pass Congress. "It was not that I disagreed with Reagan so much," he said later in assessing his years as chairman, "it is just that I did not think his budgets were doable." That is what was reported in the media the day after their January 1984 meeting.

> Domenici said he told Reagan that defense spending must be scaled back from administration suggestions and warned the President that it would be difficult to get Congress to approve additional cuts in domestic programs that have already been significantly reduced.[59]

On taxes, the chairman said, "The President prefers to maintain a position that he doesn't want to do anything to harm the recovery," and that he "wants more time to think about taxes." [60] For the moment, the president was holding to his position of 1983, but there was some small indication of "give."

When the president delivered his State of the Union address three weeks later, he gave more concrete evidence of flexibility. Emphasizing that "we must bring federal deficits down," he proposed bipartisan executive-legislative talks to secure agreement on a $100 billion, three-year "down payment" on budget reduction. The idea of the "down payment" was meant to define the scope of something that might be achievable and that "might" inoculate "against the deficit issue" in an election year.[61] Domenici was skeptical of the summit idea, predicting that "such a summit could disintegrate into the same kind of partisan bickering that doomed the gang of 17 initiative of which I was a part." [62] It did. The House-Senate-administration group met three or four times, bogged down in party differences over the incidence of cuts, and ended in the familiar game of blame between Speaker and president.

This effort and its collapse hastened the inevitable, election-year battle over partisan credit and blame. And the acceleration of partisanship virtually ruled out any bipartisan majority building. Senate Democrats, for example, began proposing a $200 billion reduction. While it may have been appealing to Domenici in terms of its magnitude, it could hardly be taken seriously by a Republican party looking for election-year unity. And, in view of the previous year's standoff, no one believed it would ever be implemented. Domenici turned to the partisan alternative—Senate Republicans and the president.

Ever since "the Domenici Plan" in the second season of 1982, Domenici's leadership strategy had centered on the idea of the budget *package*—a balanced arrangement of policies involving military spending, domestic discretionary spending, entitlement spending, taxes, and deficits. He gathered support for the package through the macro-argument that economically and politically the package was preferable to any other viable alternative. He was willing to adjust any one ingredient at the margin. But his best chance for success lay in preserving the relationships among the ingredients. All parties agreeing to the package had to believe this was the best they could get relative to the other party, that they could not get more without changing the balance, that to seek more was to risk losing much, and that the agreement among the parties would be kept.

Whenever any participant believed he could improve his position by pulling one piece out of the package, forcing attention on it, and digging in behind some change on it, the package would be undone and

Domenici's policy leadership would be threatened. That is what had happened when he lost to three Republicans on the deficit number in 1981, when he lost to the Democrats on the entitlement number in 1982, and when he lost to the president on the tax number in 1983.

In working up his proposal for 1984, Domenici emphasized again the idea of the package—especially as it would affect negotiations with the White House. "It's the congressional people putting together a package. We're looking for a package. I hope they're looking for a package. If we have to go to the President, we'll go to the President . . . [but] we ought to go to him with a full package." [63] The chairman would have to put together yet one more "Domenici Plan."

The chairman had staked out his position on the defense budget during the bipartisan talks. (See Appendix, Table A-5.) It was the same position he had taken in 1983—that a 5 percent increase after inflation was minimally adequate and maximally doable. But it meant 8 percent less and $57 billion less over three years than the president's budget request. Domenici's challenge was to shape—in the face of the previous year's defense standoff—a package that the president would accept. In consultation with the majority leader and Appropriations Committee Chairman Mark Hatfield, Domenici devised a plan that would alter the president's budget by equal dollar amounts in the three areas of controversy. If $45 billion were cut from his domestic spending budget, the president might then be persuaded to accept an equal-sized defense cut. And once that balance was struck, a tax increase of the same dollar size might also be acceptable—provided that increase did not threaten the three-year tax cut or indexing. With dollar amounts of about $45 billion in each category, deficit reduction would amount to a three-year "down payment" of nearly $150 billion—midway between the presidential and the Democratic numbers.

Lengthy, "hard" negotiations between Senate leaders and the White House produced agreement on this newest Domenici Plan. To cement the agreement, there was included a novel provision for binding limitations, or "caps" on defense and on domestic spending for each of the next three years. This was what the president and Republican conservatives demanded as insurance against any change in the balance or the amount of the two spending areas.[64] (It was, not surprisingly, opposed by Appropriations Chairman Hatfield.) With this gimmicky agreement, the impasse of 1983 was broken; and the pattern of 1982 was again made possible.

As in 1982, the president and the Senate leaders held a picture-taking ceremony. Their agreement came to be known as the "Rose Garden Package." The president went to Capitol Hill to lobby congressional Republicans on its behalf. "I believe, in this year particularly," he said, "it is essential that we appear united in our determination to get this package and stand together." [65] With the president aboard—much earlier and easier than in 1982—Domenici had regained policy leadership on the budget. "Some would argue," said the chairman to his colleagues, "that we should do more, and I could not totally disagree. But let us not be fooled into waiting for a perfect package and fail to act on the good package we have before us." [66] Domenici was committed to partisan majority building on behalf of the Rose Garden Package. The question was whether or not leadership could be translated into agreement—quickly and solidly—in committee and on the floor.

Domenici's strategic sequencing idea had the support of Majority Leader Baker. But in its most extreme form—that the Budget Committee would not even meet to consider a budget resolution until the reconciliation bill was virtually passed—the strategy provoked sharp opposition from Budget Committee Democrats and Appropriations Committee Republicans. In that form, it had to be abandoned. But the essence of the plan, that binding deficit reduction legislation should be enacted before the passage of the budget resolution, was retained. Indeed, it had to be retained, because partisan/presidential support for the Rose Garden Package depended on tangible, visible evidence that the bargain would be kept. And only binding legislation could provide such evidence. Chairman Domenici acceded to pressure by convening his Budget Committee to work on and report out a budget resolution. But he was determined to pass a budget resolution that would, in the end, simply incorporate existing legislative results. Thus he preserved his "topsy-turvy sequence." [67]

Chairman Domenici had once again faced the choice between institutional and policy goals. In 1983 he had chosen to emphasize preservation of the process. In 1984 he chose to emphasize the pursuit of policy. He steered the Rose Garden policies through the Budget Committee by the narrowest of partisan margins, 11-10. As in 1983, he was hurt by the defection of Republican Mark Andrews but helped by the absence of one Democrat. As in 1983, the victory did not come easily—which was no surprise since there had been no change in the cast of characters. Domenici had to fight off and discourage efforts within the Republican majority to join with the Democrats in mandating larger defense cuts than the president would accept. As passed by the Budget Committee, the resolution carried reconciliation instructions mandating $144 billion in tax increases and spending cuts over three years. And it was these reconciliation instructions—not the formal budget resolution—that Domenici carried first to the Senate floor.

One substantial part of the reconciliation package was already waiting there. Senator Dole's Finance Committee had been first off the mark and had passed its large share ($48 billion) of the reconciliation bill two weeks earlier. (Final figures are in Appendix, Table A-6.) The Senate tacked the remainder of its deficit-reduction package onto the Finance Committee bill. But it took "a bitter four-week debate" on the floor to complete that task.[68] It was during that time that Howard Baker formulated his frustration with the Senate. "To try to get it to move," he said, "is sort of like pushing a wet noodle. You just cannot make it go." [69] In the end Baker, Domenici, and Dole carried the Rose Garden equal parts-"down payment" compromise against various senatorial efforts to enact greater reductions—through larger defense cuts, larger tax increases, and/or a freeze in entitlement programs.

The three leaders did, however, accede to those moderate Republicans who wanted smaller reductions in domestic programs. This was the same small swing group that had held out against the leadership in 1983 and forced a bipartisan budget. In 1984 they responded to pleas of election-year party unity—after extracting a $2 billion price. This key concession passed the Senate with only two Republican defections; and the final reconciliation package passed 74-23. Most senators, it appears, wanted to go into the 1984 election with tangible evidence of having taken a deficit-reduction stance.[70] A day later, at the end of the line, the Senate passed its budget resolution, shaping it to simply conform to the deficit-reduction bill. Domenici's strategy of sequence had worked.

Next, the Senate leadership plan was to take the deficit-reduction legislation to conference with the House *before* taking the budget resolution to conference. On both measures, the House had long since done its part, quickly and in the traditional order. That is, the House Democrats, united by a desire to do something positive about the deficit before the 1984 elections, had passed their version of a budget reduction—$180 billion over three years. The military spending cut of $50 billion was the most formidable of their differences with the Senate.

Equally important, the House did not accept the glue of the Rose Garden agreement—three-year spending caps in the military and domestic areas. With their special institutional prerogatives in appropriations matters, and with a suitably stronger tradition of Appropriations Committee independence, House members were adamantly opposed to any device, such as a cap, that would jeopardize the normal appropriations process in their chamber. Indeed, House leaders had not been present in the Rose Garden negotiations where the caps were agreed upon. Domenici strongly defended the idea of caps. He considered the idea to be "historic in nature" and "a giant step in the direction of fiscal responsibility." "Without them," he said, "the budget would be 'a farce.' " To the degree that he meant what he said, his comments provide another example of Chairman Domenici's "Senate vision." The idea he lauded so profusely was, on institutional grounds, anathema to the House. To the degree that he felt compelled to defend them, the caps were the procedural price he had paid for presidential support. And the president's "vote" would be needed on any reconciliation measure.

The conferees on reconciliation legislation did what they could. They agreed on a tax increase of $48 billion and on domestic spending reductions of $45 billion. They agreed to disagree on the issue of spending caps; that is, to let each chamber follow its own wishes in the matter. This much went to the president and was signed. The conferees could not agree, however, on the matter of military spending. And so, when the conference on the budget resolution convened, that issue remained unsolved. Yet, in a sense, it was the only issue the budget resolution conference had to deal with, since the cart-before-the-horse procedure had already settled the other elements of the resolution.

Failing to reach an easy agreement with House conferees, Domenici's strategy on the military item was to let the number be settled by the deliberations of the two authorizing committees, which were by that time well along in their labors. This meant that the budget conferees did not need to meet until it was time to "ratify" authorizing committee action. And they did not meet—not much. When they did, they quickly reached an impasse. Meanwhile, with the budget resolution stalled in conference, the authorization and appropriations committees were going about their business—getting waivers and passing legislation without any direction from a budget resolution. Instead of the budget resolution coming first and shaping chamber action, it was coming last and was being shaped by chamber action. Media scorekeepers described the strategy as an "unorthodox approach to budgeting." They said that Congress had "reversed its normal budget procedures" and that "procedural requirements were essentially ignored." [71]

In the Senate, ranking committee Democrat Lawton Chiles vehemently protested the abrogation of the normal budget process and threatened to hold up as much fiscal legislation as he could until the budget conferees met and passed the regular budget. And he engaged Chairman Domenici in a lively debate on the effect of his 1984 sequential strategy for the survival of the budget process. "What we are doing in effect is trying to wipe out the mandate of the Budget Act," said Chiles. "Since the leadership has done about all it can to waive the Budget Act all year long, I think it is time we put a halt to that fast footwork." [72] The argument was, as always, partly political and partly procedural. But the procedural aspects were sufficiently serious to put Chairman Domenici on the defensive with respect to his 1984 strategy. For he had to face the question: What has this year's pursuit of my policy goals cost in terms of my longer-run institutional maintenance goal?

His answer began with the contextual argument that the unfinished policy business of 1983 and the need for party policy agreement in a presidential election year necessitated a strong policy emphasis. It moved from there to the argument that the desired policy had to be enacted as quickly as possible. And it moved from there to the need for a special sequencing strategy for producing an early outcome. "We knew from the start," he said, "this was going to be an impossible year" for using the regular budget process.[73] "This is a very difficult year. The strategy that we planned on this side was significantly different than normal." [74] Media scorekeepers claimed that the strategy was "stretching the budget process to new limits." [75] Domenici argued, however, that the budget process would not be stretched beyond recognition or usefulness by such a strategy. "We have had to be extremely innovative," he admitted. But he added, "The budget process is a wonderful process. It works. It is flexible enough to require some rather ingenious approaches from time to time." [76] From the perspective of this study, there was much truth in that assertion. In the four years that we chronicled the process, it was not used twice in the same way.

That is not to say that the 1984 strategy was without costs to the chairman's maintenance goals, because stretching the process may weaken it and/or lose support for it. Domenici admitted, publicly, that it had been "a very different kind of year, one that is very difficult for the budget process and for this chairman." [77] Privately he conceded that "This last year was a real disaster. . . . It was a basket case. The budget process very nearly died." A budget resolution was finally produced, on September 26—four months after the legal deadline and three months later than ever before. It ratified the results of the negotiations over reconciliation. It was a public indication of how much stretching had taken place. Ad hoc committees in both chambers were soon set up to consider budgetary reform. The question "Is it working?" was once again raised—more seriously than before.

For Chairman Domenici, the ultimate answer was that a budget resolution had passed, and that, therefore, the budget process had survived. On the day that the resolution passed the Senate, he argued: "The fact that the measure is still alive after all this time . . . testifies, I believe, to the strength and vitality of the budget process." [78] Further, he argued that the process had not been without an effect on outcomes. The 1983 reconciliation bill plus the 1984 Senate budget resolution had, as a matter of fact, provided the necessary guidelines for most authorizing and appropriating committees, even without a completed budget resolution. That is to say, components of the budget process had produced policy results even though the regular order had been violated. And the result was a $140 billion down payment on future deficit reduction.

Again, optimistically, Chairman Domenici predicted that deficits would soon be "on a trend line moving downward significantly and credibly." [79] He had in his own mind met his policy goals, with some incremental, but nonfatal, cost to the process itself.

The chairman had, once more, done his duty. He had pushed his fourth budget ball to the top of the hill. Neither this one nor any of the other three had been easy. Indeed, the annual budget battle is so bruising and so relentless that the chairman can take considerable pride in securing a budget resolution—any budget resolution, at any time. So long as the chairman can do this, he or she will have done nearly all the chairman can to make sure the process "works" and survives. As long as it survives it can be used to structure policy and political conflict.

But the budget process cannot, by itself, produce any particular substantive result. After four years of uninterrupted effort, Pete Domenici had probably held deficits well below what they might have been. Yet they remained enormous. On that front, he had won some battles, but he had not won his war for a balanced budget or for a predictable path to that end. He clearly understood the limits of his chairmanship and the limits of the process he had worked so hard to preserve. "I do not believe that large deficits are the result of any process. Clearly you cannot do any better than the collective will of members of the House and Senate coupled with the President regarding what they want to do, with or without a process." [80] With that summary benediction, he headed home to complete his campaign for reelection.

NOTES

1. Diane Granat, "Ruling Rambunctious Senate Proves to Be Thorny Problem for Republican Leader Baker," *Congressional Quarterly Weekly Report*, July 16, 1983, 1429.
2. Helen Dewar, "Hill Budget Process Boomerangs on Reagan," *Washington Post*, April 25, 1983.
3. *Washington Post*, April 20, 1983.
4. Helen Dewar, "Disputes on Process Complicate Recasting of Proposal on Hill," *Washington Post*, February 1, 1983.
5. Richard Cohen, "Domenici Walks a Fiscal and Political Tightrope as Budget Committee Chairman," *National Journal*, February 19, 1983.
6. Kenneth Bacon and Robert W. Merry, "Reagan's New Budget Snarled by Infighting, Faces Hostile Congress," *Wall Street Journal*, December 6, 1982; and "Reagan on the Defense," *Newsweek*, April 18, 1983.

7. *Washington Post*, March 9, 1983.
8. *Congressional Record*, March 22, 1983, H1497.
9. *Washington Post*, March 9, 1983.
10. David Hoffman and Helen Dewar, "GOP Senators Prod President on Defense Cuts," *Washington Post*, April 6, 1983; and Francis Clines [*New York Times* News Service], "Reagan Is Dug in on Defense," *Rochester Democrat and Chronicle*, April 6, 1983.
11. Albert Hunt, "Defense Request of Reagan Is Cut by Senate Panel," *Wall Street Journal*, April 8, 1983.
12. *Congressional Record*, September 23, 1987, S12544.
13. Hedrick Smith, *The Power Game* (New York: Random House, 1988), 211-212.
14. *Wall Street Journal*, April 8, 1983. For an inside description of this maneuvering, see James Miller, *Running in Place* (New York: Simon and Schuster, 1986), 40ff.
15. *Washington Post*, April 9, 1983.
16. *Washington Post*, April 21, 1983.
17. *Washington Post*, April 22, 1983.
18. Richard Cohen, "Senate Republican Control May Be Put to Test by Tough Issues This Fall," *National Journal*, September 10, 1983.
19. Granat, "Ruling Rambunctious Senate," 1431.
20. Helen Dewar, "Senate Panel Defies Reagan," *Washington Post*, April 22, 1983.
21. Dale Tate, "Senate Committee Approves Budget as GOP Members Join Democrats to Break Impasse," *Congressional Quarterly Weekly Report*, April 23, 1983.
22. Ibid.
23. *New York Times*, April 22, 1983.
24. Tate, "Senate Committee Approves Budget"; *Newsweek*, May 2, 1983; and *Washington Post*, April 25, 1983.
25. Dewar, "Senate Panel Defies Reagan." For praise of Domenici, see "The Senate and the Budget," *Washington Post*, April 25, 1983. For criticism of Domenici, see "Battle of the Republicans," *Wall Street Journal*, April 21, 1983.
26. *Congressional Record*, May 2, 1983, S5746.
27. *Congressional Record*, May 2, 1983, S5758.
28. Transcript, "The Lawmakers," WETA-TV, Washington, D.C., April 7, 1983, 5.
29. Christopher Conte, "Senate Panel Votes Tax Rises into '84 Budget," *Wall Street Journal*, April 22, 1983.
30. Cohen, "Senate Republican Control." See also Dale Tate, "Senate's Budget Resolution Stymied in Partisan Standoff," *Congressional Quarterly Weekly Report*, May 7, 1983.
31. *Washington Post*, May 13, 1983.
32. *Congressional Record*, May 12, 1983, S6587.
33. *Rochester Democrat and Chronicle*, May 14, 1983; and *Washington Post*, May 14, 1983.
34. On Weinberger, see Caspar W. Weinberger, "Yellow Journalism," *Washington Post*, June 29, 1983; and editorial, "Battle of the Republicans," *Wall Street Journal*, April 21, 1983. On Domenici, see Helen Dewar, "Domenici Scolds Weinberger for Resisting Budget Compromise," *Washington Post*, April 20, 1983. On Reagan, see Helen Dewar, "Speakes Relays Reagan Message," *Washington Post*, May 12, 1983; and David Hoffman, "Reagan Varies Approach to Congress," *Washington Post*, May 18, 1983.
35. Rowland Evans and Robert Novak, "The Budget Process Bankrupt," *Washing-*

ton Post, May 11, 1983; and Dale Tate, "Budget Prospects in Question as Senate Rejects GOP Plans," *Congressional Quarterly Weekly Report*, May 14, 1983.

36. *Congressional Record*, May 19, 1983, S7107-7108.
37. Dale Tate, "Defiant Senate Shuns Reagan, Votes Moderate Budget Plan," *Congressional Quarterly Weekly Report*, May 21, 1983.
38. Helen Dewar, "Panel Scuttles Bipartisan Budget Plan," *Washington Post*, May 19, 1983.
39. Helen Dewar, "White House Calls Bipartisan Budget Plan 'Off Target,' " *Washington Post*, May 21, 1983.
40. Associated Press and United Press International, *Rochester Democrat and Chronicle*, May 20, 1987.
41. Dewar, "White House Calls."
42. Benjamin Taylor, "Republicans Show Sharp Divisions on Budget Compromise," *Boston Globe*, June 22, 1983.
43. "A Compromise Budget at Last," *Newsweek*, July 4, 1983.
44. Dale Tate, "Congress Rebuffs President, Clears '84 Budget Resolution," *Congressional Quarterly Weekly Report*, June 25, 1983.
45. Tate, "Defiant Senate Shuns Reagan."
46. "Doing Nothing About Deficits," *Newsweek*, August 15, 1983.
47. For example, ibid.; David Broder, "Congress Gets a Lenient Grade," *Washington Post*, November 23, 1983; Helen Dewar, "GOP Leaders Seek Deficit Cuts," *Washington Post*, October 19, 1983; and Doug Harbrecht, "Domenici Hopes to Advise Reagan on Budget," *Albuquerque Tribune*, December 27, 1983.
48. *Congressional Record*, August 1, 1984, S9594.
49. *Congressional Record*, October 21, 1983, S14371.
50. Ibid.
51. *Washington Post*, November 16, 18, 1983; and *Congressional Record*, November 18, 1983, S16810-16812.
52. Ibid.
53. Helen Dewar, "Budget Agreement Called Vital," *Washington Post*, April 19, 1983; and "A Plea From David Stockman," *Washington Post*, April 20, 1983.
54. Dale Tate, "Mounting Deficits Could Spur Total Overhaul of Tax System," *Congressional Quarterly Weekly Report*, December 24, 1983.
55. Richard Cohen and Timothy Clark, "Congress Is Trying to Convince the Voters It Is Really Worried About the Deficit," *National Journal*, April 21, 1984.
56. *Newsweek*, April 23, 1984.
57. Cohen and Clark, "Congress Is Trying."
58. Dale Tate, "Finance Witnesses Back Call for '84 Action to Cut Deficits," *Congressional Quarterly Weekly Report*, December 19, 1983; and Tom Wicker, "A Showboat of a Political Content Bill," *New York Times*, November 14, 1983.
59. New York Daily News Service, "Domenici Says Reagan Wary of Boosting Taxes," *Albuquerque Journal*, January 4, 1984.
60. Ibid.
61. Elizabeth Drew, *Campaign Journal* (New York: Macmillan, 1985), 294-300; "Reagan's State of the Union Address," *Congressional Quarterly Weekly Report*, January 28, 1984; and Jonathan Moore, ed., *Campaign for President: The Managers Look at '84* (Dover, Mass.: Auburn House, 1986), 112-113.
62. *Congressional Record*, October 21, 1983, S11373.

63. Helen Dewar and David Hoffman, "GOP Leader Suggests Cuts in Defense," *Washington Post,* February 25, 1984; and "Domenici Urges $80B Arms Cut," *Boston Globe,* February 25, 1984.
64. Dale Tate, "Reagan Achieves GOP Unity by Agreeing to Deficit Cuts," *Congressional Quarterly Weekly Report,* March 17, 1984.
65. Dale Tate, "House, Senate Leaders Favor Varying Deficit-Cutting Plans," *Congressional Quarterly Weekly Report,* March 24, 1984.
66. Dale Tate, "Effort to Pass Spending Cuts Off to Torpid Start in Senate," *Congressional Quarterly Weekly Report,* April 28, 1984.
67. Dale Tate, "Hill Budget Process Working to Force Economic Decisions," *Congressional Quarterly Weekly Report,* April 14, 1984.
68. Dale Tate, "Senate Ends Deficit Marathon, Approves Reagan-Backed Bill," *Congressional Quarterly Weekly Report,* May 19, 1984.
69. Tate, "Effort to Pass Spending Cuts."
70. Cohen and Clark, "Congress Is Trying."
71. Tate, "Hill Budget Process Working"; Richard Cohen, "Looking for the Silver Lining," *National Journal,* October 20, 1984; and Dale Tate, "Effort to Reach Budget Accord Mired in Defense Money Spat," *Congressional Quarterly Weekly Report,* June 30, 1984.
72. *Congressional Record,* August 1, 1984, S9590; see also ibid., June 25, 26, 27, and August 2, 6, 8, 10, 1984.
73. Tate, "Hill Budget Process Working."
74. *Congressional Record,* August 1, 1984, S9594.
75. Tate, "Hill Budget Process Working."
76. *Congressional Record,* August 1, 1984, S9596.
77. Ibid., S9594.
78. *Congressional Record,* September 26, 1984, S11895.
79. Ibid., S11910.
80. Ibid., S11913.

A Season of Renewal

FROM GOVERNING TO CAMPAIGNING: EXPLANATORY CONNECTIONS

Throughout the last four years of his second six-year term, Senator Pete Domenici had been a leading figure in the national government. Budget politics had been at the center of all congressional politics, and he had remained at the center of all budget politics. As the last of those years began, he formally announced for reelection. He continued, of course, his work as chairman of the Budget Committee. But for that final year, at least, he and his staff became increasingly occupied with reelection. From a career perspective, what mattered most at that point in his political life was not what he did on the federal budget but what he did against a Democratic opponent. For our purposes, too, what matters at this point is to think of the governing-to-campaigning sequence, shift our attention from one activity to the other, and explore the connections between them.

Our view is that a connection worth studying is the explanation or interpretation of a legislator's governing experience that he or she makes when campaigning for electoral support. Legislators, we believe, seek votes at home on the basis of things they do in Washington. We cannot generalize on the importance of this explanatory process for election outcomes. We assume, however, that it will be present in all campaigns and will be crucial in some of them.

To a considerable degree the explanatory process is continuous. That is, a good deal of interpretive activity goes on throughout the six-year period. As each legislator accumulates governing experiences, his or her constituents will accumulate explanations about those experiences too—about their legislator's behavior in getting adjusted, making a record, adopting a style, gaining a reputation. Some of these matters get conveyed by the legislator, some by the media. In this sense, explaining—like fund raising—never stops; and, in this sense, campaigning never stops either.

On the other hand, there is a point at which the routine business of campaigning accelerates and intensifies such that "The Campaign" can be said to have begun. This point will vary considerably from contest to contest; and for each contest, it will be defined by the actions of the participants and the attention of political observers. During the "The Campaign" period, the explanatory process takes its most concentrated, most visible, and most memorable form. Explanatory material that already exists will be summed up, packaged, highlighted, lowlighted, augmented, and sold with a concentration of effort that distinguishes this period from any other in the six-year cycle. "The Campaign" focuses attention on a legislator's governing experience—whether or not the constituents learned about it early or late. It provides the most convenient focus for us, too.

As campaign periods go, we would guess, Pete Domenici's was relatively short. According to one respected classification of U.S. Senate contests, he ran a "low-key" race.[1] According to conventional criteria for assessing the quality of people who challenge incumbents, he faced a low-quality challenger.[2] Furthermore, his challenger was not designated until the campaign year was half over. This set of circumstances points to a campaign effort that was less strenuous and slower in developing than many others. We would expect, therefore, that previous explanations of Domenici's governing activity will bulk larger at campaign time than might otherwise be the case. Also, we would expect Domenici's Washington activity to be just the sort to have registered back home well before his campaign began. While this chapter will point toward "The Campaign," we shall begin by exploring the governing-campaigning connection as it developed during his time of maximum governing activity in Washington.

REPUTATION AND THE MEDIA CONNECTION

When Pete Domenici formally announced for reelection on February 12, 1984, he was about as well known in New Mexico as a public figure could be. He enjoyed 99 percent name recognition and 77 percent name recall. Only three senators in his thirty-three-member reelection class enjoyed better name recall in their states than he did in his. Not only was he very well known, he was very favorably known. Among the senators in his reelection class, he had the second-highest ratio of job approval to job disapproval, the highest ratio of favorable to unfavorable impressions, and the lowest percentage of volunteered negative comments.[3] With a job rating 45 points higher than the governor's, Domenici was undoubtedly the most popular public figure in New Mexico—and, arguably, in the history of New Mexico.[4] It was a remarkably broad base of recognition and approval from which to launch a reelection campaign.

It seems likely, therefore, that Domenici's budgetary exploits had been chronicled in New Mexico, and that these exploits and chronicles had contributed to his high standing at home. Poll results in May 1983 provide evidence that this was so. Nearly 20 percent of the state's electorate spontaneously mentioned his Budget Committee leadership when asked about him. And 37 percent of the electorate had something to say about his chairmanship when prompted. Of these, 87 percent approved of what he had done in that job and only 9 percent disapproved. There are, of course, several reasons why Pete Domenici ran so strongly in these early polls. But one of them, surely, was his budgetary performance in the Senate. In a 1983 study of Senate coverage by the three major television networks and five national newspapers, Pete Domenici ranked among the top ten senators. And more than 80 percent of these media mentions were related to his work on the Budget Committee.[5] Pete Domenici was reaping the home rewards of his Washington power.

Insofar as his approval at home was based on explanations or interpretations of his performance in Washington, the linkage was formed through his own efforts and through the efforts of the New Mexico media. We cannot determine which is more important. But we are sure that media interpretations are crucial. What they choose to emphasize and how they choose to emphasize it surely affects constituency opinion before and during "The Campaign." We shall begin with a look at the New Mexico media coverage as a connecting link between Pete Domenici's governing activity and his reelection effort.

We cannot know for sure how this linkage operates. But our working hypothesis is that the linkage occurs through a two-step, cue-taking process. Scorekeepers attached to the national media—the ones who follow Washington politics closely—make judgments about a politician's accomplishments and importance. They also make judgments about which of the politician's activities deserve coverage. Local media scorekeepers—who do not follow Washington politics closely—pick up these judgments and transmit them to their local audiences. National judgments thereby get consolidated into, or factored into, local judgments. This pattern applies particularly, we would guess, to states lacking a nationally oriented media organization of their own. New Mexico, a small (in population) state located far from Washington would therefore be especially dependent on this two-step, cue-taking linkage.

This working hypothesis is at least consistent with the perception that Domenici and his staff have of the New Mexico media. Recall, for example, his running complaint in the 1979-1980 period that his Senate accomplishments and his importance as a player there were going unrecognized and unreported at home. Granting this complaint some face validity, one explanation would be that the *national* media had not yet had anything to say about the senator from New Mexico. Recall that when they finally did take notice of his activity, in 1981, their stories invariably emphasized his emergence from obscurity, his rise from the ranks of the unknown. For eight years, it appears, the national score-keepers knew nothing about Pete Domenici. The New Mexico media had not given him his due, in our view, because there was no national media coverage for them to take cues from.

In the absence of national coverage the local media are left to their own information devices. And their own devices are simply not adequate to the reporting or the interpretive task. For most of the local media, the problem is structural. In the period under study there was very little regular, first-hand coverage of Washington politics by the New Mexico media. Only two newspapers, the *Albuquerque Journal* and the *Albuquerque Tribune,* maintained a full-time political reporter in Washington. The chief political writer of the *Journal* was the only New Mexico person who followed Pete Domenici's activity on the Budget Committee first hand. The remainder of the local newspapers relied entirely on the Associated Press (AP), on United Press International (UPI), and on the wire services of the national newspapers. None of the state's television stations had a reporter or a crew in Washington. They shared two "stringers" with a dozen or so smaller TV stations. Their coverage of Domenici was occasional, as peak events occurred. The result was that most New Mexico media people did not know first hand what Pete Domenici did. They depended upon the national media to set their agenda and supply their information on matters of Washington politics.

After the election of 1980, the national media began to pay attention to Pete Domenici. And the local newspapers (we have no record of TV or radio) began to pay attention to the national media. The first thing the local newspapers noticed was the sheer amount of national media coverage Domenici was getting. The earliest local Domenici stories, therefore, concentrated heavily on the fact that people outside of New Mexico were, all of a sudden, watching him.

"The New Mexico Senator has received considerable attention *nationally* since the election, because of his new position." [6] "Our former mayor has been catapulted from relative obscurity and has become a *national* legislative celebrity both in print and on network TV." [7]

Domenici is "in the limelight because of [his] sudden emergence from near obscurity into the realm of importance and prominence. . . . Domenici . . . has finally achieved major *national* recognition." [8] "Not since the late Clinton Anderson's hardest working days in the U.S. Senate has a New Mexican received as much *national* attention as that being poured on Senator Pete Domenici." [9] "Domenici is gaining great notoriety. He's on the tube almost as much as Lady Di these days. The *Wall Street Journal* carried a long story about him on Monday. A few days before that, Pete's picture was on the front page of the *New York Times.*" [10] The national media were, in fact, fascinated—almost transfixed—by this unfamiliar phenomenon. And their coverage meant that the local press would soon be equipped—and/or prodded—to give a new level of attention and coverage to their senior senator.

For most of the New Mexico press, most of the time, the two-step process ran through the Associated Press. AP assigned one top reporter to the congressional budget beat. And, he, along with reporters from the *Washington Post, New York Times, Wall Street Journal, Congressional Quarterly,* and the *Albuquerque Journal,* provided the nucleus of those press people who regularly watched the Senate Budget Committee. Occasionally, the work of these other reporters would be reprinted in the local press—especially feature articles involving Pete Domenici. But the basic reportage of important daily events in the budget process was provided by AP. And the AP budget story would appear, during peak events, in the *Almagordo Daily News, Artesia Daily Press, Carlsbad Current-Argus, Clovis News-Journal, Deming Headlight, El Paso Times, Farmington Daily Times, Gallup Independent, Grants Beacon, Hobbs Daily News-Sun, Las Cruces Sun-News, Las Vegas Daily Optic, Lovington Leader, Los Alamos Monitor, Portales News-Tribune, Raton Daily Range, Roswell Daily Record, Santa Fe New Mexican,* and *Silver City Daily Press.*

In Pete Domenici's first budget season, AP stories included the preliminary budget consultations between President Ronald Reagan and Senate Republican leaders, the large spending cuts passed by the Senate Budget Committee, the temporary revolt of three committee Republicans, Senate floor passage of the budget, and the passage of the omnibus reconciliation bill. Chairman Domenici was mentioned—often quoted and occasionally featured—in nearly all the stories. New Mexicans who followed these accounts received enough information to let them know that one of their senators was more deeply involved than ever before in the business of governing in Washington. Wire service accounts of his activity were widely circulated in New Mexico throughout 1981. They furnished the major corrective for the structural problem faced by the local press.

For a small, but crucial, segment of the local press, however, the problem was not structural but institutional—less the problem of acquiring knowledge than the problem of self-definition. The two largest papers, the *Albuquerque Journal* and the *Albuquerque Tribune*, after all, did have their own reporters in Washington. While they, too, relied heavily on the wire services for their day-to-day, bread-and-butter coverage of national political events, they depended less on these national sources for their interpretation of Pete Domenici's Washington activity. They had the resources and the predisposition to put a distinctive spin on their budgetary coverage. And they tended to guard their interpretive independence carefully—as an institutional matter. This posture on the part of the state's two largest and most influential papers, in what he viewed as his critical swing area politically, held another kind of potential problem for Domenici—a problem of distorted coverage or unfavorable interpretations of his work.

We have already noted Domenici's worried concentration on his treatment at the hands of the Albuquerque press. A member of his staff gets to his Albuquerque office at 7:00 a.m. (9:00 a.m. Washington time), clips articles of interest from the two local papers, and sends them immediately by fax machine to the Washington office. The clippings are kept in the office for a couple of weeks. Sometimes, articles about key events are read over the phone to the Washington staff. Press clippings from the rest of the state filter into the Albuquerque office later and are sent, in large month-sized batches, to Washington. For the senator and his staff, therefore, the *Journal* and the *Tribune* are objects of special watchfulness. In their eyes, the two papers—the *Journal* much more than the *Tribune*—constitute a special problem.

For their part, we would argue, the larger papers construe their job in a way that makes them inordinately suspicious of self-aggrandizing politicians. They want to cover the news as it affects the broadest community of readers; and they do not wish to distort their coverage with excessive attention to politics. When they do attend to politics, they wish to be as objective and neutral—in the sense of reporting all sides of a question—as possible. They do not wish to be, or appear to be, acolytes of, or cheerleaders for, any political figure. Thus, even when they knew what Pete Domenici was doing—and despite the efforts of the Domenici staff enterprise to keep them apprised—the institutional tendency of the Albuquerque papers was to bend over backward not to reward him with coverage that might seem overly extensive or overly favorable.

In the case of the *Journal*, this institutional tendency was buttressed, perhaps, by the opinion of its political reporter that Pete Domenici has "a short fuse and a deep seated need for approval," that he is "driven by his own insecurity," and "needs constant reassurance." [11] And, of course, the more the *Journal* reporters and editors saw themselves being badgered by the senator and his staff, the more likely they were to dig in behind their occupational defenses. From their perspective, too, there were numerous instances when they did give the chairman his due.[12]

From the perspective of the Domenici enterprise, the desire of the largest local papers to maintain their institutional independence often resulted in local interpretations that were different from, and less favorable than, the prevailing interpretation in the national media. As one veteran Albuquerque staffer put it,

> The local papers don't do him justice. We've made the point many times that he gets good coverage in the Chicago papers or the Los Angeles papers, but when you look for the same story in the local papers, it isn't there. Pete will say, "I don't know what's the matter with the Albuquerque papers. I'm treated better by the national press than by the press at home."

In the fall of 1981, after the budget success of his first season had been widely recognized in the national media but not, his staffers felt, in the Albuquerque papers, one of his press aides voiced their frustration and offered an explanation—partly structural but mostly institutional.

> [In the beginning] the papers here thought, "He's just a freshman senator, not worth covering." And they were right. The problem is that now that Domenici is an influential senator, they still don't give him the coverage he deserves. They don't know what they've got. They don't realize how important he is. They are so parochial here.... Sometimes his picture is in the *New York Times* and the *Washington Post* and it won't make the local paper. If I call and complain they say, "We print his picture all the time." They don't want to be thought of as boosters of his. They are paranoid about that. Not the small-town papers. They are proud of him; and they'll print his picture. But the *Journal* thinks of itself as a big national paper that isn't about to be taken in by a senator. They don't consider his national activity anything special unless they can see him being "senatorial"—chairing a hearing or coming out of the White House.

From the "senatorial" perspective, of course, there was a lot more to see.

A friendly, state-based political columnist commented similarly in the fall of 1981. After praising Domenici, he wrote that he had done so on the basis of observing what "the *national media* are saying about Domenici."

> *They* think he is an outstanding Senator—not just because he happens to have power as Chairman of the Senate Budget Committee, but much more because of the way he has exercised that power. *So, how come the New Mexico media haven't quite recognized that?* Maybe a little of that prophet without honor in his own country syndrome? Maybe a little because the *Albuquerque Journal, most powerful single medium in the state,* is still hesitant to admit his importance (for reasons in the

minds of its editors it would take a good psychiatrist to understand)?[13]

Thus, the *Journal*'s posture as a self-defined, all-purpose, national newspaper was characterized, even locally, as overly parochial and insecure.

Sometimes it seems the word should be "perverse." Consider, for
example, the treatment by the *Journal* of Chairman Domenici's most
acclaimed coalition-building effort—the winning-over of President Reagan and a twelve-man Republican committee majority on May 5, 1982.
Faced with several decisions as to how to treat this triumph of
leadership by their state's senior senator, the *Albuquerque Journal* divided
its treatment between a minimal acknowledgement of his role and a
concentration on the views of his opponents.

The problem was not one of knowledge. The *Journal*'s Washington
reporter had followed the budget drama day in and day out—side by
side with the national media scorekeepers. But he and his paper
reported something very different from what the others did. Recall that
the *New York Times* editorial of May 6 was entitled "President Domenici?". And recall that the *Wall Street Journal*'s feature story of May 11
was headlined "In High Stakes Fight over Budget, Domenici Just
Outmaneuvered Democrats." *Newsweek*'s substantial story of May 17 was
headlined "Domenici's Budget Deal"; and it featured a picture of
Domenici with the caption "The Chairman: A Gang of One Forges a
Compromise." By comparison with the national media, the *Journal*'s
interpretation ranged from bland to begrudging—and, one must assume, deliberately so.

The *Journal*'s May 6 story, written by its Washington reporter, was
headlined "Reagan Gives Go Ahead to Domenici Budget Plan." It
described Domenici's announcement of presidential support as "a
dramatic move" but gave no credit to him for putting together the
winning coalition. Indeed, it deliberately gave all the credit to
Howard Baker. Without a doubt, Baker's support was crucial. But
Domenici was being credited in the national media as the architect of
the victory.

On May 7 the *Journal* carried a front-page picture of Domenici and
Howard Baker shaking hands with Reagan, with the caption, "He
congratulated them at news conference for coming up with budget
compromise." A press conference with the president of the United States
clearly qualified as "being senatorial"; and the paper acknowledged it.
The accompanying front-page story, however, carried the headline
"Panel OK's Budget Plans Trimming Social Security"; and the inside
carry-over section of the article was headlined "Budget Seeks $40 Billion
Social Security Savings." The article mentions Domenici only once—in

paragraph eight of its thirty-one paragraphs—simply as "author of the new budget proposal."

The picture surely carries a message of Domenici's legislative leadership; but the accompanying article deflects all attention from that fact. What the paper gives with the picture, it takes away with the article. Indeed, considered together, the front-page picture and story convey the negative message that Domenici is tampering with Social Security. And that is exactly the way the senior citizen groups in New Mexico interpreted it.[14] Another effect is to highlight the one aspect of the budget agreement most vulnerable to attack—and already under attack—by Democratic party senators. While it is true that the Social Security provision surely warranted attention, the decision to make it the centerpiece of the story while at the same time deciding to ignore Domenici's coalition-building activity struck this observer as perverse.

The *Journal's* singularly downbeat coverage of Domenici's Washington triumph became even clearer, two days later, when its Washington reporter presented his analysis of the May 5 agreement. It, too, was written more from the perspective of the chairman's political opponents than from the perspective of the chairman himself. Under the headline, "The Republicans Are Not Through Yet," he saved his skimpy description of Domenici's coalition-building effort until the twenty-first of his twenty-five paragraphs. And in his next-to-last paragraph he called the budget "an important breakthrough." But he gave Domenici no credit for his substantive accomplishment. Quite to the contrary. He devoted most of his Domenici-related paragraphs to echoing the complaints of committee Democrats concerning Domenici's procedural tactics. He began, "Domenici's handling of the budget committee on the days leading up to the surprise agreement was amazing to watch. For one thing, he threw away the rule book." And he concluded, "let's hope it is the first and only time Domenici sees fit to play loose with the rules."[15]

The writer's decision to put a dominantly negative spin on Domenici's performance reflected the viewpoint of the most petulant of the committee's "outmaneuvered" Democrats. The article made no effort— as the *Wall Street Journal* had, for example—to dig into the intricacies and delicacies of Domenici's coalition-building maneuvers. It showed no interest in the key relationship of the chairman with his Republican committee members. Nor did it give the slightest hint of the kind of influence implied in the *New York Times* editorial that Domenici was, de facto, setting the government's agenda. In short, the *Journal* made no effort, at a time of the chairman's greatest legislative accomplishment to date, to give him his due. The *Wall Street Journal* article is one of only two that hang on the wall of Domenici's outer office, where every visitor will see it on the way in to talk with the senator. It is a clear reminder of how the chairman viewed his May 5 budget agreement. His home state's largest paper saw it very differently—or, better perhaps, chose not to see it at all.

Pete Domenici's "institutional problem" with the media was less tractable than his structural problem. But, over time, both problems were ameliorated by the two-step process. The structural problem became less severe as the national media fed increasing amounts of information about Domenici to the local media. The institutional problem was mitigated because the two Albuquerque papers could not dominate statewide New Mexico opinion or insulate themselves from the tidal wave of favorable national attention flowing into New Mexico. A total statewide opinion formed about Pete Domenici in the face of which any single newspaper could have only a minor effect.

Consider the previous example. While the *Albuquerque Journal* chose to downplay Domenici's May 5, 1982, accomplishment, the *Albuquerque Tribune* gave him full credit for it. And it did so by taking cues from the national press coverage of the event. The *Tribune*'s Washington reporter presented the story of the May 5 agreement under the title "Senator Domenici the Compromiser"; and he called the chairman "the Henry Clay of the 1980's." He devoted his fourth and fifth paragraphs to quoting the *New York Times*'s "President Domenici?" editorial.[16] The *Carlsbad Current-Argus* reprinted verbatim a highly complimentary May 9 editorial from the *Los Angeles Times* describing Domenici as "the cool hand from Albuquerque" who "held the budget process together in his soft spoken obstinate way."[17] The political columnist for the *Santa Fe New Mexican*, a paper with a statewide circulation, devoted an entire column to the *New York Times* editorial, under the headline "Domenici Knows How to Use Powerful Post." He used the praise and recognition provided by the *Times* to remind New Mexicans of the national stature and recognized talent of their senator. And he closed on a note of national-local press relations.

> Maybe someday the folks at home will come to understand that we have an exceptional opportunity. Maybe we can even shift into high gear, *as the press from the rest of the nation has,* and come to appreciate that this is no ordinary lawmaker.[18]

The two-step process takes time. But, with the national press giving Domenici constant and favorable attention, and with most of the local press transfixed by the national attention, the rest of the local press would sooner or later, most of the time, follow.

After a year in power, that was Pete Domenici's considered viewpoint, too. In New Mexico, in October 1981, he made a comment that he could never have made earlier. "This senator at this stage of his career wants people to know what he's doing.... People do know what I'm doing. By the grace of AP, UPI, CBS, ABC, NBC, the *New York Times,* and the *Washington Post,* people know that I'm in the middle of things." If this two-step, two-stage hypothesis holds, local coverage will, over time, come to more closely approximate national coverage—in tone, if not in amount. That proposition, too, is consistent with Pete Domenici's own view. He believes that the national media exerts, over time, a beneficial effect on the local media and brings about a convergence in their coverage.

Reflecting on his press relations in the aftermath of the 1982 budget battle, he said,

> I wouldn't want you to think that I have reached the state that every politician dreams of, where the press back home gives him all the coverage he thinks he deserves and interprets what he does the way he wants it interpreted. I haven't. I still fret when a story in New Mexico carries the headline "Domenici's Budget Committee Cuts Social Security $40 Billion...." But overall, there has been an enormous change.... The exposure I get from the national press, from the *New York Times* and the *Washington Post,* has begun to creep into New Mexico—not a lot, but enough. I get lots of exposure from national television and radio.... That kind of publicity has had a big effect on the local media. It has forced the New Mexico press and television to take me seriously and pay more attention to what I say and do.... When I'm on TV or radio, in the national weekly magazines and the national papers, it gives a legitimacy to what I say when I'm back home. The local people are less suspicious that I'm just feeding them some flak.... I don't have the anxiety about the press that I used to have. A lot of it takes care of itself now.

There is a sense conveyed here that not only does the local press need the national press but that the local press will not stand against the national press over the long run. The tide of national publicity washes over the local media as relentlessly as the budget process itself rolls over more particularistic items on the political agenda. In Pete Domenici's case the net effect in his home state brought him to the highly favorable poll ratings with which we opened this section.

BUDGET SEASONS AND THE MEDIA CONNECTION

Our earlier description of Chairman Domenici's governing activity emphasized his changing relations with President Reagan over the first three budget seasons—from dependence through transition to independence. For New Mexicans who were interested, this developmental theme could easily be followed in the local media. And to the extent that it came to be discerned locally, it gave the people at home a particularly favorable perspective from which to view Senator Domenici. They saw him as a person who, while generally in tune with President Reagan, was willing to disagree with him in pursuit of certain policy goals. Domenici came across as an independent senator—as someone who is his own man, willing to think for himself and for his state. He came across not as someone rigidly ideological or slavishly partisan but as someone tenacious in pursuit of his view of good public policy.

Independence in relation to a president who was widely considered to be very conservative probably had the added effect of making him appear less conservative, or, moderate. "I think I'm sort of a moderate to a moderate conservative," [19] said Domenici in defining his place on the ideological spectrum. When asked to describe him, New Mexico voters approximated that view. Asked in May 1983, "Would you say he's ... very conservative, somewhat conservative, somewhat liberal, very liberal?", 15 percent of New Mexicans opted for the first label, 50 percent for the "somewhat conservative" label, 12 percent for the "somewhat liberal" label, and 2 percent for the fourth label. Moreover, 7 percent spontaneously suggested the term "moderate" to describe Domenici, and 16 percent had no opinion. At the same time, the chairman's job approval rating ("strongly approve" plus "somewhat approve") was 82 percent among Democrats, 86 percent among self-styled moderates, 80 percent among independents, and 73 percent among liberals. It was 89 percent among Republicans and 90 percent among conservatives.

In the same poll, respondents were asked, "What is the first thing that comes to mind when you think of Pete Domenici, is there anything you particularly like or dislike about him?" Only 8 percent answered negatively and 16 percent had no opinion. It was, and it had always been, Domenici's most noteworthy characteristic that he drew so few "negatives" from his constituents—fewer, we have noted, than any other senator running in 1984. There never had been much "not to like" about him. And his work on the Budget Committee had not changed that image. Of the positive opinions, 28 percent answered (in several forms) that he had done a good job, 21 percent mentioned favorable personal characteristics, 18 percent mentioned his Budget Committee performance, 5 percent liked his stand on certain issues, and 3 percent were generally positive. Among the personal characteristics mentioned were strong and decisive, 6 percent; honest and sincere, 5 percent; qualified and capable, 3 percent; and senatorial-political skills, 3 percent. By July 1984, when asked whether certain phrases better described Domenici or his opponent, the chairman received his highest marks on "can best handle future problems facing New Mexico" (68 percent), "gets things done" (67 percent), and "is consistent" (64 percent).[20] All could be related to his work on the Budget Committee.

In his first budget season, Domenici was viewed locally, and correctly, as a loyal lieutenant on the Reagan team and as a spearhead of the Reagan program in Congress. Whatever disagreement might have existed regarding the full plate of Reaganomics, it was hidden beneath the two leaders' surface agreement on balanced budgets and growth economics. The Washington reporter for the *Tribune* stated (and shaped) the local view saying, in February, that the chairman's "commitment to the administration is cast in concrete. Domenici has been calling for a balanced budget and an end to deficit spending so long he can't very well turn back now."[21] A month later, he wrote that,

> Senate Budget Committee Chairman Pete Domenici is certain to be remembered as the man who wielded President Reagan's budget cutting ax with discipline, precision, and dispatch.[22]

As we said earlier, however, the major message conveyed locally was mostly one of Domenici's involvement in Washington. It was conveyed in large part by the sheer amount of local attention being paid to national attention and in part by the daily reporting by the wire services of important budgetary events.

In the second budget season, however, signs of the senator's open disagreement with the president began to be reported locally, as Domenici talked about immediate congressional action to balance the budget and Reagan decided to wait. As local coverage increased, the theme of Domenici's growing independence began to develop.

Some significant Associated Press reports, all widely printed in New Mexico during Domenici's second, or transition, budget season, began with the paragraphs quoted below. These *first paragraphs* do not convey the subtlety of Domenici's activity, as we described it earlier, but they do convey the sense of change from the early months of 1981:

> *September 14* "Congress likely will want a larger cut in the defense budget than the $13 billion, three-year package proposed by President Reagan," Senate Budget Committee Chairman Pete Domenici said Sunday.[23]
>
> [*September 24* the president, in a nationwide television speech, quotes Domenici by name as saying, "You can run but you can't hide," regarding deficits.]
>
> *September 25* Senator Pete Domenici's reaction to President Reagan's speech on the economy was that Congress should show as much courage as the President in facing up to the country's economic problems.[24]
>
> *October 22* The Chairman of the Senate Budget Committee said yesterday that without further Congressional action, the nation faces

an accumulated deficit of $20 billion to $25 billion over the next three years.[25]

November 5 After months of cooperation, President Reagan and some of his GOP Senate Allies are moving in opposite directions—the President ruling out big tax increases and Republicans ruling them in—to balance the 1984 budget.[26]

November 11 Some Senate Republicans, resisting President Reagan's request to wait until next year, want to push ahead immediately with a three-year budget balancing plan that includes large tax increases and cuts in benefit programs.[27]

November 13 Republicans on the Senate Budget Committee are pressing ahead with $114 billion in tax increases and budget cuts despite a clear signal that the House wants to go along with President Reagan and put off action till next year.[28]

[*November 16* The Domenici Plan loses, 12-10, in the Senate Budget Committee.]

[*December 8* Although administration economists have taken to declaring that record budget deficits of $100 billion won't fuel inflation or high interest rates after all, the Senate Budget Committee chairman, Senator Pete Domenici, insists that much red ink will be "devastating to the economy." [29]]

Sometimes these AP reports highlighted Domenici, sometimes not. Since AP reports are used nationwide, their tendency is to generalize, that is: "Senate Republicans," or "GOP Allies." Still, careful readers could infer, if they were not told later in the article, a growing disagreement between the president and the chairman.

The interpretive local press, operating under no nationally imposed constraints, could, and did, convey a much sharper sense of disagreement. The *Albuquerque Journal's* page-one, November 13, 1981, story—with the headline "Domenici Leads Budget Rebellion"—began:

> Republicans on the Senate Budget Committee, led by Senator Pete Domenici, rebelled against President Reagan's wishes and prepared a plan to balance the budget by 1984. Domenici submitted his $160 billion plan just a few hours after Reagan called him to the White House to ask him to hold off.[30]

The *Journal* covered the season's story to its end with the same tone of heightened personal conflict. "Senate Panel Rejects Domenici Plan" was the headline on November 17; and the story began,

> The Senate Budget Committee handed President Reagan a victory Monday when it voted down three plans to balance the budget by fiscal year 1984, including one by Senator Pete Domenici.[31]

On November 20 the *Journal* headline read "Senate Committee Clears Outdated Budget Resolution: Domenici Yields to Reagan." The story began,

> The Senate Budget Committee Thursday bowed, albeit reluctantly, to

White House demands and reported out without a recommendation the outdated first budget resolution, a move one panel member called "a sham." [32]

The tone of this *Journal* article dismayed Domenici, whose posture was that he was trying to help the president with his program, and who realized he must stay within the reach of the president to influence him.

A staff member grumbled about the November 13 headline that "It might just as well have been written by the liberals at the *Washington Post*." The net effect of the Albuquerque stories surely was to highlight, if not open conflict, then at least Domenici's growing independence in his relations with the president. There was, of course, some reality behind this scorekeeping angle. But there was also some evidence of the media's occupational attraction to political conflict.

The local, end-of-the-season assessment of Domenici's first-year-chairman performance continued to focus mostly on the fact that he was now playing on the national stage. The focus began to shade, however, away from sheer fascination and toward a sense of local pride. The assessment of the *Tribune*'s top local political reporter was that,

Domenici's star is rising nationally though his role as Chairman of the Senate Budget Committee, the point of greatest focus as Reagan's fiscal plans unfolded throughout the year. Pete's photo was often seen on the front pages of national newspapers, in the major news magazines, and on the nightly news of the major television networks. He has received high marks for his work and deservedly so.[33]

No available evidence suggests that informed local opinion held otherwise. But another strand of the local assessment—the changing relationship with Reagan—could also be heard. A columnist for the *Santa Fe New Mexican* wrote in December:

The deficit for next year is now expected to be $109 billion, then rise the following year to $162 billion. . . . What worries him [Domenici] is that the Reagan administration is beginning to act as though those numbers could be lived with. . . . If Pete is getting weary of carrying Reagan proposals, both in committee and on the floor, that's understandable.[34]

The local story was becoming more than just Domenici's notoriety and involvement.

As Chairman Domenici entered his third budget season, in 1982, the local media convincingly carried home, to anyone who was interested, both his independence and his influence. In April the news director of a Santa Fe radio station wrote,

Many political professionals [at the state capitol] are openly proud of the job being done by Republican U.S. Senator Pete Domenici of New Mexico. A leading figure in the battle to develop a budget with lower deficits than predicted by the White House, Domenici has won the admiration of both sides of the political aisle. Last year when I visited Domenici in Washington, I wrote a column for the *Santa Fe Reporter* on his evident muscle in the Senate. *But it wasn't until this year that the average New Mexican received, via national news accounts, a first hand indication of his power.* Even some of the Washington news people are giving him high marks. . . . It's no secret that I do not favor many of the changes being made in Washington, but Domenici is a bright spot for us all.[35]

The pivotal event in producing this view was the Conference Board speech of February 23, in which the chairman said that the president's budget proposal "accepts almost benignly what are malignant deficits" and asserted that "Congress just won't pass it in its present form." Domenici's Washington activity was now capturing the direct interest of the local media.

His speech was reported throughout New Mexico in an AP story that began:

The Republican chairman of the Senate Budget Committee is making what his Democratic counterpart in the House calls "an extremely significant" step toward a bipartisan rewrite of President Reagan's deficit ridden budget. It calls for less military spending and more taxes than Reagan has proposed.[36]

The *Albuquerque Journal* carried the article under the front-page headline "Compromise on Budget Proposed by Domenici: Rejecting Reagan Plan." The story called it "the sharpest defection yet by a GOP leader." The story also described Domenici as "one of President Reagan's most consistent supporters" and reported that the White House reaction was that his proposal was "serious and deserves attention." [37] It thus emphasized Domenici's attack on the deficit rather than on the president. But the difference of opinion, and the bid for bipartisanship, remained prominent. Indeed, Domenici's independence was highlighted when New Mexico's other Republican senator, former astronaut Harrison Schmitt, stated flatly that "I personally would not have taken on the president publicly." That story was circulated statewide, also courtesy of AP.[38]

Editorial interpretation at home picked up on Domenici's increased independence. The *Portales News-Tribune* said that "the most prominent among his [Reagan's] outspoken critics now is Senator Pete Domenici." [39] The *Santa Fe New Mexican* entitled its editorial "Domenici's reasoned break." [40] In the *Artesia Daily Press,* a columnist said that Domenici had "walked away from the man in the White House over that budget full of deficits." [41] The *Albuquerque Tribune* wrote that "A familiar name has jumped off the Good Ship Lollipop." [42] The *Carlsbad Current-*

Argus gave Domenici "an 'A' for effort, guts and sincerity.... It takes guts to be a good senator."[43] Back in Washington, we recall, Domenici was convinced that his action "doesn't play well in my state." But, so far as media comment was concerned, the reaction was entirely favorable.

The *Albuquerque Tribune* used the Domenici-Schmitt difference to highlight the chairman's independence. Under the heading "Domenici Is Right," it editorialized:

> New Mexico Senator Pete Domenici is embattled with the White House over his proposed changes in the next federal budget.... There is no question in our mind that Domenici tried in every way possible behind the scenes to persuade Reagan to moderate his position.... We don't feel our two senators have to agree on every issue, but neither do we want our representatives in Congress to be a rubber stamp for the President's administration. And, on this issue, Schmitt looks dangerously like such a device.[44]

The *Tribune*'s political columnist summed up the post-Conference Board relationship this way: "Reagan and his point man have taken different paths in their quest for economic progress ... [and] Reagan needs Domenici more than Domenici needs Reagan."[45] For the remainder of 1982, Domenici was viewed locally as an independent actor, bargaining on an equal footing with the president of the United States. And that, as we have described in Chapter 3, was exactly what was happening in Washington.

The progress of the Washington negotiations was reported back home more in terms of Domenici than in terms of "Senate Republicans." And this was a distinct, noticeable change from 1981. Consider the flow of battlefront headlines in the two Albuquerque papers beginning with the first meeting of the Senate Budget Committee:

March 5 Domenici Says Reagan Deficit Must Be Cut
March 8 Domenici Admits Budget Plan Needed: Hopes Consensus Is Near
March 8 Reagan Applauds Domenici Proposal
April 3 Senate Republicans to Write Own '83 Budget Resolution
April 12 Domenici Stops Work in '83 Budget
April 19 Domenici Says Deficit Will Near $180 Billion
April 30 Reagan-Congress Budget Efforts Collapse in Orgy of Finger Pointing
May 4 New Domenici Plan Seeks Spending, Tax Cut Freezes
May 4 Domenici Proposes Bold Plan
May 6 Reagan Gives Go-ahead to Domenici Budget Plan
May 7 Panel OKs Budget Plans Trimming Social Security
May 12 Seniors Unit Raps Domenici's Budget
May 18 Domenici Admits Social Security Cut Can't Pass
June 3 Domenici Raps House on Budget
June 11 Domenici Ready to Fix Up Budget

June 16 Domenici Says Senate Plan a "Major Accomplishment"
June 18 GOP Agrees on '83 Budget with Tax-Hike

By the end of Pete Domenici's third budget season, the local media had joined the national media consensus in emphasizing the chairman's independence and his influence.

An AP poll named Domenici as "the most influential person in New Mexico." [46] And one local commentator, at least, proclaimed him New Mexico's best senator ever. [47] The *Albuquerque Journal*'s Washington reporter wrote in late 1982 that,

> Domenici is not just another senator. He's on the evening news night after night, on weekend interview shows, on the front pages of newspapers all over the world. New Mexicans are proud of him. [48]

In early 1983 AP feature writer Mike Shanahan's profile of Domenici was published statewide. His judgment was that,

> Over the last three years, the 51-year-old Domenici has won respect in his own right as a fair-minded and independent—some say stubborn—spirit, who has more than once challenged Reagan when he thought the president had gone too far in cutting taxes or not far enough in reducing the Pentagon budget. [49]

At the same time, the *Albuquerque Tribune*'s local reporter wrote,

> His importance in the Senate . . . his role as a national leader . . . and the notoriety he has brought to his home state of New Mexico have combined to give him an unparalleled stature in the eyes of his fellow New Mexicans that crosses party lines, ethnic boundaries and socio-economic class barriers. People in New Mexico are just plain proud of Domenici. [50]

These New Mexico judgments—supported by the national media and based on national performance—provided an impressive underpinning for a reelection campaign.

HOME STYLE AND THE MEDIA CONNECTION

As the local pundits began to contemplate Domenici's reelection effort, one further subject engaged their interest—the senator's home style. The problem here was the obverse side of the picture of national success. It could be stated in two forms. First, would New Mexicans, for all their recognition of his independence and influence as a legislator, get the sense that Domenici had not given them tangible services in exchange for their support? Second, would New Mexicans, for all their pride in his national performance, get the sense that Domenici had lost touch with them? That is, would the home folks come to feel that their senator had, in one form or another, "gone Washington?" Indeed, it was only March of 1981 when the *Tribune*'s politics writer began his column, "Will fame spoil Pete Domenici? That is a question that is crossing people's minds as they watch the New Mexico Republican Senator's actions as Chairman of the powerful Senate Budget Committee." [51]

In a self-consciously small, neglected, and distant state like New Mexico, this question poses a constant danger to any elected federal office holder—more so, we would guess, than in a large state, close to Washington and filled with the nation's elites. New Mexicans are prone to see themselves as "virtual industrial vassals of the older eastern states" or as "an energy colony for the eastern states" or as "neglected by that portion of the nation east of the Mississippi" or as "frequently overlooked ... and suffering from an identity crisis." [52] Politicians sent to Washington are expected to maintain strong local attachments. Local pride is expected to be requited.

The successful 1982 campaign of New Mexico Democrats to unseat the state's other Republican senator had as a major theme the charge that Harrison Schmitt was insufficiently interested in, or in contact with, the people he represented. "I accuse Schmitt of being more dedicated to representing NASA than he does to representing New Mexico," said one of his opponents. "He hasn't lived in New Mexico since he was 18. He never had any investments or businesses in New Mexico. He doesn't know the state and its people." Or, "He has no working relationships with the people of New Mexico." [53] Schmitt's other opponent said, when he announced for the seat, that Schmitt was not "close enough to the everyday concerns of this state." "I think we get in trouble," he argued, "when we allow a federal representative to disappear back in Washington, keep in touch with us by mail or come back now and then to hold office hours." [54] The prominence of the "he's 'gone Washington' " charge in the campaign against Schmitt illustrates its potency as a campaign theme in New Mexico.

It was an electoral theme that, if it could be used, would spell trouble for Pete Domenici. As the *Journal*'s columnist speculated in early 1983, "It would be foolish of Domenici ... to assume he's a cinch for reelection and not pay proper attention to the folks back home. . . . That would almost guarantee defeat in New Mexico." [55] And as the *Tribune*'s columnist predicted in late 1982, "It's a safe bet that Domenici will spend much of his time next year in New Mexico, talking to the voters and will be carefully shaping his legislation and efforts to the benefit of New Mexico." [56]

As we know from the May 1983 poll results, Pete Domenici's relationship with the home folks was not a problem. Voters were asked to rate Domenici—"excellent, good, only fair, or poor" on three parts of his job. Combining the top two categories, Domenici got 79 percent approval for "taking leadership on important national issues," 72 percent approval for "helping solve the problems of New Mexico," and 71 percent approval for "keeping in touch with the voters back home." The sense that he was a legislative leader was remarkably strong; the sense that he was looking out for the home folks was close behind.

His campaign manager commented on those poll numbers, in January 1984:

> People are proud of his influence in Washington, but they also believe he looks after New Mexico. We see no evidence that people think he's "gone Washington." He's been on all the right TV shows, but he's not on the Washington social circuit. It seems he has managed both sides of his job well. [Governor] Anaya is getting a lot of criticism now on just those grounds, that his desire to become a national Hispanic leader has taken him away from New Mexico. We have bumper stickers that say—after ET—"Toney Anaya, call home." Pete has not received that criticism.

Domenici had, apparently, achieved the local reputation he had set for himself in his 1979 post-mortem—a blending of his established image as a "caring for," "sympathy with" person and a newer image as having a national outlook on the issues. Indeed, just as he had hoped in March 1979, this very combination would become the theme of his 1984 campaign.

Some of what he had done to maintain his ties to New Mexico was deliberate. He continued to go home regularly—for as much time in the first year of his chairmanship (sixteen trips, forty-five days) as in the year preceding it (ten trips, forty-five days).[57] After Schmitt's defeat, Domenici sought and won an assignment to the Appropriations Committee, the Senate's premier spot from which to watch, protect, and fund local projects of all sorts. A top staffer said in 1983 that "Our list of appropriations for the state is so long nobody can believe it." Domenici was active in publicizing his funding achievements—for example, money to repair the historic irrigation system (acequias), money for the protection of the water rights of non-Indians, money for the Raton water supply, and aid for a veterans' hospital, all in Hispanic northern New Mexico. "I've done a lot as far as the government is concerned," said Domenici. "New Mexico is first in return from the government per tax dollar and fourth in per capita federal dollars coming into the state. I didn't do all that; but I've been able to help."

He worked to relate his budget work to local concerns whenever possible. On the day that the 1982 budget resolution finally passed Congress, for example, he highlighted for the Associated Press the resolution's benefits for New Mexico. The next day, the local press carried two AP stories throughout the state—one that the resolution had passed, the other that the Budget Committee chairman had been looking out for the home folks. The second story carried headlines such as: "Domenici Sees Compromise Budget Plan Kind to the State" (Hobbs), "Compact Pleases Domenici" (Santa Fe), "Domenici: NM Will Fare Well" (Portales), "Domenici: It's Good for State" (Carlsbad), "NM Fares Well in Budget Compromise, Domenici Says" (Albuquerque), "Senator Says Compromise Provides for New Mexico" (Las Cruces), and "Pete Says Plan Kind to NM" (Roswell). In this manner, Domenici worked to keep his national leadership tied to, not separated from, the concerns of his constituents.

A speech to 250 people at New Mexico State University in the fall of 1981—early in the second budget season—illustrates the small and subtle ways in which Domenici could use his chairmanship in Washington to cement his relationships at home. The situation was structured by the university's president in his introduction, which stressed the senator's Washington performance and local pride in that performance:

> ... I don't know anybody who has gone onto the national stage in Washington with more national attention, has created a better climate, has brought more vision and logic and judgment into the political situation than Senator Pete Domenici. I had a chance, coming back on the airplane from Washington about a month ago, to pick up a *Washington Post* and there on page three was a two-thirds page article on Senator Domenici. And that very week, Jack Anderson, senator, also had an article and when you get Jack Anderson to agree on anything it must be good.
>
> So I think you and I and all of us are very fortunate to have this kind of a senator working for us there in Washington and looking out after not only our interests in New Mexico but interests across the United States. Of course here at the University we are very pleased with our range caterpillar laboratory that Senator Pete Domenici helped inaugurate a few months ago and also in the Coyote research program. In both cases he's been very much interested in the agricultural sphere....

Spurred by these references to his national activity, Domenici moved easily to let his listeners savor and share with him the personal rewards of his governing exploits:

> I want to tell you about Jack Anderson. Knowing the kind of people you are, you never believe Jack Anderson, so I don't know why you ought to believe him when he says I'm good [laughter].... You know, it's fine to be mentioned in Jack Anderson's column ... but it's really superfine when the president delivers his speech to the American people and he quotes you like he did me last time.
>
> Let me tell you how all this occurred.... My job is not only to convince the president when I think he ought to do something.... I

have to work up through Howard Baker who is our leader. So I started two weeks before that, being a pest. I'd camp out in Howard Baker's office and just lecture him on—for just as long as he'd stay there—about the fact that we had to convince the president to make a second address and that he had to go on and get on the record that we ought to start right up there in Washington and make a second round of cuts contemplated by his budget and not wait until next year.

Now that was a pretty tough job to get Howard convinced that what the money markets were saying was not "we don't like the Reagan plan" but rather "we like the first phase but we're not convinced Congress is going to adopt the second phase. . . ." Anyhow, I was trying to convince Howard of that and I got him that far. . . .

Then I said, "Leader, you're just half way. Next thing is you've got to convince the president—first yourself—that that great big part of the American budget called entitlements which, with interest on the debt, is now 57 percent of the budget and growing at 11 percent per year, most of which is automatically increasing because we built in a consumer price index to add to it every year—that we can't make that second step of cuts or reductions credible without taking off some of that." "Oh," he said, "I don't think that's doable. That can't be done. But keep trying to convince me."

Well I got him so angry at me by showing him the numbers that he told me one morning about 10 o'clock, "Pete, just go to your office, please. And you in your own words, write me a memo no longer than one page and convince me you're right."

I went to my office. I called my budget director. . . . I sat him down and I said, ". . . I'm preparing a memo for Senator Baker. He destroys me because he always opens these serious discussions with some old Tennessee saying or some hillbilly joke or something about when he was a lawyer that sort of makes the point. And I need *something* from history that's sort of catchy. So you be thinking about that." He said, "I've already got something." He said, "Do you know what Joe Louis said when he was fighting Max Schmeling . . . that 'he can run but he can't hide?' " I said, "That's super; that's what we're going to build the Baker memo around."

Well we did that. We convinced Baker, and to make a long story short, it was my privilege to be called upon by the leader to tell the president not where to make the detailed cuts, but to try to explain what I explained to you—that we ought not kid ourselves, if we can't produce the next round of cuts we haven't done any better than those other guys at controlling the deficits. . . . Well, you know the president wrote down on a little yellow pad as I was talking; and then about five days later, they called my office and they said, "We would like to read a paragraph out of the president's speech." And they read me my quote. They said, "We're calling you, senator, because we don't want the president to quote things that aren't true. So we want to make sure that in fact that occurred. . . . Would you verify?" I said, "Oh my God, yes I will."

And I called Steve Bell and I said, "Steve, you'd better be right." [laughter] The White House would like confirmation or verification that Joe Louis said, 'He can run but he can't hide.' " Well I didn't hear much on the other side [laughter] and he said, "I'll find out" [laughter]. Well, I saw him in the hall that afternoon and he wasn't too willing to talk [laughter]. . . . Finally I cornered him and he said, "It's all right, I called"—I guess there's an archive of famous quotations of boxers [laughter]—"and what I found was that we were almost right [laughter]. Joe Louis said that. But, senator, we should have known Max Schmeling was a great big heavy guy who could hardly move. It was Billy Conn." So you now understand why the president had it right when he said that Joe Louis fights Billy Conn in 1933 as quoted to me by Senator Domenici.

The session then proceeded to more serious discussion. But, again, Domenici acted so as to bridge the distance between his national activity and his New Mexico constituents.

Reflecting on this particular speech, as compared with the twelve other events during his four-day trip home, Domenici ranked it the most "enjoyable" of all. "There was a good representation of people there," he began.

> The vibes were good. I could be funny; and it's hard for me to be funny. Things just popped out right. It was the first time I had told the Howard Baker story in public. A lot of people came a long way, up to a hundred miles. They came to bitch. But they thought it was important enough to come all that way to talk with me. That made me feel good.

Assuming some mutuality of feeling, the event was a perfect example of how home relationships can be built on the basis of Washington activity. And the basic building block was, of course, the chairmanship.

Because of his chairmanship, too, the Domenici staff enterprise was afforded more opportunity than ever to address the individual concerns of his constituents. Legislators, we know, actively solicit casework so that they can build up the credits associated with efforts to help both individuals and groups with their specific problems. For the chairman, there was no need to solicit. He got more chances than he could handle. Domenici, we recall, described himself in his first term as "acting like a congressman" in providing personal service to his constituents. And his staff agreed that their efforts in this regard intensified as a result of his new position. His Washington staff doubled their letter output, from eighteen thousand in 1980 to thirty-six thousand in 1981—exclusive of mass mailings.

In New Mexico, the post-1980 workload of his four field offices grew. "Our casework has tripled since Pete became chairman," said one field director.

> People think that because he's influential in Washington he can do more for them with their problems. So we get cases that would otherwise go to other members of the delegation. Who wants to go to

a freshman senator when they could go to the chairman of the Budget Committee? Of course, we can't always do anything to help; but we try awfully hard.

And it is "trying hard" that reaps benefits.

The new caseload was not all beneficial. Another field director talked about projects:

My workload has gone up ten times since he became chairman. I'm invited to come and consult more than I ever was. . . . People want to be sure we know everything they are doing. . . . I get to visit many more places on behalf of the senator. They know now, more than before, he may be able to help. Or they think he can. Actually a lot of people have very unrealistic expectations.

The latter theme was common to all staffers. "We get more complex problems now," said a third director. "People began to say, 'If Pete can't do it, nobody can. Let's give Pete a try.'" The first director concluded, "What's made it more difficult for us is the nature of the requests."

They used to come in and ask if he could do this. Now they come in and demand. They say, "I know he can do it. I know he has the clout. . . ." We have to explain to them that he does not control these federal agencies. But they don't believe it. Pete's ability to help them hasn't changed as much as their expectations of him have.

Still, the increased opportunities to try to help with individual cases and with group projects are of net benefit to an elected official.

In assessing Domenici's job performance in "keeping in touch with the voters back home," the state's Hispanic voters—its poorest citizens—gave him a job approval rating (in May 1983) of 71 percent—only four points below the statewide total. And 60 percent of this group said later that year that they would vote to reelect him no matter who ran against him. In a small, word-of-mouth state the marginal benefits of casework are greatest. For whatever constituency service is worth in terms of staying close to the home folks, Pete Domenici's second term probably brought greater rewards than his first.

More important than what he and his staff did deliberately is what Domenici himself did naturally. It is simply impossible to see him, meet him, or read about him—to have any contact direct or indirect with him—and imagine that he has "gone Washington." In this respect, Domenici's normal presentation of self at home is his greatest political asset. And it is sufficiently consistent so that it cannot be distorted and pictured otherwise. A long-time associate emphasized "natural" aspects of his behavior that the observer notices immediately:

He hung around with the gang on Park and Fourteenth, played baseball, basketball, the whole thing. It's natural for him to put his

arm around a guy without it seeming to be forced. "Como está, Jose?";
"Como está, Pete?" People call him Pete. They think of him as a
senator, but not someone with a big head. You know how he
dresses—no fancy clothes. He'll keep the big shots waiting in his
office while he chases after the janitor. It's natural for him.

He seems perfectly comfortable with his position. But he also seems a
little surprised that he has achieved it. "It's fair to say they are proud of
me," he says of his constituents. "But I didn't plan all this stuff." The
result is someone who engages easily in the ordinary, unexciting routine
of politics at home.

People who have known him a long time approach an observer
with the comment, "He hasn't changed a bit." They mean it in two
senses—conveyed by two women who went to school with him. Said
one,

Everyone likes Pete Domenici. They always have. I went to college
with him and he has not changed one bit. He was very popular in
college and he's very popular now. I've never heard anyone say they
didn't like him.

Said the other,

What I like about Pete Domenici is that you would never know he's
one of the most powerful people in Washington. He hasn't changed
one bit. It hasn't gone to his head. He comes back and gets right
down to the level of the ordinary person. You can tell it's natural for
him.

He has not lost his likability, and he has not lost his common touch. One
imagines that New Mexico's national legislators always undergo critical
scrutiny on both points. They are Pete Domenici's natural attributes.

In the state's large Hispanic community, this natural modesty helps
account for the fact that he gets as much support there as it is possible
for an Anglo Republican to get. At a private meeting of one hundred
Hispanic Democrats at La Puenta in Albuquerque's solidly Democratic
South Valley, a man rose at the conclusion of Domenici's informal talk
and said, "I have known you all my life, and you have always talked to
us on our level. When we need you, you are always there. We have got
to vote for you." This is the image that encourages all New Mexicans
who know him to think of him as "Pete." [58]

He is also known to many of those who do not know him, as "Pete,"
or "our Pete," or "Senator Pete"—or so he is frequently labeled in
newspaper headlines throughout the state. Indeed, his ordinariness is an
essential ingredient in the story line that has followed him everywhere
since November 1980—the "unknown senator catapulted out of obscurity. . . ." His is a political Horatio Alger story; and there seems to be no

end to the fascination with Horatio Alger stories. There is "the rise" or "the climb" or "the emergence" of the individual, and then there is the question of how far away from "the background" or "the roots" or "the origins" the individual has moved. With Domenici the story line invariably is that he has risen far and fast—"Pete Domenici: From Stock Boy to Senator" headlines one page of his 1984 campaign brochure—but that he has not outgrown his hard-working, humble, religious, immigrant roots. Which means of course that he has not gotten out of touch with the people of his state.

"Behind the Scenes With Senator Pete," reads the headline of the feature article in the slick monthly publication *Albuquerque Living*. And the subheading reads, "Despite the pressures of life in Washington's fast lane, Albuquerque native Pete Domenici remains remarkably unscathed and down to earth." [59] When driven in limousines, he sits in the front seat so as not to be conspicuous. He often takes the subway to work. There are nearly mythic elements to the tale. Feature writers are attracted to the theme of the strapped financial circumstances and the unpretentious life style of a man with eight children, worn-out automobiles, unfashionable clothing—and power. Their stories bring readers (and viewers) who do not know him to the same conclusion that others have reached by observation.

The most widely circulated profile of Domenici's second term began this way:

> One day last year, slow talking, chain-smoking Senate Budget Committee Chairman Pete Domenici stepped from his battered blue Volkswagen into the White House driveway and surveyed the scene. [60]

The story profiled a man in power who remains "one of us." It ran under headlines such as: "Austere Domenici in Midst of Budget Fray" (Farmington), "Frugal Domenici's Star Rises in Washington" (Carlsbad), "Domenici Leads a Frugal Life" (Clovis), "Domenici Steps into Front Rank" (Las Cruces), "Senator Pete Domenici Has Risen to National Prominence" (Las Vegas), "Austere Minded Pete Domenici Now Has Powerful Senate Role" (Hobbs), "Domenici In Midst of Budget Fight" (Artesia, Lovington), "Senator Domenici in Midst of Budget Fight" (Portales), "State's Senator Gains Washington Power" (Silver City), "Domenici's Star Rises Still" (Roswell), and "Domenici Disarming in Midst of Budget Fights" (Grants). The theme is that Pete Domenici is important in Washington but has not "gone Washington."

The senator himself put it this way in April 1983:

> I think the people in the state are proud of the fact that I'm in a leadership role.... That creates a good feeling toward me. So long as

I continue alongside of that to take care of New Mexico's needs and to make sure that they understand here in New Mexico that I'm doing that. . . . I'm sure that I don't always vote the way [they] would want me to on everything, but I try my best and I am genuinely concerned about everyone in my state.[61]

That is both the personally established and the media-assisted reputation he carried into the reelection campaign of 1984.

THE SECOND REELECTION CAMPAIGN

Pete Domenici won reelection in November 1984 with 71.9 percent of the vote. He carried every county in the state. His vote total and his vote margin set all-time records for statewide contests in New Mexico. The size of the victory was not more than a mild surprise to the senator and his campaign staff. From the time they saw the results of their May 1983 baseline polls, they knew they would win. And the numbers revealed in that poll did not change significantly over the next year and a half.[62] His triumph, we would argue, was based on twelve years of governing activity in Washington and twelve years of presentational activity in New Mexico.

Though they did not believe their eventual opponent was the strongest one available, the Domenici enterprise never really feared any other candidate either. If there was any fear at all, it was of some unforeseen catastrophe—economic collapse, a scandal, or a health problem—totally beyond their control. They set a goal for themselves that effectively ensured against their only other fear—overconfidence. Their goal was to win by the largest possible margin. They were determined to do nothing that might contribute to a disappointing victory like that of 1978. They kept their expectations modest but their aspirations high. They directed the campaign not toward the win-or-lose outcome, which seemed foreordained, but toward the *margin* by which the winning outcome would be measured. Their target was the statewide record 63.4 percent vote of Senator Clinton Anderson in 1960; and they fixed their hopes on a 65.0 percent total. Measured against their goals, the Domenici campaign was a smashing success. In the senator's view, it was "the best campaign this state has ever seen."

Campaigns can be directed to goals beyond winning. One of these is to win by a huge margin. And winning by a huge margin was deemed to be immensely consequential for Pete Domenici's political future—personal, partisan, and governmental. Assuming, that is, that the consensus electoral interpretation would emphasize the size of the victory.

In September 1983 one of Domenici's top campaign aides explained the *personal* rationale.

> I know what the outcome will be, he said, and that's probably dangerous. But the important thing is that we max out in this election. We don't just need to win, we need to win big. If we do, Domenici will be in the clear. He will be able to do anything he wants. It would cut the last cord that ties him down. When you open the book where people write about these things, it says, 'He only got 53 percent last time; he isn't the horse he's supposed to be.' The people who can kill that idea are not the ones who write the book, but the people back home.

A large vote would free the senator to entertain new political goals or pursue old ones.

Domenici discussed at length the *partisan* rationale for an overwhelming victory. "Whether I got 72 percent or 52 percent would make no difference in how I behaved in the Senate," he said in answer to a question.

> But if I got 72 percent or even 62 percent, it would make a big difference in how I behaved here in New Mexico. Because I would start working to see that our state begins to share in the prosperity it deserves. . . . If I couldn't work with the governor, I'd work to bring new leadership to the state. I think we could take over the governorship. . . . If I got a big vote, I'd be willing to give it a try, to give New Mexico a real two-party system.

Near the end of the campaign, a top aide elaborated the possible *governmental* consequences of a big vote margin. "I want to beat Reagan by 15 points," he exclaimed.

> I don't care what else we have to do, we've got to lead him. We don't want him to lead us. I know it counts here, but it counts a hell of a lot back there. . . . I want us to go over 70 percent. . . . We want the president to understand that it's the moderate senators who lead the ticket. Otherwise, he'll come in with this big mandate and beat his chest. Someone has to go back and keep the fingers in the dike, and the only place to do it is in the Senate.

This comment strikingly measures the long road Chairman Domenici had traveled from his postelection, mandate-driven lieutenancy of 1981. The campaign was run to "max out" and, by maxing out, to help the senator achieve, if he wished, a variety of his own political goals.

In some respects, the senator running in 1984 was the same senator who had run in 1978. And in some respects he was different. He was the same senator in the sense that his public image contained exceptionally few negative references and very many positive ones. Therefore, both campaigns made him their centerpiece. And the overall strategy of both campaigns was to make the election a judgment on his past performance. The difference in the campaign themes, however, reflected the six-year difference in Domenici's performance.

In 1978 the campaigners emphasized the senator's personal characteristics and his local connections. They paid scant attention to his governing activity in Washington. They did not think it significantly prominent or appealing. They ran a home-oriented, congressional-style campaign. In 1984 the campaigners had to pay a lot of attention to the senator's extensive, influential, and highly publicized governing activity. They had no intention of giving up the 1978 theme of Domenici's home connections. But they had to devise a theme that would complement the home aspect of his performances with the newly prominent Washington aspect of his performance. The election would then be structured as a referendum on both.

"In his last campaign," summarized a long-time aide, "you had a first-term senator grasping or thrashing to find a record. This time the problem is distilling his record of national accomplishment. And now with [the] Appropriations [Committee], we have been shoveling grants into New Mexico.... So, up here [one hand held high] we've got the national record and down here [one hand held low] we've got the record of things done for the state." The campaign theme was a combination of the two levels of accomplishment. The campaign slogan became: "What he's doing on Capitol Hill makes an important difference here in New Mexico."

On the cover of his 1978 campaign brochure had been a picture of "Pete Domenici" leaning back in a chair, smiling, tie unfastened—in no particular context. On the cover of the 1984 brochure is a picture of "Senator Pete Domenici" talking seriously as he presides, in shirtsleeves, over a committee meeting. The 1978 brochure is filled with examples of his honesty and integrity. Its theme is: "When Pete tells you he stands for something, you know he really does." The 1984 brochure is filled with testimonials to his effectiveness in various fields from fourteen different local and national sources. Its theme stresses "What New Mexico's senior senator [has] done in critical state and national issues."

In 1978 Domenici's longest, kickoff TV ad had been a paean to the state, its people, its resources, its future. The theme was "a good senator for a good state," with a focus on the good state. In 1984 his longest, kickoff TV ad was a series of testimonials to "the good senator" and his Senate performance. It was comprised of a series of pictures that showed him, first, shaking hands with citizens, then mingling with Howard Baker, and then giving a speech. As a voiceover read a series of testimonials, the words rolled up the screen: "a Godsend . . . a realistic, thoroughly non-doctrinaire approach to his job" (David Broder, *Washing-*

ton Post), "in an atmosphere of extremes ... consistently provides a needed breath of sensible compromise" *(Las Cruces Sun News)*, "a power in the Senate ... a quiet grace that is unusual in a body of 100 politicians" (Eleanor Randolph, *Washington Monthly*). The emphasis on his power and on his independence is noticeable.

A related TV testimonial to his qualities featured citizen comments such as: "a very active senator doing all he can for New Mexico," "placed New Mexico on the map," "gets results," "a very powerful person in the Senate who never forgets he's first and foremost a New Mexican," "one of the best senators America has," and "done wonderful." His 1978 TV campaign contained nothing like either one of these ads. In 1984 he was presented—however vaguely—in terms of his Senate performance to a degree that he was not and could not have been six years earlier. The difference lay, of course, in his chairmanship.

Drawing the contrast between the flagship commercials of 1978 and 1984 should not obscure the effort, common to both years, to focus on Domenici's attractive personal qualities. If anything, the effort was more extensive in 1984—with five different testimonial-type commercials, compared with only one six years before. The 1978 testimonial had been all-purpose. The 1984 package featured slightly more differentiation, as befit the more complex senatorial activity it was advertising. The testimonial ad described above focused on his importance as a senator. Another one focused on his attention to New Mexico, with the message that he had not "gone Washington...," "what he's done for New Mexico is tremendous," "has done a lot for the people of New Mexico," "knows the people around here and what we need," and "represents the people of New Mexico."

A third ad invited a look at the senator as a person, especially his independence: "I don't vote the party, I vote the man," "down to earth," "says what he believes, what he really believes and sticks by it," "not a politician, a human being," "a good person, we can trust him," "he votes for what the people want," and "I don't think he's just a politician, he really cares." Another focuses on his caring attitude toward people: "cares about the citizens of New Mexico," "has helped the people in many, many ways," "has brought clean employment to New Mexico," "has own state's interests at heart," and "sincere and honest person." In total, the commercials were designed to advertise the Washington performance, the home performance, and the easy integration of the two.

The 1984 package of commercials reveals, also, the one issue-area in which the integration was not so easy, the one issue-area where Domenici believed that his Washington performance created a political weakness at home—Social Security. Chairman Domenici had spent four years trying to force the administration, his fellow senators, and the

House to slow the growth of entitlement programs, particularly by postponing or reducing the cost-of-living adjustments for Social Security and other pension plans. In 1982 he had argued that solvency required the $40 billion Social Security "plug" number, but he did not specify how the money was to be obtained. He worried about how that would play at home; and his commercials reflected that.

In a set of four, targeted, testimonial-type ads, people spoke about his good work for veterans, education, working men and women, and the elderly. He made another, special commercial directed at the last group; and it was the most explicit commercial of the campaign. Against a background of pictures showing Domenici talking with senior citizens in various settings, the voiceover and the words on the screen said,

> 176,000 New Mexicans will receive Social Security checks this month, as always. They will, because of Senator Pete Domenici's courage. He helped lead the fight in the Senate last year to keep Social Security from going bankrupt. Concerned senior citizen groups have praised his work to keep Social Security truly secure. So, when those Social Security checks arrive this month, we can say thanks to our Senator Pete Domenici.

It was the argument regarding solvency that he had lost in Congress. But he took the offensive with it at home.

In 1984 the Domenici people planned a more extensive effort in Hispanic, Democratic, northern New Mexico than they had in 1978. This change in strategy was directly related to their 1984 goal of a record-breaking electoral margin. The campaign aide who spoke in 1983 of "maxing out" continued his discussion of their plans, by arguing that the strategy of 1978 had been wrong:

> I knew last time that the ethnic factor would be very strong in the election. But the official strategy was: hit 'em hard in Albuquerque, hit 'em hard in the south, and the hell with the rest. Anything north of Interstate 40 didn't count. The strategy was to go with your strength and forget the rest. But what is Interstate 40 except an artificial line? It doesn't mean anything. Don't you think there are Hispanics in Belen? That's south of Interstate 40. Actually the Hispanic strength is in Albuquerque, and they care very much what happens up north. The network in the Hispanic community runs all over the state.

By not pressing hard in the north, he argued, the 1978 campaigners had weakened Domenici among Hispanics statewide.

The argument of the 1978 campaigners had been that it would be both fruitless and counterproductive to hit hard against a popular, Spanish-surnamed candidate (Anaya) in northern New Mexico. Domenici had campaigned there, as we saw earlier, seeking support via constituency service and via personal attributes displayed in small groups—but without any effort at organization. In the nine "northern counties" he got 39 percent of the vote. Domenici's aides remained split on the wisdom of the 1978 strategy because they remained uncertain of their strength in the north against a Hispanic candidate. Domenici's own view, in 1982, was more sober than it had been in 1978. "I hate to have to admit this because they are so dear to my heart, but the fact is that I have very little reliable support in the Hispanic area. They are not bastions of strength for [me]." And, he commented in 1984, "If I ran against a Hispanic in the north—like last time—I'd lose a lot of my support there just like that." But, with their polls showing a favorable image among Hispanics, with the strong likelihood that their opponent would not be Hispanic, and driven by this desire to win big, they changed their strategy.

"The strategy of this campaign has been different from 1978," said one aide a week before the election. "In 1978 we had an Albuquerque and southern strategy. We wrote off the north.... This year we are contesting everywhere in the state. We could see a chance for a big victory, so the strategy is to wash over the entire state." Unlike 1978, they assigned a full-time organizer to the north early in 1984 to work aggressively among Democrats. And Domenici campaigned at full speed in the most heavily Democratic, Hispanic areas of the state. His theme was that their future lay outside the traditional *patron*-dominated political and economic structure. It was an anti-*patron* theme he had hit hard in a major speech two years earlier.[63]

As we flew to the most Democratic, and the most *patron*-dominated, county in New Mexico ("It's the only county in the state where literature is printed in both English and Spanish telling people to vote straight Democratic."), Domenici said, "I want to deliver a message if I can, to the people of Rio Arriba that the days of the *patron* are numbered and that they should join the rest of the state in supporting me." [64] In his speech in Espanola, he began,

> I've had a great month. People have been great. . . . I don't know what it is. Maybe hard work pays off. Maybe they are saying I've done a good job. I'm going to win. I'm not going to stop working. I hope people up here aren't misled by anyone. I hope they won't be told by political leaders who they have to vote for, but will go out, look at the candidates, pick and choose. No more of this 'vote one way.'

In his speech he tried, in other ways, too, to sever the attachments between local leaders and followers.

He told his listeners that "regardless of what the politicians around here tell you, an expanding private economy is the only hope for the "attacked Domenici's record in the U.S. Senate at every opportunity." [73] But she was unable to structure the election contest in her terms or to receive the kind of one-on-one consideration she wanted. Some people, including her primary opponent and many of Domenici's campaigners, believed Pratt was "too liberal for New Mexico" or "removed from the mainstream of a conservative state like New Mexico." [74] But it cannot be said that either she or her views were rejected in the election. That is because her views were never considered and she was never judged. Her candidacy may—as the Domenici people believed—have cost the Democrats approximately 5 percent of the vote among some Hispanics and some ideological centrists. But, on the whole, the challenger had no impact on the election. As the Domenici people said over and over, "She has not been able to get it all together." The election was structured and conducted exactly as the Domenici people wanted it to be—as a referendum on his performance as a senator.

Of course they did what they could, once their opponent was known, to make it come out that way. They moved quietly but aggressively to solicit support within her natural constituencies; and second, they pointedly ignored her. "She was not able to take the constituencies she had in the primary and bring them into the general election," said one Domenici campaigner.

> We very consciously infused ourselves into each of its elements—labor, environmentalists, women. We held off the labor endorsement for seven months, too late for them to come together and give her any strong support.... With the environmentalists, we put together our own committee chaired by the national vice chairman of the Sierra Club.... With women, we have had less success. The strong feminists have been with her from the first. But a lot of other women are with us.... She never regained the momentum she had in the primary.

The Domenici organizer in northern new Mexico told a similar story of their preemptive strategy among Hispanic Democrats there:

> As soon as Judy Pratt won the [Democratic] nomination, we went to the key Democrats in the northern counties—not the chairmen but the second-level people in the party—walked right up on their front porches and asked them to commit themselves. By the time Pratt could get her act together up here, we had a huge number of Democrats lined up in the "Alliance for Domenici."

By their own actions, they believed they had helped to prevent the organization of opposing constituencies.

"There is simply no organized opposition to him anywhere in the state, no group around which the opposition can rally," exclaimed one aide. "In a state with so many varied elements as this one, that is simply

future of the area and its young people." And he told them that, contrary to the intimations of their leaders, individual welfare payments (Social Security, food stamps, medical care) "do not come from county government," "[not] from the benevolence of local politicians, but from the people of the United States and the Congress." "The rules of the United States of America say you get these benefits.... Nobody's rules locally give people these things." It was a frontal attack on the Democratic organization in the area. To which his local supporters added a constituency service argument, by printing and circulating a broadside in English and Spanish, citing Domenici's work in funding the local irrigation system—"We need Pete for our acequias."

After his trip, Domenici said, "There's more action in that county than ever before. But the rural areas will vote straight Democratic. We'll carry Espanola, but all the little towns will kill us." But he carried Rio Arriba county—by 50.5 percent, an increase of 14.1 percent over 1978. In the nine northern counties he received 63 percent of the vote—a 24 percent increase over 1978. We cannot know whether the newer, northern strategy had any more effect than, say, the eventual presence of an Anglo woman on the Democratic ticket. But the results are at least consistent with the intentions and the efforts of the Domenici campaigners.

Domenici campaigned hard, too, in other Hispanic, Democratic strongholds. At Archie Metzger's in Albuquerque's South Valley, which he had lost by 36 percentage points in 1978, he argued, again, that the people there should join the mainstream.

> It's hard for you to vote Republican. I understand this. I'm finishing twelve years and I think I've done a good job for New Mexico and the United States [applause]. Wouldn't it be wonderful if we could look down here election night and see that the Valley was just like the rest of New Mexico, if we could say, "My gosh, a Republican named Domenici won the Valley?" That would make me happiest that night—if we could say, "We weren't told how to vote, that's not right. We looked at the people and Pete Domenici won"—if I got your votes just like the other counties in New Mexico.

Asked, afterward, what he thought the response was, he said, "I learned that I have a lot of votes there and that they can't take them away." He wanted them all. He got 60 percent.

In other respects, the campaign strategy was very similar to that of 1978. It was the classic strategy of a popular incumbent who starts with a substantial lead. And, in Domenici's case, that lead was not put under sufficient challenge during the 1984 campaign to necessitate any change. In the preparation and preemption period before his challenger was known, he recruited an organization and raised money. In the comparison and confrontation period after his opponent was known, he ran an aggressive but low-key campaign—quietly pressing his record and his familiarity while ignoring his opponent and shunning publicity. It was the strategy used—and also criticized—in 1978. But it was deemed appropriate to the changed circumstances of 1984—namely the far greater popularity gap separating the senator from his new opponent.

There is some evidence, as in 1978, that Domenici himself had to be persuaded. Late in the campaign an aide commented that "We have deliberately run a low-key campaign so far, and we are just peaking. One person—whose name I won't mention—wanted to come out early with guns blazing." But Domenici did make himself visible as soon as the reelection effort of the other New Mexico senator ended. In November 1982 the *Journal*'s political writer headlined his column "Domenici Already Running for 1984." He began, "Since dawn broke on November 3, Senator Pete Domenici has been off and running for reelection with a singlemindedness that has startled even colleagues . . . [and] he has already made it clear, he'll run as his own man, not President Reagan's." [65]

When I first dropped in on the New Mexico campaigners in January 1984, the chairman's notoriety was clearly a main source of strength in early maneuvering. "We're working primarily on fund raising," said one. "It's been real easy—so easy it's scary. People just come up to me and offer to contribute. Sometimes they want to contribute more than is allowed. We set a goal of $1 million in 1983 and we have just about reached it." A month later the *Journal* headlined, "Domenici's Team Puts Together $907,960 Campaign War Chest." [66] They had also signed up organizational leaders in every county. "People are flattered when we call and ask them for help," said a staffer. "People have a lot of pride in Pete Domenici. There's a great deal of residual emotional support for him left over from past campaigns; and we tap that. But I would say at least 50 percent of the people are new."

In the words of another aide, they had also succeeded in "icing down" some very prominent Democrats. "We are better off today than we were at a comparable time six years ago," summed up one campaigner. "For one thing the average man in the street knows who Pete Domenici is and thinks he's going to win. For another thing we have a very strong 'Democrats for Domenici' going. They are the kind of people who talk; and they should be causing the Democrats a lot of worry." A subsequent *Journal* analysis of this group and of the senator's "unprecedented" Democratic support carried the headline, "Domenici's Budget Committee Role Attracts Democrats." [67]

By design, all of this preparatory activity went forward quietly. "Pete gets so much free publicity as a senator," said one staffer,

that we are going to do everything we can to play up Pete Domenici the senator and play down Pete Domenici the candidate. Once people see you as a candidate, the newspapers get real bad about giving you any publicity without also mentioning your opponents. . . . Pete will announce on February 12. But we will not play it up. We have a headquarters going, but it's tucked away where no one else can see it—or find it.

All the natural advantages accruing to an incumbent were substantially augmented in Domenici's case by the activities of his chairmanship. His campaigning cannot be understood apart from his governing.

As campaigns become more expensive and more complex, these early, preparatory activities have a preemptive impact—discouraging potential challengers from entering the contest. In 1978 that apparently happened. In 1984 it apparently did not. If anyone was driven out of the race it was due more to the lopsidedly discouraging poll results than to early displays of financial or organizational strength. The two candidates who sought the Democratic nomination were Nick Franklin, the state party chair, and Judy Pratt, a three-term state legislator. Until fairly late in their contest, the Domenici campaigners assumed that Franklin, the better known, more centrist candidate would be their opponent. But the primary campaign was, instead, dominated by the activist enthusiasts of the more ideologically defined liberal, Judy Pratt. And she won a classic primary victory. [68]

Local scorekeepers declared that the Domenici-Pratt contest would "give New Mexicans as clear a choice of political philosophies as the state has ever seen," and "be as clearly defined a race on political issues and philosophy as has been offered in a long time." [69] This was doubtless an accurate prediction—assuming that the campaign would, indeed, be fought out "on the issues" that separated them.

Pratt focused on, and played up, the sharp philosophical differences between them and used strong campaign rhetoric to force Domenici into an issue-oriented confrontation with her. It was the classic strategy for an unknown, underfinanced underdog. "Our strategy is to expose him," she said. "The image that he's tried to create is that he's good for New Mexico, that he's a nice guy, and that he's a moderate. Probably the last is the worst, because he is not a moderate." [70] Calling him "a Wall Street senator," she held a press conference displaying piled-up money bags and a computer printout of Domenici's political action committee contributions as props. [71] "Domenici's full support of Reaganomics," she said at another point, "made him the architect of a budget that has devastated human services and jobs in the country." [72]

In their two debates, reporters said, she was "feisty, aggressive and [she] elaborated her position clearly and forcefully"; and, they said, she

amazing. Of course he has his enemies, but no group." It was another way of stating the near absence of "negatives" in his case.

To further preclude the appearance of any rallying point, the Domenici campaign paid as little attention to the opposing candidate as possible. In five days of traveling with the campaign, I never heard Domenici mention her name. Twice he alluded to her views. Once he commented, "My opponent and I disagree on just about everything." The other time he said, "My opponent and I wouldn't agree on a clear day that the sun was up." But that was all, in five days of nonstop talking.

Privately, he said that if need be he would attack her views—which he viewed as extreme ("She wants to change the country's economic system, she really does."), but he saw no need to do so. A campaign aide added,

> We could have used overkill in attacking her fringe views . . . and that would have gone over well in some parts of the state. It could have brought a backlash. Our policy is not to pay any attention to her, not to give her any publicity. It could only help create a sympathy vote. That's the main thing we've had to worry about all along.

On the campaign trail Domenici said, "That's another difference from 1978. There is absolutely no press of any kind following us. You don't see any stories in the newspapers about us, do you? That's just the way we want it. We don't want to give her any publicity." Unlike Toney Anaya, Judy Pratt could not generate it by herself. Indeed, she often had to introduce herself with, "I'm the one running against Pete Domenici."

During their unavoidable personal encounters, the debates, Domenici's strategy was to present himself as a national leader, and to acknowledge his opponent without tangling with her or patronizing her. Thinking about it in advance, he said that "In my opening statement I will not pay any attention to my opponent. I'll just go 'over the top.' " And an aide had warned, "She's going to come after you like a flaming banshee. You have to be nice to her." The press reported that "Domenici remained cool and calm despite verbal assaults from Pratt" and "Domenici answered some charges specifically, but generally steered clear of heated exchanges." He "kept his cool . . . and was articulate in putting his largely familiar ideas forward." [75]

Before the debates, he expressed two worries: The "frightening" prospect that "the debate is not judged on issues; it's all judged on style," and the more specific concern that his opponent would zero in on his stands regarding entitlement cutbacks, especially Social Security. On the matter of style, his "cool" demeanor apparently kept Pratt from gaining either "publicity" or a "sympathy vote." On the matter of the retirees, he noted, "The one issue we did not want to see in the next morning's headlines was Social Security. . . . Once I realized she was not going to use it, I knew we were not going to be in trouble." The debates illustrate Domenici's preventive strategies; but they changed nothing.

On the positive side, the campaign took on the flavor of a triumphal tour. The first thing he had said to me in 1978 was, "I act like a congressman." But the first thing he said when I arrived in late October 1984 was, "It sure is nice to have a campaign like this. After losing one and having two close ones, this one is a joy." I heard him introduced by turns as "the only real budget balancer in the federal government," "the future president of the United States," "the next majority leader of the United States Senate," and "the only true statesman in the history of New Mexico." He was greeted with "Good luck, but you won't need it," or "You're going to win by the biggest margin in history." He invariably began his presentations by describing the campaign as "magnificent" and "wonderful" and "gratifying," as one "I never expected I would ever have if I served thirty years," and as one in which "people have been gracious and kind, volunteers by the hundreds, contributors by the thousands." "I really am not quite sure yet why," he would say with appropriate modesty. "Maybe after sixteen years, you have to be a nice guy. I'm not sure what I've done. . . . In any event it's tremendous and something I'll never forget."

Wherever he went, people wanted to associate themselves with him. Local candidates clung to him. Two Republican congressional candidates introduced him in their districts. Said one, "We have a saying in New Mexico: 'Tell me who you're with and I'll tell you who you are.' I'm with Pete Domenici." Said the other, "I'm here for the same reason as everyone else is, to help Pete Domenici get reelected. He's a great man and he's like a brother. I love him." In their pitches, Republican candidates for lesser offices always mentioned Domenici—their previous association with him, their desire to reelect him, his presence on the ballot; in other words, "Vote for Pete at the top of the ticket and don't forget me at the bottom."

In the regions of his greatest strength, Democratic candidates, too, grabbed at his coattails. "I'm in hot water with my people in the south," he said, "because the Democratic candidates show up at my events. We usually have one event at Republican headquarters. If an event is open, all the Democrats come." In some southern counties, echoed a staffer, "the local candidates of both parties have pictures of Domenici on the cover of their brochures—the Republican candidate says, 'Pete Domenici says of me' . . . and the Democratic candidate says, 'Pete Domenici says of me. . . .'" The perception of him as a winner was universal; and the desire to climb aboard was irresistible.

The phenomenon was new to 1984. Domenici turned it doubly to his advantage by making light of it as he discussed the development of his career. "I went into politics on a dare," he told one group.

> Five people met with me in Magidson's Restaurant. Now, everywhere I go, people tell me they were at that breakfast. I've concluded I was in a rally and didn't know it! It's the same with my pitching career. Everywhere I go, all over the state, I find people who say they played baseball with me. If it's ten o'clock, they all say they batted against me. If it's after midnight, they all say they hit home runs off me!

With one deft stroke, he touched upon his local roots, his growth in popularity, his ability to laugh at himself—all the while calling attention to his bandwagon.

The substance of his message was in keeping with the exhilaration of the campaign itself. It was an optimistic message that concealed all his private worries. He emphasized the turnaround in the country during the past four years, in the national spirit, in the attitudes and allegiances of the younger generation, in economic opportunity, and in military preparedness. He claimed the country was still "taking care of its moral and social responsibilities at home." For New Mexico he claimed that "we've got a great future; we've just got to be sure that we share in America's prosperity and that we bring it to every community and every area." He cited examples—a new factory in San Miguel, a school program in Wagon Mound—that this was beginning to be so. The message was upbeat and hopeful.

He did not mention the federal budget or the Budget Committee. Nor did he evoke the atmosphere of frustration, or the constraint and scarcity that characterized his life inside the budget process. He drew from the success of the president and the administration without stressing any binding personal association with the administration. His message assumed widespread support for Domenici and for what he had done; it was totally noncontroversial. "I don't have any litany of pledges," he said. "If New Mexicans don't know me yet, there's absolutely no way they are going to."

Beyond this general message, Domenici elaborated his campaign theme that what he did and said in Washington and what he did and said in New Mexico represented a single, integrated pattern of ideas and actions. He did so by crediting the New Mexico input for his Washington performance. It was his own way of saying that he had not "gone Washington." During a series of house parties called "the blitz" in Albuquerque's Northeast Heights, he constantly associated his national success with local influences:

> The best place to start is local government. You deal with people's problems and you get into a mold of solving problems. When you get to national problems, you have local problems and local people in your mind's eye.

Or,

> I've been lucky. I've been in some big meetings, made lots of important decisions, made a lot of policy in some big rooms. But the start I got on the Albuquerque City Commission has taught me how to be a senator—how to deal with problems, how to visit with people, listen to people's problems, follow through on their problems.

Or,

> I know more about New Mexico than any New Mexican—from Raton to Las Cruces, from Tucumcari to Hidalgo County. You remember those things when you sit around the room with five people and maybe the president.

He acknowledged, yet played down, his Washington success; but he emphasized, and played up, the local antecedents of that success.

The turnout and the vote for Domenici in the populous, mobile, middle-class Northeast Heights had been one of the biggest disappointments of the 1978 campaign. As we left the last of the blitz events there, the senator summed up his mood and his expectations for 1984.

> There's a lot of support for Pete Domenici in the Heights. I can feel it. I'm not fooling when I say I have never felt anything like this, ever—the enthusiasm, the respect. We've been getting crowds all day like we've never had up here before. Usually these people hide and you can't find them. They have too many other things to do than to come to rallies. I talked to two couples tonight who said it was absolutely the first political thing they had ever done. In 1978 it was Toney Anaya that was having enthusiastic parties like ours have been. He was just coming off a successful term as attorney general. Everywhere he went, people were taking his picture. He was taking away from our strength. And we had trouble turning out people in the Heights. This year it's the other way around. We keep adding to our strength. There are eight thousand Republicans in that district we were just in. We might just get 75 percent to 78 percent of them. We could win this whole thing by 62 percent to 65 percent. There's only seven or eight days left for them to turn it around. I don't see how they could win. But, you know the old Domenici.

Searching for something to worry about, no doubt. No need. He got 84 percent in the Heights area, an increase of 21 percent from 1978.

With his reelection campaign fully under control, there was time for the senator to reflect on his longer-term goals and his future career. Mostly he did so in private; mostly he concerned himself with the matter of institution building within the Republican party in New

Mexico. Pete Domenici had not begun his career within the party organization. Party building had been no concern of his in 1978. But in 1984 he was the acknowledged leader of the Republican ticket. He saw the party, badly defeated in 1982 and still split by factionalism, as in need of and perhaps ready for, new blood and new leadership. And gradually he had come to see himself as the most likely agent of a Republican resurgence and, hence, of a two-party system in his home state. He talked often about the new situation in which he found himself, about how and whether he could exploit the opportunity it presented.

Domenici's flirtation with party building was not dissimilar from his cautious behavior in other instances. "I started thinking seriously about it two years ago," he said.

> I had thought about it for a long time, but never did anything about it. I didn't think it was doable. Or, at least, I didn't think I could do it. But we took a big licking in 1982 and the party was badly divided. I thought I could win, by myself, in 1984. But I also thought I could provide a little leadership in bringing the party together.

So, party defeat and personal popularity were two elements in the altered context.[76] The third element was the recognition by Domenici that the raw material for a revived party was at hand and was especially amenable to his leadership—because he had brought many of them into politics in the first place. — "Did you see where the *Journal* endorsed Don Davoti [a former staffer] this morning?" he asked.

> One of the amazing things that has happened over the past twelve years is the number of people who have worked for me or helped me and are now starting careers of their own. Invariably, they are associated with me. When the *Journal* endorsed Lou Gallegos, they said, "worked for Senator Domenici." When they endorsed Davoti, they said "worked for Pete Domenici." Everywhere you go, there are people who came into politics with me. There's a network of Domenici people all over the state. Those people can be the future of the Republican party in New Mexico.

After three statewide campaigns and two terms in the Senate, Pete Domenici had become, de facto, the recruiter and the leader of a significant segment of his party. He drew encouragement from this fact. "A big difference this time," he said, "is that a lot of my friends, people who have been with me a long time, are running themselves, all over the state. If we took over the governorship now, we would have a lot of talented people who could run the state, fill the high appointive offices. We haven't had that, in our party, in New Mexico, for a long time."

For most of two days in late October, Domenici acted as the umbrella for gatherings of Republican candidates during the blitz. In his brief opening remarks, he always made room for a party-building pep talk. "I know some of you here are Democrats," he began.

> We welcome you. But I hope you will understand that we believe America works best when two parties compete; and that we are proud that the Republican party is getting strong enough—not yet perhaps—to bring a two-party system to New Mexico. When one party controls everything, that is not right. I can remember, when I first ran, going to Republican rallies that produced seventeen people. I can remember going to Republican county committee meetings when four or five people showed up. That was not right and it was not healthy for democracy. We couldn't get people to run. So we are proud of the progress we have made and proud of the entire slate of local Republican candidates who are with us tonight. We are proud that so many people in New Mexico are coming our way.

In evaluating the blitz meetings afterward, Domenici felt he had, indeed, provided party leadership.

> Those events in the Heights were great. The local candidates felt like they were part of the team. They appreciated the fact that I was there. I think I've been able to give a little leadership, by making them feel they've got a chance and drawing people to the events. The blitz had an impact. It'll help give us some action in this area; the local candidates picked up some votes; the Democrats know there are no more free rides.

But it would take a much more persistent concentrated effort than that. And, from what one could observe, it was not clear that Domenici was going to move much quicker or further on the institution-building front.

He said that if he won a big victory, he would undertake the task. And he did win big. But there was some hesitation and a characteristic aversion to risk. Contemplating the long-term task, he commented that,

> It's tough. Some of those people are real mean. They have never forgiven me for helping Jerry Ford. They kept me off the delegation. They don't think I vote with Reagan enough. . . . I'm going to try; but I'm not going to beat my head against the wall. That's not a senator's role. And I can't give it a lot of time. It will have to be done by surrogates. I now have a lot of surrogates. What gives me hope is that we have brought a whole new generation into the Republican party and they are waiting to take over—the young business and professional types. If someone asks those people they will respond.

Whether Domenici would ask them, or be in a position to ask them, remained an open question as his campaign came to an end.

In moments of reflection, the senator from New Mexico entertained yet another personal goal—the leadership of his party in the Senate. From the day Majority Leader Howard Baker announced his retirement,

Pete Domenici had been mentioned as a possible successor. Public mention was often made of this possibility during the reelection campaign, and Domenici openly acknowledged the likelihood of such an effort. But he refused to elaborate or speculate. Privately, however, he discussed his strategy and his chances. And he sounded very much like a candidate. Still, he held back from any total commitment to try for the office and from any active campaigning among his colleagues. Both would be required if he were to have a chance to succeed. Whether or not he would make an all-out effort remained one more open question as his campaign came to an end.

About the achievement of his electoral goals, however, there could be no doubt. As Pete Domenici prepared to return to Washington, he could savor his electoral accomplishment as he had not been able to do in 1978. He had beaten Democrat Clinton Anderson's statewide record by 8 percentage points—72 to 64. And he had led popular Republican president Ronald Reagan by 12 percentage points—72 to 60. His historic victory at the polls was a capstone reward for the exercise of his chairman's power. And it was an invigorating renewal of his license to help govern the country.

NOTES

1. Mark Westlye, "Competitiveness of Senate Seats and Voting Behavior in Senate Elections," *American Journal of Political Science* (May 1983): 253-283.
2. Pevrill Squire, "Challenger Quality and Voting Behavior in Senate Elections," paper prepared for delivery at the Electing the Senate Conference, University of Houston and Rice University, December 1-2, 1989.
3. Polls taken for Domenici by RSM Inc. in 1983-1984. Unless otherwise noted, poll data are taken from this series of polls.
4. Poll by Zia Associates, October 21, 1983. Domenici's "excellent" plus "good" job rating was 80.6 percent. Governor Anaya's was 34.6 percent. On Anaya's low standing, see John Robertson, "Anaya," *Albuquerque Journal*, January 1, 1984; and T. R. Reid, "Say, Does Toney Annoya?" *Washington Post Weekly Edition*, Spring 1985. See also Richard Williams, "Who'll Run Against Domenici?" *Albuquerque Tribune*, February 12, 1983.
5. Stephen Hess, *The Ultimate Insiders* (Washington, D.C.: Brookings Institution, 1986), chap. 2. Taken from a 1981-1982 study of coverage by the three TV networks only, "Network Evening News Visibility of Congressmen and Senators," paper prepared for the 1984 annual meeting of the Association for Education in Journalism and Mass Communication.
6. Eric McCrossen, "Domenici: Cuts Will Come Gradually," *Albuquerque Journal*, November 16, 1980.
7. Bill Tanner, "For Pete's Sake—New Image, New Car," *Albuquerque Tribune*, January 3, 1981.

8. Bob Duke, "Domenici, Skeen in the Limelight," *Albuquerque Tribune,* January 23, 1981.

9. Eric McCrossen, "Domenici Committed to Fight for Reagan's Economic Package," *Albuquerque Journal,* April 19, 1981.

10. Richard Williams, "Pete Domenici Is Gaining Notoriety Nationally," *Albuquerque Tribune,* March 21, 1981.

11. Paul Wieck, "Budget Cut Reviews Will Be Critical Test of Domenici's Clout," *Albuquerque Journal,* March 15, 1981; and Paul Wieck, "Has Domenici Overextended Himself?" *Albuquerque Journal,* January 1983.

12. For example, Paul Wieck, "Budget Committee Lands Domenici," *Albuquerque Journal,* March 22, 1981. But even this article describes the praise as a chairman's "customary accolade from his colleagues for a job well done."

13. Fred McCaffrey, "The Observer," *Santa Fe New Mexican,* October 8, 1981.

14. "Seniors Unit Raps Domenici Budget," *Albuquerque Tribune,* May 12, 1982; Bob Duke, "Domenici Running into Criticism," *Albuquerque Tribune,* May 17, 1982; and Marvin Tessner, "Domenici Defends Budget Here," *Las Cruces Sun News,* May 9, 1982.

15. Paul Wieck, "Republicans Are Not Through Yet," *Albuquerque Journal,* May 9, 1982.

16. Bob Duke, "Senator Domenici the Compromiser," *Albuquerque Tribune,* May 10, 1982.

17. "Cool Head on Budget," *Carlsbad Current-Argus,* May 21, 1982.

18. Fred McCaffrey, "Domenici Knows How to Use Powerful Post," *Almagordo Daily News,* May 12, 1982.

19. Transcript "The Lawmakers," Washington: WETA-TV, April 7, 1983, 6.

20. The "no opinion" category for these three items was 14 percent, 17 percent, and 18 percent, respectively.

21. Bob Duke, *Albuquerque Tribune,* February 20, 1981.

22. Bob Duke, "Domenici Wields Ax with Even Hand," *Albuquerque Tribune,* March 19, 1981.

23. *El Paso Times,* September 14, 1981.

24. *Grants Beacon,* September 25, 1981.

25. *Carlsbad Current-Argus,* October 22, 1981.

26. *Artesia Daily Press,* November 5, 1981.

27. *Lovington Leader,* November 11, 1981.

28. *Lovington Leader,* November 13, 1981.

29. *Grants Beacon,* December 8, 1981.

30. Paul Wieck, "Domenici Leads Budget Rebellion," *Albuquerque Journal,* November 13, 1981.

31. Paul Wieck, "Senate Panel Rejects Domenici Plan," *Albuquerque Journal,* November 17, 1981.

32. Paul Wieck, "Senate Committee Clears Outdated Budget Resolution: Domenici Yields to Reagan," *Albuquerque Journal,* November 20, 1981.

33. Richard Williams, "Politicking in N.M. at a Slow Pace in 1981," *Albuquerque Tribune,* January 4, 1982.

34. Fred McCaffrey, "Domenici Worries About Course," *Santa Fe New Mexican,* December 11, 1981.

35. Bob Barth, "Microphone," *Santa Fe Reporter,* April 14, 1982. See also Barry Casebolt, "Putting the Heat on Pete," *Carlsbad Current-Argus,* April 22, 1982.

36. *Raton Daily Range,* February 24, 1982.

37. *Albuquerque Journal,* February 24, 1982.

38. *Raton Daily Range,* February 25, 1982.
39. Gordon Greaves, "By the Way," *Portales News-Tribune,* March 3, 1982.
40. *Santa Fe New Mexican,* March 5, 1982.
41. Fred McCaffrey, "Budget Suggestions Valid," *Artesia Daily Press,* March 7, 1982.
42. Steve Cameron, in *Albuquerque Tribune,* February 26, 1982.
43. "Domenici's Budget Plan," *Carlsbad Current-Argus,* February 26, 1982.
44. *Albuquerque Tribune,* March 4, 1982.
45. Bob Duke, "Reagan Needs Domenici's Help," *Albuquerque Tribune,* March 8, 1982.
46. Val J. Halamandaris, "Senator Pete Domenici: Champion of the Elderly—Advocate for Home Care," *Caring,* April 1984.
47. Fred McCaffrey, "Inside the Capitol," *Grants Beacon,* September 1, 1982.
48. Paul Wieck, "Domenici Already Running for 1984," *Albuquerque Journal,* November 21, 1982.
49. For example, Mike Shanahan, "Austere Domenici in Midst of Budget Fray," *Farmington Daily Times,* February 14, 1983.
50. Richard Williams, "Who'll Run Against Domenici?" *Albuquerque Tribune,* February 12, 1983.
51. Richard Williams, "Pete Domenici Is Gaining Nationally in Notoriety," *Albuquerque Tribune,* March 21, 1981.
52. As quoted from *Albuquerque Journal* in David Nyhan, "Sagebrush Rebels Feel Their Victory Is Near," *Boston Globe,* August 18, 1981; and Pete Domenici, "Where Texas Is a Suburb," *Washington Star,* May 8, 1979, as reprinted in *Congressional Record,* May 14, 1979, S5817.
53. Former governor Jerry Apodaca. "Apodaca Slaps at Schmitt's Record," *Clovis News Journal,* October 18, 1981; "Apodaca Stumps Belen," *Valencia County News Bulletin,* October 26, 1981; and "Apodaca Criticizes Schmitt, GOP Policies," *Carlsbad Current-Argus,* October 14, 1981.
54. Attorney General Jeff Bingaman, the eventual winner. Wally Gordon, "Bingaman Announces for U.S. Senate, Attacks Schmitt Record," *Albuquerque Journal,* January 15, 1981.
55. Paul Wieck, *Albuquerque Journal,* January 1983.
56. Richard Williams, "Domenici Worried About His Future," *Albuquerque Tribune,* November 20, 1982.
57. From Domenici files. "Days" are defined as days in which he had at least one engagement. For Domenici's first-term record of trips and days, plus an analysis of his itinerary at home, see William Taggert and Robert Durant, "Home Style of a U.S. Senator: A Longitudinal Analysis," *Legislative Studies Quarterly* (November 1985): 489-504.
58. An article with this as its theme is, Linda Vanderwerf, "Domenici's Star Burning Brightly," *Las Cruces Sun-News,* March 13, 1983.
59. John Curran, "Behind the Scenes With Senator Pete," *Albuquerque Living,* August 1985.
60. Mike Shanahan, "Austere Domenici."
61. Transcript, "The Lawmakers," April 7, 1983.
62. In Domenici's own polls, favorable replies to the question "Do you think Pete Domenici has performed well enough to deserve reelection or is it time to give a new person a chance?" were 66 percent in March 1982, 70 percent in May 1983, and 71 percent in July 1984. Polls by Zia Research Associates in October 1983 and September 1984 found that 77 percent and 80 percent of

the respondents respectively planned to vote for Domenici.

63. Mark Nassutti, "Domenici Bitterly Attacks Patron System," *Albuquerque Journal*, August 12, 1982.

64. A recent look at Rio Arriba can be found in Dennis Farney, "Courting Hispanic Vote Becomes No Minor Event as Swelling Ranks Translate into Potential Clout," *Wall Street Journal*, September 13, 1988.

65. Paul Wieck, "Domenici Already Running for 1984," *Albuquerque Journal*, November 11, 1982. See also *Albuquerque Tribune*, November 20, 1982.

66. *Albuquerque Journal*, February 3, 1984. On the early campaign, see also Robert Beier, "Domenici Drive Picks Up Steam," *Albuquerque Journal*, April 4, 1983; and Robert Beier, "Domenici Letter Hints Jitters over Campaign Fund Raising," *Albuquerque Journal*, October 26, 1983.

67. Robert Beier, "Domenici's Budget Committee Role Attracts Democrats," *Albuquerque Journal*, August 8, 1984.

68. John Robertson, "Would Be Democratic Opponents Span Democratic Spectrum," *Albuquerque Journal*, May 1984; and Douglas McClellan, in *El Paso Times*, May 21, 1984.

69. Fred McCaffrey, "Judy Pratt Sure to Run Good Race," *Las Cruces Sun-News*, May 1984; and *Albuquerque Journal*, May 27, 1984.

70. *Las Cruces Sun-News*, October 14, 1984.

71. *Albuquerque Tribune*, October 9, 1984.

72. *Las Cruces Sun-News*, November 9, 1983.

73. *Albuquerque Journal*, October 16, 1984; and *Albuquerque Tribune*, October 16, 1984.

74. *Albuquerque Journal*, August 8, 1984.

75. *Albuquerque Journal*, October 16, 1982; and *Albuquerque Tribune*, October 16, 1982.

76. Richard Williams, "Domenici Worried About His Future," *Albuquerque Tribune*, November 20, 1982.

The Chairman: Last Seasons

FROM CAMPAIGNING TO GOVERNING: THE ELECTORAL INTERPRETATION

My personal on-and-off observation of Pete Domenici's political activity ended with his 1984 campaign. But his reelection victory in New Mexico, I believe, had an immediate impact on his activity in Washington—specifically on his candidacy for the leadership of his party in the Senate. And that impact demonstrates anew the force of the governing-to-campaigning-to-governing sequence in shaping senatorial careers. We do not know for sure what his post-1984 electoral interpretation was. An educated guess, however, would be that he and his campaigners attributed the historic proportions of his victory very largely to the publicity and the accomplishments that flowed from his Budget Committee chairmanship. Certainly they had structured his campaign to promote that kind of retrospective judgment on his performance. Most probably, therefore, the "constructed explanation" of 1984, in sharp contrast to the one in 1978, had a substantial Washington component to it.

Our guess is that the huge victory margin, together with its Washington component, was interpreted by Domenici as convincing proof that he had achieved the goals he set for himself in 1979—that is, he had added success as a policy-oriented national senator to his previous success as an honest, caring, New Mexico-oriented senator. Such an interpretation, in turn, would place him in a position to think about, to develop, and to pursue his personal political goals wherever they might lead him. His campaigners had believed that if he "maxed out" he would be free "to do anything he wants." Our guess is that that is exactly the interpretation he placed on his reelection results. It is our further guess that his electoral interpretation helps us to understand his candidacy for majority leader.

When Howard Baker announced his retirement plans in January 1983, Pete Domenici's name surfaced as a possible contender.[1] That early development was more a testimony to the esteem of his colleagues than to the palpability of his ambition. Given the four-year primacy of budget matters on the Senate's agenda and given the satisfaction with his leadership in that area, the idea of a promotion for Domenici came naturally to his fellow Republicans. In 1984 he had been voted by his colleagues as "the most effective" committee chairman and the second "most respected" member of the Senate.[2] For an individual accustomed to "filtering up" to the top of whatever organization he belonged to, and for a senator who had gradually accumulated ever-larger shares of governing influence, the idea of reaching for the most influential position in the Senate could not have been a novel or uncongenial one.

The point is not that Domenici had always wanted to be party leader; he hadn't. It is just that he found himself in a situation where the position of leader could be considered, by him and his supporters, as a logical, credible next step. An opportunity had presented itself. Ambition theory tells us that whatever higher office an ambitious politician can try for, he or she will try for.[3] And Pete Domenici was no stranger to progressive ambition. It is, therefore, no surprise that he decided to try for it. He did not succeed. But his efforts to achieve that goal are instructive for our broader analysis of his behavior and of his career.

It is not clear when Chairman Domenici first entertained the prospect of running for the majority leader. But it is clear that his candidacy developed more slowly and conveyed more uncertainty than did that of the other four contestants. And in that regard Domenici's behavior followed a familiar pattern of cautious forward motion. In March 1983 he told an interviewer that he had read about himself as a possible contender but that "Nothing I do in the foreseeable future is going to be overtly directed at that." In this same interview, Domenici discussed his "natural inclination to worry a great deal about myself, to worry about and second guess my abilities and argue with myself about my basic capabilities." And he applied this introspection to the majority leader's job by acknowledging his success as a legislator but wondering about the transferability of those talents. Being a good majority leader, he said, takes "a huge amount of time, tremendous patience, a real understanding of the various senators' needs." And he added, "None of that sounds like a good legislator, which I think I may be." [4]

He was not yet as comfortable with the idea as he would have to be to wage a determined campaign for the job. And he was slow to move. By mid-1984, at a time when Bob Dole had admittedly talked to twenty-five or thirty colleagues about his candidacy, Domenici was willing to say that he was "seriously interested." But he added that he was "not out actively attempting to gather support." [5]

In all the preliminary speculation, a constant theme was Domenici's lack of aggressiveness in pursuing the job. In June one reporter said that "he has been somewhat hesitant about pushing his own candidacy, which some senators interpret as ambivalence." [6] In October another journalist's assessment began with: "One of Domenici's biggest problems in the leadership race is that some senators are not convinced [he] seriously wants the job. . . . This perception stems from a perception that Domenici has frequently changed his mind about whether to seek [it]. . . . In campaigning for the job, his style has been less aggressive than the other candidates." [7] A third observer added another recognizable element to this pattern of caution and uncertainty—the push of his staff. "There were no 'staff promoted' candidates in the contest," he wrote, "but Domenici came close to qualifying." And he described top staffers urging Domenici to accelerate his efforts, telling him that "Unless you get in and work at it, you can't last." [8] Another writer said that Domenici's "eager aides" were "promoting him." [9] This pattern, too, was familiar. Domenici's top staffers were reacting to and countervailing against his instinctive caution.

Our central notion is, however, that it was Domenici's election victory that fixed his determination to run hard for the job and, further, that his election victory together with his constructed explanation of it was a necessary ingredient in overcoming his caution. Without an utterly convincing electoral victory, he would not have continued in the race. During the campaign, I asked him whether a victory margin of 72 percent, 62 percent, or 52 percent would make any kind of difference to his future behavior. His first reply was that "If I won by 72 percent, it would help me in the majority leader's race—for reasons I can't tell you." An educated guess would be that 72 percent would serve to resolve whatever doubts he entertained about his capacities and would serve to make him a more credible, attractive candidate to his colleagues. He got 72 percent. And on that basis, he became a resolute and unambivalent candidate.

As his reelection campaign neared its close in New Mexico, his comments indicated that he still had much to do in Washington in the race for majority leader. "I got started late," he said. "If I hadn't been so tied up with the budget falling to pieces the last three months, I would have started talking to people earlier." And he expressed modest expectations for success. He claimed five committed votes plus his own and calculated that he needed two more to survive the first ballot, in a succession of low-man-drops-out ballots. "I have a good shot at six people to get those two I need," he said. "Those aren't bad odds. And I think if I get by the first ballot, I've got a chance." He did not explain further.

It was not expected, by the handicappers, that he would survive the first ballot. It is further evidence of his accelerating postelection efforts, however, that on the eve of the vote it was reported that "one last-minute development [is that] Domenici seemed to be picking up strength . . . [and has] 'suddenly come to life.' " [10] He survived the first ballot, with nine votes. But he was the low man—with ten votes—on the second ballot. By running better than expected, he was judged to have run a credible race; he sustained no reputational damage in his loss. And he remained free to pursue his progressive ambitions another day.

Leadership decisions are so personal on the part of the voters that one can only speculate why Domenici failed. There are some clues. Press observers, for example, described Domenici as: "hard working but lackluster," "a skillful and gregarious practitioner of the legislative art . . . [who] may lack pizzazz," "well liked but carrying the scars of his seemingly endless budget battles," "vastly respected and liked but . . . duty bound to deliver the bad news and be bossy." [11] In comparison with the eventual winner, Bob Dole, Domenici was described variously as the tortoise to the hare and the hedgehog to the fox. The interpretation of the first comparison was that "Dole will take a position much earlier than Domenici, but will change it more often. Dole is usually quicker out of the box, but sometimes runs in the wrong direction. Domenici is slower, but stays the course." The interpretation of the second comparison was that "The fox knows many things. The hedgehog knows only one thing, but really knows it." [12] Altogether, media commentary conveyed the suspicion that Chairman Domenici might not be sufficiently aggressive and might not be sufficiently broad-gauged for the job of party leader.

The perceived lack of aggressiveness matches our own observation of Domenici's cautious approach to decision making, his instinctive aversion to risk. This characteristic had, of course, been displayed in the majority leader's race itself. With respect to an insufficient breadth of view, the interesting feature of this commentary is how closely his perceived drawbacks dovetail with the demands of his chairmanship. Its institutional maintenance tasks, we have continually noted, are highly constraining. And in this sense, the same job that propelled Domenici to prominence in the Senate probably worked to prevent him from further advancement in that body. The budget chairmanship is an imprisoning as well as a liberating job. It pins its occupant to a perpetual grindstone, envelops him in procedural and numerical entanglements, associates him with economic woe, ties him to institutional frustration, and denies him fashionable legislative victories. It demands a responsible performance; it prohibits a popular performance.

Maintaining the budget process and leading the legislative party are not naturally compatible tasks. As broad as the budgetary field is, the party leader plays on an even larger field, institutionally and politically. We have commented on Domenici's "chairman's vision," his "Senate vision," and his reliance on leader Baker's perspective in navigating beyond the confines of his committee. Domenici's total investment in his chairmanship had made him a good chairman—by some accounts, the Senate's best chairman—substantively knowledgeable and procedurally adept.[13] But it had also saddled him with some chairman's liabilities. Whether or not they were decisive, they surely hurt him.

Domenici himself recognized that. Reflecting on his chances in late October, he said,

> I know you can tell, from traveling with me and listening to me, that I would make a good spokesman for the party. I can get up and talk intelligently about any subject. But I don't think my colleagues see me that way. They know me in a very limited role. That hurts me, I think.

This self-assessment, as far as it went, seemed accurate. The constraints of the chairmanship as well as the cautiousness of his political style combined to frustrate his effort to use his campaign strength at home to enhance his governing strength in Washington.

A SEASON OF ECLIPSED LEADERSHIP: 1985

In terms of any future political ambitions, Pete Domenici's unsuccessful leadership race placed him, temporarily at least, in a Catch-22 situation. He had to return to his chairman's role and engage, once more, in the very same Sisyphean labors that militated against his success in the leadership contest. He was, of course, returning to a central position of influence in the Senate. But the context had changed once again. And no change was more consequential for the chairman than the one brought about by the contest for majority leader. For the effect of the contest was to turn what had been a constant factor throughout five budget seasons into a variable for the sixth season. It was the majority leadership itself.

A shorthand expression of any committee chairman's relationship to the Senate as a whole is his relationship with the majority leader. Leader Baker had given Chairman Domenici all the operating freedom he wanted in shaping budgetary policy. Baker had stood ready to help at critical negotiating junctures; but he did not act in ways that diminished

Domenici's influence in budgetary matters. That preeminence was about to be changed. For Domenici would now have to share influence over budgetary matters with a party leader who was less patient, less conciliatory, less mild mannered, and less deferential than Howard Baker.

One widespread interpretation of Bob Dole's election was that it reflected a desire for more assertive leadership. Senators wanted institutional independence externally and institutional action internally.[14] Understandably, Dole wanted to respond to these expectations as soon as possible. He was, by temperament, an assertive person. He would enjoy something of a honeymoon with his colleagues. And he had presidential ambitions. Predictably, his earliest opportunity would come at the beginning of the 1985 budget cycle. So, Pete Domenici returned to the fiscal fray only to find his party's leader unusually anxious to get out front and to make his own mark in the budgetary arena. Having just been decisively defeated for the leadership, Domenici was in no mood to fight against the newly elected leader and "split the party right down the middle."[15] So, for the time being, he could neither "filter up" nor govern more.

Despite the built-in competition for turf between the Budget and Finance committees, the basic relationship between Chairman Domenici and Chairman Dole and their staffs had been cooperative and supportive. They were strongly motivated by the belief that the Senate Republicans had to demonstrate their ability to govern. From 1981 on, they helped each other in the spirit of team play. And they would continue to do so in 1985. But, beginning in 1983—at about the time of Howard Baker's announcement—they began a gentle sparring for the title of deficit-reducer-in-chief of the Senate.[16] One observer wrote in 1984, "Dole and Domenici ... have been parading their skills as champions of deficit reduction, with occasional needling of Domenici by Dole that has stretched but not broken the no-combat rules."[17]

By 1985 Bob Dole was well credentialed as someone who had "focused on cutting the federal budget deficit ... with the zeal of a crusader for several years."[18] He was not bound by his institutional position to preserve, protect, and defend the congressional budget process—to answer the question "Is it working?" Pete Domenici was. Dole could distance himself from the process to a degree that Domenici could not. With Domenici battling to exhaustion over budgetary formulas, for instance, Dole could engage in irreverent asides to reporters: "It's all sort of a game anyway," or "It's all going to be decided in conference so we just ought to put a zero in there."[19] The two men worked together, but with different perspectives on the process. Dole's perspective would enable him to play a prominent role in guiding the process;

and his prominence would be freshly constraining for the Budget Committee chairman.

Pete Domenici returned to his chairmanship to follow a familiar and well-worn path. The day after his leadership defeat, he and the Republican team made their yearly kickoff pilgrimage to the White House. There, they received their yearly confirmation of the substantial gap in thinking on defense spending and taxes between themselves and the president. Domenici left the meeting with his yearly comment that "we're willing to help him, but it's a two-way street." [20] He suggested, once more, his strategy for dealing with the president on the defense budget. "Unless Congress puts together a domestic reduction that's very large, there won't be much to negotiate with the president with." [21] A few days later he advocated a similar strategy in coping with the president's adamant stand against taxes; that is, "put one package together with no taxes in it and see how much you get and then go back in a while, three months or four months, and say it isn't enough." [22] He went to work, once again, preparing a congressional budget package—one with, as always, "a different mix" than the president's.

It was a familiar sequence. Media scorekeepers recorded their own sense of déjà vu. "This is after all, the fourth year in a row that Congress has had to take the lead." [23] "Congress will have to save Reagan from himself again." [24] "Once again, Mr. Reagan has refused to send a serious budget to Congress. Once again, he has left the initiative to a small group of courageous Republican senators—most prominently Pete Domenici . . . and Robert Dole." [25]

In the new leadership context, however, Domenici began work "under the aegis" of the party leader.[26] Dole, wrote one journalist, "has grabbed center stage on Capitol Hill in a daring bid to . . . put together a package of spending bills that pales by comparison with anything passed during Reagan's first term but is still palatable to Congress." [27] Dole's first initiative as leader was to announce, early in January, that the Senate Republicans would put together a budget *before* the president announced his. "We want to get out front on this," he said. "We want to tell the president not to pull us; we want to go." [28] He said that "Senate Republican leaders and committee chairmen would submit proposals to him by February 1st." [29]

Dole was unable, however, to forge an early consensus, mostly because of intraparty differences over the defense numbers. "Defense has become almost a wall," said Domenici later. "To some extent, until you get that wall down, you can't get anything done." [30] On the other hand, the president's budget did not command a consensus either. So Dole withdrew temporarily and turned the problem over to Chairman Domenici and to the normal budget process. "He's the chef now," said

Dole. "He's sort of got to put it together. Let's see what he can cook." At the same time, Dole described the Budget Committee's all-too-familiar dilemma. "If the president is not going to be for what we finally agree upon, it's going to be tough." [31]

Domenici was a good deal less than enthusiastic about the task of consensus building—not because it seemed any different from his earlier efforts, but because it seemed so much the same. In a February 5 speech to the National Press Club, the chairman showed signs of war-weariness. "I understand the distinguished majority leader of the U.S. Senate has said that he passed me the ball, as far as putting together a package, and passed it over to the Budget Committee and me," Domenici began.

> And without going into a big long story about a great fullback named Leroy who ran the ball twenty-six consecutive times, let me just say that I called him up. As you know, when they asked him to run the twenty-seventh time, he said, "Leroy don't want the ball." Well, I called the distinguished majority leader and said that I kind of felt like Leroy.

He did not want the ball. But, as usual, the team player accepted his responsibility.

He took the lead by preparing and presenting yet another "Domenici Plan." He labeled this one the "promised land" budget, because it was calculated to reach goals originally set by the Senate leaders and agreed to by the president—a cut of $50-$60 billion for fiscal 1986 and a deficit level reduced to $100 billion by 1988. He first scouted the possibility of bipartisan support for his plan. But when a series of committee votes showed this strategy to be unworkable, he negotiated out a consensus package among the committee's Republicans and passed it out of the committee—as he had in three of the previous four years—with a partisan majority.

For fiscal 1986, Domenici's committee bill called for an increase in defense spending equal only to inflation, as opposed to the president's request for 6 percent above inflation. (See Appendix, Table A-7.) It provided $55 billion in domestic spending cuts as opposed to the president's request for $50 billion. It called for a one-year freeze on cost-of-living adjustments for Social Security recipients and other federal pensioners, as the president had not. It projected a deficit of $172 billion as against the president's $180 billion. Neither it nor the president's budget called for any tax increases. Where the 1988 deficit was $144 billion in the president's proposal; it was $102 billion in the committee's plan.

The *New York Times* editorialized in familiar, supportive fashion about "The Domenici Budget."

> For tenacity and stamina, Senator Pete Domenici's performance is remarkable. The president wouldn't make the hard choices in the budget. The Republican senators couldn't agree on a version of their own. Once again, it has been left to Senator Domenici as chairman of the Budget Committee and once again he has produced a budget that is both fairer and sounder than Mr. Reagan's. Inside his Committee Domenici once again demonstrated his negotiating skill, "cajoling, compromising and fine tuning" his package to construct his partisan majority.[32]

The chairman called the final product "a pretty good budget . . . pretty much consensus." [33] It was a very shaky consensus. But, once again, the chairman had done his institutional duty. He had passed a bill out of his committee and sent it to the Senate. "One thing happened," he said, "that made all the turmoil and difficulties of producing a budget worthwhile. We succeeded. We did report out a budget." [34] It was another major accomplishment. But it was his peak performance for 1985. And it was followed by a time of eclipse for his budget leadership.

To the point of committee passage, the pattern of activity bore many similarities to Domenici's triumphal year of 1982—the agenda-setting Domenici Plan, the partisan passage of the committee bill, the effort to show the president a large amount of domestic spending restraint, and the praise for the chairman's leadership. But in one major respect the sequence of 1985 differed from that of 1982. The committee bill did not have presidential support. Further, the president was on the sidelines making menacing threats—"go ahead and make my day"—whenever a tax notion surfaced.[35] If his support was to be negotiated, it would have to be negotiated outside the context of the Budget Committee. And there was, of course, a new majority leader ready, willing, and eager to do just that.

Majority Leader Bob Dole was described as saying that the budget "needs some work," and as "hinting at the possibility of three way negotiations with the White House and congressional Democrats to assure its passage." [36] His first priority was to work on the president. To that end, he set up a "working group" (including Domenici) to negotiate a new agreement with the White House. "If we go off on our own in the Congress, and the president is not on board, then we can't get anywhere." [37] Domenici wanted to take his committee's budget resolution to the floor; and he was described as "plainly anxious for Senate action" and "frustrated" by the working group. But Dole simply observed that "The Leader often has a different perspective than the committee chairman." [38] It was the leader's perspective that dominated from that point forward. With the leader's perspective went credit from the scorekeepers. And credit for the majority leader carried with it a decline in the chairman's influence on budget making.

Agreement on a new budget was struck between the working group and the president. It called for a 3 percent increase above inflation in the defense budget, a fixed 2 percent COLA for Social Security, and the elimination of, rather than cuts in, several domestic programs. Domenici supported it, despite its difference from his committee's budget; and he went to the White House with Dole to announce the agreement. But Majority Leader Dole, Budget Director Stockman, and Treasury Secretary Donald Regan were credited as "mainly responsible for the compromise"—not Domenici.[39]

Subsequently, Dole took the revised budget resolution to the Senate floor. Using his prerogatives as majority leader and fortified by a very complex procedural arrangement, he controlled first, the introduction of his bill, second, the amending process and, third, the introduction of a substitute package. As various elements of the leadership-White House agreement began to be altered on the floor, often initiated and supported by Republicans, Dole reopened negotiations with the White House in hopes of producing a more viable package. He succeeded. It was reported that "Dole won critical concessions from the administration." [40] "His Lyndon Johnson-style maneuvering and brokering," wrote one reporter, "achieved a stunning compromise on the budget, persuading senators and the administration to backtrack on their positions." [41]

The final agreement, called "the Dole Package" or "Dole II," bore a close family resemblance to Domenici's original Budget Committee bill. It called for a defense increase equal only to inflation and for a one-year freeze on Social Security and other federal pension adjustments. On intellectual grounds, it should have been called Domenici II. Indeed, the Social Security freeze was exactly the kind of strong medicine on entitlements the New Mexican had been advocating since 1981.

Domenici was thrilled when the budget resolution passed in the Senate by the whisker of the vice president's tie-breaking vote, 50-49. The next morning he said that,

> I never saw such emotion, tension, and so much attendance by every senator. We were all on the floor of the Senate for five or six hours. I think we ended up without a lot of acrimony. Everyone knows that we have a very big deficit problem and when we finished, everyone felt good. And we were very proud of what we were able to accomplish.[42]

It was a mark of the policy-oriented team player that the chairman should have taken such pride in the outcome when the credit was going elsewhere. The majority leader generously said that "there are three or four winners in this and one of those is Pete Domenici." [43] But the big winner was Bob Dole.

One close observer wrote that "Dole's stock soared when the Senate voted 50-49 to pass the resolution designed largely by him." [44] Other journalists called the budget's passage "a noteworthy victory for Dole" and "a tactical victory for Dole ... who has staked his reputation as leader on making a significant start on deficit reduction this year." [45] Pete Domenici acted as loyal cheerleader: "It was the most exciting evening I've had in the U.S. Senate in 13 years, because we really accomplished something historic." [46] And "We have achieved what I'm sure the cynics thought was impossible—significant deficit reduction." [47] He was a member of the "we" team. But the team once described as "Domenici and Dole" was now more often described as "Dole and Domenici." Or just "Dole." Their product was now described as "the Dole-Domenici budget." Or just "the Dole budget." [48] Indeed it was now said that "more than any other single member of Congress, Dole has held the Reagan administration's feet to the fire on cutting the deficit." [49] "Never before," wrote Budget Director Stockman, "had the game of fiscal governance been played so seriously, so completely and so broadly as it was in Bob Dole's office in the spring of 1985." [50]

A week later, the House passed its budget—no Social Security freeze, bigger defense cuts, fewer domestic cuts. In the conference committee, Domenici became, once more, the central Senate player. But the train of events surrounding the conference led to a substantial and potentially long-term diminution of the chairman's influence on governing.

The budget conference opened with Domenici insisting on Social Security restraints and with the House group insisting on a freeze in defense funds. Soon, things reached an impasse. Several Senate conferees, with Domenici's private support, decided to implement his strategy and introduce a tax proposal into the deliberations. At this point President Reagan intervened to change the entire bargaining context. Under pressure (as always) from House Republicans on Social Security and fearful that a stalemate would produce tax increases, he backed away from his agreement with Dole and the Senate Republicans on Social Security and cut a deal with the House Democrats. They promised him no taxes plus the higher defense number and he promised them full COLA adjustments.

Shades of 1981 and 1982, or "déjà vu all over again" surfaced except that in those earlier years, the presidential retreat took place *before* the budget reached the Senate floor, and, therefore, with most senators uncommitted. This time, it came with the Senate Republicans almost unanimously committed. This group—sixteen of whom were the Reagan freshmen of 1980 facing a critical reelection—were left hanging in support of a highly unpopular position in favor of a COLA freeze. They were described variously as "embarrassed," "apoplectic," "outraged," "betrayed," "abandoned," "seduced," "blindsided," "shot down," "undercut," "deserted," "left high and dry," "sold down the river," and with "the rug pulled out from under" them. Dole's own metaphor was that "There was an agreement under an oak tree, and it was Dole's limb they sawed off." [51] Chairman Domenici recorded no public reaction. But given the euphoria with which he had greeted the Senate outcome, he could only have felt anger and frayed attachments to the team.

The president's about-face had two short-run effects with possible long-run consequences. First, it damaged his relationship with his most loyal allies, and, by weakening them, may have put Republican control of the Senate in added jeopardy. Second, it changed the short-run bargaining context inside the conference; and that, in turn, may have led to some far-reaching changes in the politics of budget making. "At that moment, when Reagan undercut his own Republicans' plan," a Democratic budget staffer said years later, "all hope was dashed of ever having a serious, dramatic effort against the deficit." [52] And Domenici's top budget aide agreed. "[When] Ronald Reagan pulled the rug out from under Senate Republicans in 1985, we lost an historic opportunity." [53] The subsequent Gramm-Rudman-Hollings initiative in the Senate must be viewed as the unfolding of a sequence begun by the president's reversal.

The president's turnaround undermined the Senate's bargaining position by removing Social Security and taxes from the set of negotiable items. The Senate conferees lost the leverage that came from their ability to insist on entitlement changes. At that point Domenici was "strongly urged by House Republicans, the White House, the president, some of my own people" to work out some kind of compromise with the House conferees because "it didn't matter all that much." [54] "I was told," he said afterward, "to get off my stubbornness and get a budget. I said, 'One more time.' " [55]

A veteran reporter described the outcome as the first budget victory for the House Democrats during the Reagan presidency.[56] In the words of David Stockman, "sooner or later the Senate was going to be forced into concession after concession after concession until you got this limp rag." [57] Those verdicts on the product were widely shared in the Senate. No one felt more frustrated by the end product than Domenici. Privately, he told his fellow Republicans in and out of the Senate, "That's it. Don't count on me to produce another budget [by] biting around the edges." [58] He was serving notice on "the team" that 1986 would be different.

Nonetheless, Chairman Domenici brought the conference agreement to the Senate floor and defended it publicly in familiar, loyal fashion. First and foremost, a budget was necessary and a budget had been produced. He called this accomplishment "against overwhelming odds, a minor miracle." For him as chairman, of course, it meant that his institutional maintenance goal had been met once more. Whatever the criticism might be, any budget was better than no budget.

> We just happened to think we could not give up.... I could have chucked it to you four weeks ago.... But to those who are saying ... that is just what you should have done, I ask you what would you have gotten by the end of the year, and what would you have gotten next year and the next year.... You would have gotten nothing.

To have walked away would have been, in the chairman's view, irresponsible, not to mention a dereliction of his special institutional duty.

Second, Domenici argued that the agreement represented "the largest deficit reduction effort in the history of Congress." And it came close to meeting the goals set earlier in the session. It projected cuts of $55 billion as opposed to $63 billion in Domenici's first budget. It projected a deficit in fiscal 1988 of $112 billion as opposed to the leadership goal of $100 billion. "I'm not gung ho," he said. "I do not think it is marvelous, because we could have done better. But ... we are talking like it is nothing. It's only the biggest budget cut in the history of this nation." But he added, "The deficits it applies to are also the largest ever."

Third, he argued that the budget was "the best that could be done under the circumstances." Specifically, "when revenues and true entitlements were taken off the table ... no process no matter how ingenious could have produced the savings that were lost." And, generally,

> If the Congress will not act to cut deficits more, then no process will make up for the lack of will. If the president will not cooperate in areas that are absolutely vital for his support, then no Congress can be asked to do more.

Domenici concluded: "There is only one issue. Have we done the best with what is there?" [59] The official Senate answer was, overwhelmingly, yes. Pete Domenici had done the best possible job. His conference report was agreed to 62-37.

Formal approval of the product did not mean, however, satisfaction with it. And the feeling was widespread in the Senate that "the best possible" result was simply not good enough. Beyond the disappointment with the terms of the budget, there was a lack of confidence in the assumptions that lay behind it and in anyone's willingness to undertake the hard implementation that lay ahead. Indeed, Congress did fail in that year to enact the reconciliation measure necessary to guarantee much of the prescribed action.

Among the earliest critics, Majority Leader Dole, unconstrained by the institutional imperatives of the budget process, was the leader. He described the budget as a "watered down, nothing budget." He described it by turns as "marginally better ... than no budget at all," or "better than no budget all ... a step, a very small step, in the right direction." He also called it "a copout by all of us. When we voted for the budget resolution, we in effect said, 'We give up.' " [60] The difference between the Domenici reaction and the Dole reaction was large—and predictive of what was to come.

From the vantage point of an outside observer, the 1985 budget season was business as usual. In one sense, every budget season we studied had been different from every other one. But in another sense, 1985 bore a strong resemblance to the other three postmandate years. In every case a budget had been produced. But the people most involved, such as Chairman Domenici, had skated constantly on the thin edge of stalemate to produce it. This condition of near stalemate—inside the committee, between committee and floor, between Senate and president, between Senate and House—prevented the decisiveness in action necessary to radically affect deficits. Accordingly, deficits remained high. In Domenici's words,

> We have political gridlock at this point, and the existing processes of our government, executive and legislative, invite the continuation of gridlock.... In many quarters, there is tacit encouragement for the gridlock to remain and so long as that attitude is unchallenged, the deficit does not go down; it goes up.[61]

His explanation was correct. The budget stalemate was political.

GRAMM-RUDMAN-HOLLINGS

Chairman Domenici's traditional argument had been that no alteration of the budget process could change an outcome held in place by politics. He had been imaginative—in 1981 and 1984—in utilizing the flexibilities of budget procedures and sequences to affect outcomes. But he had been willing, in the end, to sacrifice outcomes to save the process. He was not opposed to changing the process. But he believed in gradual change— undertaken only when the process was not under serious challenge—lest the process be lost.[62] Few of his colleagues shared this sense of guardianship—this chairman's vision. Other senators were moved by repeated disappointment and frustration with the annual budget outcome and with the prospect of more of the same in the future. And they were in a mood in 1985 to accept suggestions of radical change.

Four years after the August 1981 congressional recess had marked a major turning point in budget politics, the August 1985 recess marked another. And the sequence of precipitating events was the same. When senators went home to their constituencies in 1985 to explain their budget, they encountered enormous skepticism and great explanatory difficulty. A May Gallup poll had found "a growing public perception that the current deficit poses a very serious threat to the nation." It found that 58 percent saw the deficit as a "very serious" problem, with 23 percent more calling it "fairly serious." [63] Yet budgetary politics remained business as usual. No senator could guarantee his or her constituents that the yearly deficit would fall much below $200 billion anytime soon. And whatever the projections of their recently passed budget resolution, senators knew from the failure of past projections that their budgetary promises were no longer credible. They had, in short, no satisfactory answer to the question "What are you doing to bring down the deficit?". And the question had grown increasingly insistent.[64]

When the senators returned to Washington, three of their colleagues—Republicans Phil Gramm and Warren Rudman, and Democrat Fritz Hollings—awaited them with a vehicle for budgetary reform. Just as the budget legislation of 1974 was a reflection on the perceived failure of the existing appropriations and taxing process, so was the Gramm-Rudman-Hollings proposal of 1985 a reflection on the perceived failure of the existing budget process.

We will not examine or assess the Gramm-Rudman-Hollings reform here. The only points of interest for our career analysis are Pete Domenici's attitude toward the reform and its potential effect on the chairmanship. The legislation provided statutory targets for progressively lower deficits, with a procedure for mandating the necessary spending reductions when Congress and the president could not agree on a budget resolution. Spending cuts were to be divided equally between defense and (with a number of exceptions such as Social Security) discretionary nondefense programs. It was predicated on the assumption that Congress and the president had not and could not, through the normal budget process, agree upon the reductions necessary to meet the targets. Hence, the automatic budget-cutting process would come into play, and Budget Committee discretion would bow to an automatic process of "sequestration." With the committee's hands thus tied, the chairman's influence on process and on outcomes would be substantially diminished.

Bob Dole and Pete Domenici were both described as "cool" and "dubious" when the plan was first introduced. The party leader—lacking any strong commitment to the post-1974 process—followed "the political wind" almost immediately.[65] Domenici's choice quickly became one of supporting the new plan or fighting it.

One option, of course, was to defend the status quo. But that would not have satisfied those senators who wanted a new, more credible answer to give their constituents. Domenici knew, better than any of them, the "political gridlock" he was in. And his own level of frustration—"don't count on me" and "one more time"—was at a new high. He could hardly deny the rationale for change. Furthermore, to conduct an all-out fight would have been to desert the team-playing pattern he had followed for so long in favor of behavior that seemed self-serving and obstructionist.

A second option was to interpose a less radical reform. Our guess is that, left alone, he would have preferred this characteristically cautious course. He had often entertained the idea of incremental change. His devotion, after all, was to the give and take of the normal political process, not to hand-tying, save-me-from-myself circumventions of that process. But he was either unwilling or unable to intervene. He may have been unwilling to act because, like "Leroy," he was simply weary of carrying the ball. It would be remarkable if four years of endless and earnest endeavor had not brought on some budgetary burnout. Or, he may have been unable to act because Gramm-Rudman-Hollings had gathered too much momentum too fast. The proposal may simply have seemed, as one of its sponsors said, "a bad idea whose time had come."

The third option was to support the reform. That is what he did. Soon after Bob Dole had seized the lead, Domenici decided to follow. As chairman, he would have to play a large part in making the new plan work. If he endorsed the plan early, he apparently reasoned, he could shape the legislation to make it compatible with the existing process. After the favorable Senate vote, a committee colleague reflected on his chairman's decision:

> I think the budget thing has worn him down. The Gramm-Rudman amendment took the play away from him. He should have been out front with some proposal. I was surprised when he voted for it. I know his staff thinks it's worthless. But it was the only game in town. I guess he felt he had to go along.

He added, "Dole, not Domenici, grabbed the lead."

Domenici, however, became active in working out the details; he helped negotiate it in conference; he stoutly defended it on the floor. "Could it be any worse than what we have? I concluded no," he said.[66] "I started the Gramm-Rudman-Hollings process," he said,

> as a constructive player in these temporary emergency procedures. I remain convinced that . . . it had to happen because of the frustration that set in after all of the gridlock that has occurred in the last two years. . . . It is in that record that I offered many amendments and changes . . . and frankly I think it has a chance of working.[67]

He saw his decision, ultimately, as one more effort to preserve the congressional budget process. But clearly the reigning reform idea had not been his idea. And, for the time being at least, the budgetary leadership he had held for so long had passed to others.

In supporting Gramm-Rudman-Hollings, Chairman Domenici expressed the view that the new plan would not supersede the give and take of the normal budget process, but that its presence would force the old process to work better. With the automatic device pointing at their heads, he prophesied, the regular players would work out their differences. The trigger would never have to be pulled, because no one would risk the alternative. "If Congress and the president do not come up with a game plan," he argued, "everyone's favorite program is going to get clobbered. . . . Tell us, how can there be more incentive for the president and these two houses of Congress?" [68] That was his public, optimistic view. It was, of course, an expression of his own strong preference for the normal budget process, and for the scenario in which the Budget Committee and its chairman would retain the maximum possible influence.

A SEASON OF REVIVED LEADERSHIP: 1986

The final year of Pete Domenici's chairmanship was very little affected by the crucial sequestration procedures of the Gramm-Rudman-Hollings reform. First in February and finally in July, the courts struck down the automatic spending cut procedure; and the threat of sequestration was not legally restored until after Domenici's chairmanship had ended.[69] However, the Gramm-Rudman-Hollings legislation was discussed extensively throughout 1986. And the fiscal 1987 budget did meet the deficit target set by the law. But the reforms did not receive a fair test of their effectiveness and their impact until later. Nor did Domenici have to render a considered judgment on the matter. An evaluation lies beyond the scope of this study. For our purposes, however, it is worth noting that a substantial body of recent opinion holds that the reforms have not substantially altered the budget-making processes and problems of the Domenici era. The new hurdles of sequestration and budget targets have spawned several new bookkeeping gimmicks and a few new procedural manipulations. But the "normal" budget process, the political gridlock, and the large budget deficits remain.[70]

A brief look at Domenici's seventh budget season reveals a familiar picture. It can be placed within the same parameters as all the others and can be discussed in terms of the same variables as the others—even though, as usual, the precise patterning of the various factors would be somewhat different.

In overall context, 1986 was most like 1983. Both featured a temporarily defused public concern for deficit reduction,[71] an immovable president on defense and tax matters,[72] and a now-fractious group of Senate Republicans.[73] The main difference from 1983 was that the motivating external factor was the onset of an election year. Twenty-two Republican seats—including those of the sixteen Reagan freshmen— were at stake. Driven by diverse electoral concerns, the Republican incumbents were unable to coalesce behind any budget package. The president, who was not running, persisted more adamantly than ever in sticking with a budget that was, in a now routine congressional response, "dead on arrival." [74] In these circumstances, without sufficient economic or political pressure to sustain a partisan budget resolution, Domenici moved, as he had in 1983, to put together a bipartisan coalition. Working closely with ranking Democrat Lawton Chiles, that is what he did.

The result brought another strong assertion of his independence and restored his influence close to the level it had reached before 1985. (Data in Appendix, Table A-8.) When the budget—supported by seven of twelve Republicans and six of ten Democrats—passed the committee, media scorekeepers described the group as "in open revolt against President Reagan" and said that the vote "marks a new break between the White House and the Senate leadership." [75] They described Chairman Domenici as "a rebel ... going against Reagan in the most public manner" and "in public defiance" of the White House.[76] It was, of course, only the newest resolution of the governing dilemmas of team play and independence that he had been struggling with since 1981.

In other respects, too, the outlines of his 1986 performance were familiar. "The budget problem is back where they always drop it off this time of year," summarized one reporter in late March, "with Domenici Chiles and Co., the steady soldiers of the Senate Budget Committee.... Leadership falls by default to the senators. The Republicans have to bring along their president, the Democrats their party." [77] In 1986, unlike 1985, Majority Leader Bob Dole surrendered the limelight and played at best a private, supportive role.[78]

When the budget passed the Senate 70-25, it was interpreted in the press as "a significant victory for Senate Budget Committee Chairman Pete Domenici." [79] And a long-time observer concluded that, "Budget Committee chairman Pete V. Domenici of New Mexico has been saving the administration from itself for years with budgets that bear a reasonable resemblance to reality. This year, his Senate budget steers a useful course between ... the president ... and the House." [80] In the end, Domenici was forced to back down on his and the committee's tax proposals to get a budget that the president could pronounce "generally acceptable." [81] (See Appendix, Table A-9.) And the budgetary outcome, once again, produced familiar media summaries of congressional action: "Lawmakers Look Back on Two Years of Partisan Fights, Missed Deadlines: Congress Does Little About Deficit Which Looms as Its Main Problem in '87," and "99th's Record Was Good—But That Deficit's Still There." [82]

As the chairman guided this last piece of legislation through the Senate, he looked back on his years of effort and generalized about his budgetary leadership. "In my office," he said at one point,

> I have an old print depicting the ancient Greek Sisyphus, who was destined to spend his after-life pushing a rock up a mountain—only in this print he is pushing a budget instead of a rock. One will recall that every time he reached the top of the mountain, the rock came rolling down over him. [83]

At another point, he reflected that,

> The senator from New Mexico is not a newcomer to negotiation. In the past five years, because of the nature of this process, I think I have probably negotiated more times on more issues, produced more negotiated budgets out of the back room of the leadership or out of the committee room of the Senate Budget Committee or in a conference room of the House and the Senate, than any other senator here, and probably more than any Member of the House. [84]

When he brought the conference report to the floor, he said,

> I am not here tonight as I have been on perhaps three of the five budgets I have managed on the floor—I am not here tonight extremely proud of this product, but I am satisfied. [85]

Each of these final reflections contained summaries of his six years as chairman—the unremitting burden, the endless negotiation, and the uncertain outcome.

The three budgets of which the chairman *was* "extremely proud" were those he negotiated in 1981, 1982, and 1984. The first of these carried the promise of the Reagan revolution. The second one was most genuinely his own. The third one featured an election-year agreement with the president. Each one was a partisan Republican budget. As his friend and ranking committee Democrat Lawton Chiles noted in 1986, "[He] was always ready to jam his budgets down our throats when he had the numbers." [86] And he "had the numbers"—inside the committee and out—only when he had the president.

It is ironic that in his last year as chairman, Domenici returned to the bipartisan committee tradition he had inherited. But the election of 1980 and the subsequent interpretation of the election had thrown the president and the Senate Republicans together as the dominant governing force. Chairman Domenici could best satisfy his policy preferences and his institutional duties, in combination, when he could keep the president with him in a partisan alliance.

Sustaining a working relationship with the president was, however, the chairman's most persistent and burdensome problem. The very concern for party, policy, and governance that drew them together could just as easily keep them apart. So much depended upon context. Pete Domenici always wanted to work with the president. But he wanted to help govern even more. And, governing meant producing a budget through the congressional budget process. So, if a working relationship with the president proved impossible as it did in 1983, 1985, and 1986, he would do what was necessary to keep the budget process working. As chairman, he construed that institutional maintenance goal to be his special responsibility—whether or not he was "extremely proud" of the budgetary outcome.

CONCLUSION

In November 1986 the Democrats recaptured the Senate. And Pete Domenici lost his chairmanship the same way he had won it—by a concatenation of election contests and election results in which he did not participate and over which he had no control.[87] His career path took another huge turn—from the majority party to the minority party—shrinking his resources, diminishing his opportunities for leadership, and removing him from the national spotlight.[88] Whatever the Senate elections of 1986 represented, they were not a referendum on Pete Domenici's record as Budget Committee chairman. Whatever factors influence votes for Senate candidates, a desire to affect party control of the Senate is not one of them. The only public vote of confidence *Chairman* Domenici would ever receive came from the voters of New Mexico in 1984. So the broadest kind of concluding judgment on his performance is not available from within the American political system.

The account in this book warrants the conclusion, at least, that it was no ordinary performance. It took place on the center stage of domestic politics, and it held that place for six years. It required extraordinary devotion to duty, grueling policy struggles with powerful people, countless reassessments and restructurings of "the Domenici Plan," and the ceaseless construction and reconstruction of majorities. It produced some defeats and some successes. But, mostly, it produced a series of half-defeats and half-successes, an unending sequence of decisions that provided temporary pauses on the way to the next decision. Finally, it was a performance that brought more than an ordinary share of admiration and praise.

By way of a conclusion, the 1986 judgments of the country's leading journalist of American politics—neither a conservative nor a Republican—will serve us well. David Broder conducted, in print, the performance referendum he knew the voters would not.

As the 1986 Senate elections approached and with party control of the Senate at stake, Broder concluded that the Senate Republicans had turned in "a performance of considerable distinction." He followed with an expression of concern about the voters' willingness "to dismiss this question of party control too casually." Were they to consider this question, he continued, they would find in the performance of Pete Domenici and two of his colleagues (Robert Dole and Richard Lugar) "three of the best reasons for voting Republican in the states with Senate contests this November." "These men," he wrote, ". . . are of such exceptional quality that their performance ought to weigh in the voter's calculus."

He praised all three for their "largemindedness, their ability to see beyond their personal ambitions . . . and beyond the parochial interests of their states." He praised Domenici particularly for "his tactical skill, sound judgment and political courage on tough issues of budget policy, opposing the dogmatists of the administration and in both parties."[89]

When the 1986 elections were over, Broder returned to the same theme: that congressional elections do not turn on the issue of party control and, therefore, that Pete Domenici and his colleagues had been removed from their chairmanships without anyone focusing on their performance—removed "accidentally" as Broder put it.[90] Early in his chairmanship, Domenici had hoped otherwise. But it was an unrealistic expectation. "The effect of the election," Broder wrote, "was to say there is no reward for being as responsible as . . . Pete Domenici . . . [has been. He] balanced the obligation of party loyalty to the president with courage in efforts to resolve the contradictions in the administration's fiscal policy. . . ." There is plenty of praise for any United States senator in Broder's conceptualization and in his judgments.

There is, also, in Broder's discussion enough recognition of Pete Domenici's achievement to close our description of an eight-year segment of his political career.[91] For a freshman who had aspired only to claim some share in governing, there was exceptional influence. For a newcomer who had wanted to "filter up" within his organization, there was a leadership position just below the topmost rung. For someone who "yearned to be courageous," there was testimony to his courage. For "the player" who wanted to be credited for his policy ideas, there was widespread acceptance of them. For the man who fretted about lack of media attention, there was a surfeit of it. In these changes we can indeed follow the development of a career. And the necessary condition that underlies all these developmental changes was, of course, the assumption of the chairmanship.

It was the chairmanship that, in turn, allowed Pete Domenici's most distinctive personal quality to emerge—his sense of responsibility. His personal goal (to gain legislative influence and to help govern the country) and his style (cautious and earnest) combined to exude that sense of responsibility. It was displayed in the web of obligations he felt and enacted toward others—partisan loyalty to serve the president, subject-matter competence to serve his Senate colleagues, budget-process guardianship to serve the legislative institution, and policy judgment to serve the republic.

In all of these relationships he had constantly weighed the competing claims of team play and independence. The fact that he worried so continuously and so openly about all these matters of obligation imparted an obvious sincerity to the weighing of his responsibilities. Even his political shortcomings—his chairman's vision, his Senate vision, his lack of aggressiveness—were manifestations of what one participant called his case of "terminal responsibility." From what we have seen in this study, Pete Domenici was, above all, a responsible chairman. As much as we value a responsible performance by our legislative leaders, for that much Pete Domenici was an exemplary leader of the United States Senate.

NOTES

1. Diane Granat, "Ruling Rambunctious Senate Proves to Be Thorny Problem for Republican Leader Baker," *Congressional Quarterly Weekly Report,* July 16, 1983, 1429.
2. In a *U.S. News and World Report* poll. *El Paso Times,* April 16, 1984.
3. Joseph Schlesinger, *Ambition and Politics* (Chicago: Rand McNally, 1966).
4. Linda Vanderwerf, "Domenici's Star Burning Brightly," *Las Cruces Sun-News,* March 13, 1983.
5. Helen Dewar, "The Clubby Little Race for the Senate GOP Leadership," *Washington Post Weekly Edition,* June 11, 1984.
6. Ibid.
7. Diane Granat, "GOP Scramble on Senate Leadership Jobs," *Congressional Quarterly Weekly Report,* October 6, 1984.
8. Robert Peabody, "The Selection of a Senate Majority Leader, 1984," unpub-

lished manuscript. Excerpted with permission of the author.

9. Richard Cohen, "The Race Is on to Replace Howard Baker as the Leader of Senate Republicans," *National Journal,* October 6, 1984.

10. Steven Roberts, "Five Senators in Tight Race to Be Chosen Republican Leader Today," *New York Times,* November 28, 1984.

11. Granat, "GOP Scramble"; Cohen, "Race Is On"; Dewar, "Clubby Little Race"; and George Will, "The Struggle to Succeed Baker as GOP Senate Chief," *Boston Globe,* March 24, 1984.

12. Paul Houston, "If Congress Slashes Deficits, Give Credit to Tortoise and the Hare," *Los Angeles Times,* February 5, 1984.

13. See references in Val Halamandaris, "Senator Pete Domenici: Champion of the Elderly—Advocate for Home Care," *Caring,* April 1984.

14. Norman Ornstein, David Rohde, Robert Peabody, "Party Leadership and the Institutional Context: The Senate From Baker to Dole," paper prepared for the annual meeting of the American Political Science Association, Washington, D.C., 1986. Andy Plattner, "Dole on the Job: Keeping the Senate Running," *Congressional Quarterly Weekly Report,* June 29, 1985; and Norman Ornstein, "Dole as Majority Leader: An Early Assessment," *Dirksen Congressional Center Report,* December 1985.

15. Jonathan Rauch, "Pete Domenici Stands at Center of Storm as Budget Crisis Comes to a Head," *National Journal,* February 1, 1986.

16. Granat, "GOP Scramble."

17. Dewar, "Clubby Little Race."

18. Plattner, "Dole on the Job."

19. *New York Times,* May 3, 1983; and *Washington Post,* May 3, 1983.

20. Dale Tate, "Legislators Offer Conditions for '85 Budget-Cutting Effort," *Congressional Quarterly Weekly Report,* December 1, 1984.

21. *New York Times,* February 4, 1985.

22. Transcript, "Newsmaker Sunday," Cable News Network, December 2, 1984.

23. Jodie Allen, "Tom Sawyer's Budget," *Washington Post,* January 28, 1985.

24. Lou Cannon, "Weinberger's Temporary Defense Budget Victory," *Washington Post Weekly Edition,* January 7, 1985.

25. "A Republican Compromise," *Washington Post,* April 22, 1985.

26. Elizabeth Wehr, "Deficit Reductions: The Search Continues," *Congressional Quarterly Weekly Report,* February 2, 1985; and Helen Dewar, "Enter the Fightin' 99th," *Washington Post Weekly Edition,* January 14, 1985.

27. Helen Dewar, *Washington Post,* February 9, 1985.

28. Pamela Fessler, "GOP Senators Take Budget Cutting Lead," *Congressional Quarterly Weekly Report,* January 5, 1985.

29. Tom Redburn, "Senate GOP Producing Own Budget Plan," *Los Angeles Times,* January 5, 1985.

30. Pamela Fessler, "Senate GOP Laboring to Salvage Budget Pace," *Congressional Quarterly Weekly Report,* February 23, 1985.

31. Bernard Weinraub, "President Depicts Budget as Chance for a New Course," *New York Times,* February 5, 1985; and *Washington Post Weekly Edition,* February 11, 1985.

32. "The Domenici Budget," *New York Times,* March 6, 1985.

33. Elizabeth Wehr, "Senate GOP Budget Plan Spreads Uneasiness," *Congressional Quarterly Weekly Report,* March 23, 1985.

34. *Congressional Record,* April 30, 1985.

35. *Newsweek,* March 25, 1985.

36. Helen Dewar, "Split Panel Approves '86 Budget," *Washington Post*, March 15, 1985.
37. Helen Dewar, "Just How Many Rabbits Are in Dole's Hat?" *Washington Post Weekly Edition*, February 11, 1985.
38. Jacqueline Calmes, "Much Talk, Little Action on Fiscal 1986 Budget," *Congressional Quarterly Weekly Report*, March 30, 1985.
39. Elizabeth Wehr, "FY '86 Budget Struggle Moves to Senate Floor," *Congressional Quarterly Weekly Report*, April 20, 1985.
40. Elizabeth Wehr, "Budget Squeaks Through Senate Floor Vote," *Congressional Quarterly Weekly Report*, May 11, 1985.
41. Hedrick Smith, "Bob Dole's Big Gamble," *New York Times Magazine*, June 30, 1985.
42. John Curran, "Behind the Scenes with Senator Pete," *Albuquerque Living*, August 1985.
43. Ibid.
44. Plattner, "Dole on the Job."
45. Wehr, "Budget Squeaks Through"; and "At Long Last, A Budget," *Newsweek*, May 20, 1985.
46. Curran, "Behind the Scenes."
47. Wehr, "Budget Squeaks Through."
48. Stockman, *The Triumph of Politics* (New York: Harper and Row, 1986), 389-390.
49. Plattner, "Dole on the Job"; and Wehr, "Budget Squeaks Through."
50. Stockman, *Triumph of Politics*, 389.
51. *Newsweek*, July 22, 29, 1985, August 22, 1985; *New York Times*, July 23, 1985; *Congressional Quarterly Weekly Report*, July 27, 1985, August 3, 1985; *Washington Post Weekly Edition*, August 12, 19, 1985; *Congressional Record*, August 1, 1985, S10736, November 14, 1985, S15481; and *National Journal*, January 4, 1986.
52. Jacqueline Calmes, "Gramm-Rudman-Hollings: Has Its Time Passed?" *Congressional Quarterly Weekly Report*, October 14, 1989, 2686.
53. Ibid.
54. Elizabeth Wehr, "Pete Domenici: A 'Reluctant Revolutionary,' " *Congressional Quarterly Weekly Report*, May 3, 1986.
55. Dorothy Collin, "When You Cut Pete Domenici, He Bleeds Black Ink," *Chicago Tribune*, June 29, 1986.
56. Helen Dewar, "Remember Reagan's Tight Grip on Congress? Well, Forget It," *Washington Post*, August 19, 1985.
57. "Stockman Critical of Congressional Budget Plan," *Boston Globe*, August 15, 1985.
58. Wehr, "Pete Domenici."
59. *Congressional Record*, August 1, 1985, S10731-S10749.
60. "At Last, a 'Nothing Budget,' " *Newsweek*, August 12, 1985; *Congressional Record*, July 30, 1985, S10300, August 1, 1985, S10756; and "Rough Going for Reagan," *U.S. News and World Report*, August 19, 1985.
61. *Congressional Record*, December 11, 1985, S17386.
62. Elizabeth Wehr, "Budget Decisions Still Breed Discontent, but Fewer Calls to Restructure the Process," *Congressional Quarterly Weekly Report*, August 31, 1985; see also Jonathan Rauch, "Politics of Deficit Reduction Remain Deadlocked Despite Balanced Budget Act," *National Journal*, January 4, 1986.
63. *Congressional Record*, May 6, 1985, S5455.

64. Elizabeth Wehr, "Support Grows for Balancing Federal Budget," *Congressional Quarterly Weekly Report*, October 8, 1985.
65. Dick Kirschten and Jonathan Rauch, "Political Poker Game over Deficit Bill Calls Bluff of Reagan and Congress," *National Journal*, December 14, 1985.
66. *Congressional Record*, December 11, 1985, S17386.
67. *Congressional Record*, April 9, 1986, S3918.
68. *Congressional Record*, December 11, 1985, S17431; and Jonathan Rauch, "Pete Domenici Stands at Center of Storm as Budget Deficit Crisis Comes to Head," *National Journal*, February 1, 1986.
69. Elizabeth Wehr, "Budget Puts Congress in a Combative Mood," *Congressional Quarterly Weekly Report*, February 8, 1986; and Jonathan Rauch, "The Thickening Fog," *National Journal*, July 12, 1986.
70. From fiscal 1987—fiscal 1989, deficits were $149.7 billion, $155.1 billion, and $152.1 billion. Congressional Budget Office, "The Economic and Budget Outlook," 1990, Table E-1. Some recent informed judgments will be found in: Jacqueline Calmes, "Congress Is Already Hedging on Deficit-Reduction Plan," "Bipartisan Pact Set the Stage for Easy Going in the Fall," and "Gramm-Rudman-Hollings: Has Its Time Passed?" in *Congressional Quarterly Weekly Report*, July 27, 1989, September 2, 1989, October 14, 1989; John Yang, "Ever-Growing Deficits Establish the Failure of Gramm-Rudman," *Wall Street Journal*, October 3, 1989; and Steven Mufson, "Missing the Broad Side of the Barn: Gramm-Rudman's Target Practice Has Balanced Out as a Big Zero," *Washington Post Weekly Edition*, May 28-June 3, 1990. See also chap. 2, note 2.
71. David Shribman and Ellen Hume, "Election Paradox: Deficit Is a Vital Issue to Voters Yet Seems to Affect Few Votes: Candidates Fail to Tackle It and Public Isn't Willing to Back Specific Actions," *Wall Street Journal*, October 10, 1986.
72. *Wall Street Journal*, February 6, 1986; and Wehr, "Budget Puts Congress."
73. *Congressional Record*, April 4, 1986, S3918.
74. Helen Dewar, "Chicken and Egg: Budget and Tax Revision," *Washington Post Weekly Edition*, March 17, 1986; and Elizabeth Wehr, "Bipartisan Budget Heads for Senate Floor," *Congressional Quarterly Weekly Report*, March 22, 1986.
75. Wehr, "Bipartisan Budget"; and Jonathan Fuerbringer, "Senate Panel Cuts Reagan's Request for Military in '87," *New York Times*, March 20, 1986.
76. Wehr, "Pete Domenici"; and Wehr, "Bipartisan Budget."
77. *Washington Post Weekly Edition*, March 24, 1986. See also *Washington Post Weekly Edition*, April 4, 1986.
78. *Congressional Record*, April 14, 1986, S4192; and Adam Pertman, "Dole Channels Energy Toward White House," *Boston Globe*, August 24, 1986.
79. Elizabeth Wehr, "Senate Adopts $1 Trillion Fiscal 1987 Budget," *Congressional Quarterly Weekly Report*, May 3, 1986.
80. Lou Cannon, "Saved By Senate," *Washington Post Weekly Edition*, June 2, 1986.
81. *Boston Globe*, June 11, 15, 28, 1986.
82. Steven Roberts, *Rochester Democrat and Chronicle*, October 1986; and David S. Broder [Washington Post News Service], *Philadelphia Inquirer*, October 22, 1986.
83. *Congressional Record*, April 21, 1986, S4580.
84. *Congressional Record*, April 9, 1986, S3917-S3918.
85. *Congressional Record*, June 26, 1986, S8681.
86. Wehr, "Pete Domenici."

87. See Jonathan Fuerbringer, "The Spotlight Shifts from Domenici," *New York Times*, May 14, 1987.

88. Three glimpses: As a member of the minority (1987): "Anybody who was as active as I was, who liked it as much as I did, finds it difficult to adjust. I like to get things done. I like to be part of the action," as quoted in Jonathan Fuerbringer, "The Spotlight Shifts from Domenici," *New York Times*, May 14, 1987. As part of George Bush's short list for vice president (1988): "He said he felt he would 'add a lot' to the Republican ticket. . . . In the past two years, he has receded even further into the shadows of the Republican minority, but it is clear from his comments here this week that he would welcome the opportunity to become more of a national figure," Curtis Wilkie, "Domenici Ready for Limelight," *Boston Globe*, August 16, 1988. As a participant in the 1990 budget summit: "The exception [to Republican 'carping'] is New Mexico's Sen. Pete Domenici, who knows more of the details than most others in the room . . . [his] obvious frustration with the creaky budget process has abated as he sees a chance to forge a significant deficit-reduction package," David Wessel, "With the Exception of Domenici, GOP Lawmakers Limit Role in Deficit Package to Playing Spoiler," *Wall Street Journal*, June 25, 1990. Pete Domenici was easily reelected to the U.S. Senate for a fourth term in November 1990.

89. David S. Broder, "The Senate's Leading Lights," *Washington Post Weekly Edition*, June 9, 1986.

90. David S. Broder, "Pitfalls for the GOP," *Washington Post Weekly Edition*, December 1, 1986. See also, "Change in the Senate," *Washington Post Weekly Edition*, November 17, 1986.

91. For two days, in November 1990, I observed Domenici's third reelection campaign in New Mexico. It was noncompetitive and barely visible. Its moments of maximum concern and activity had occurred much earlier in a successful effort to discourage Domenici's strongest potential opponent— Democratic representative Bill Richardson—from challenging him. Domenici hired a part-time professional organizer in August 1988 and began raising money in January 1989. In the first six months he raised $750,000. From January to June he "ran against Bill Richardson," who decided, after some polling of his own, to stay where he was. The man who did challenge Domenici was a state senator severely lacking in accomplishment, money, visibility, seriousness, and strategy.

The atmosphere of the campaign, locally as well as nationally, was one of voter concern about the future direction of the country, disenchantment with Congress, and discontent with incumbent politicians. Much of that pessimism and anger had been generated by the lengthy, frustrating, divisive, and much criticized season of budget making, in which Domenici was a prominent negotiator and an eventual supporter. It was, he said, "the most frustrating six months of my eighteen years in the Senate."

Due largely to the widely deplored "budget fiasco," the number of New Mexicans believing that "the country was on the wrong track" had jumped from 40 percent to 66 percent between June and late October 1990. Seventy-one percent of them listed the budget (40 percent), the economy (23 percent), or taxes (8 percent) as the country's number one problem. The ratio of their disapproval to approval of Congress stood at an all-time low of 75 percent to 18 percent. But these opinions had no effect on the voters' attitude toward Domenici.

At the same time—late October—the ratio of favorable to unfavorable voter opinion of Domenici stood at a remarkable 86 percent to 6 percent. His name recognition stood at 99 percent. Voters were asked to agree or disagree with the statement, "Pete Domenici has been in Washington longer than any other New Mexico politician. He has been there so long that he is now more a part of the problem with Washington than the solution." Seventy-one percent disagreed, and twenty-one percent agreed. When asked to approve or disapprove of "the job Pete Domenici is doing *to solve the budget crisis,*" 64 percent approved and 18 percent disapproved. These figures presaged a strong vote of confidence in the budget committee's top Republican.

Domenici's soft, positive television ads never mentioned his budget work. Neither did they mention national issues or picture him in Washington. With the slogan "He Stands for New Mexico," the television ads treated only his contributions to the state: saving two thousand jobs for potash miners, bringing three Canadian polar bears to the Albuquerque Zoo, sponsoring math-science training programs for teachers, and protecting high-tech industries against unfair Japanese competition. "The role of a senator in his home state," he intoned, "isn't found in a textbook. It's what you make of it." In all respects, these ads represented a reversal of his 1984 campaign. Now, his success on the national stage was taken for granted.

Editorial endorsements, however, praised him for his blend of local and national service. Calling him "a towering political figure in New Mexico and nationally prominent to boot," the *Albuquerque Tribune* said, "He is powerful and he has used his power to benefit the state." "He's carried New Mexico to heights of influence in the Senate and the nation seldom seen by a small ... state," echoed the *Roswell Daily Record*. "[And] through it all, he's never forgotten New Mexico, its needs and priorities." The *Albuquerque Journal* praised him as "an expert and a power on matters of federal budget policy ... [who] keeps close tabs on the state's needs and priorities [while] concerning himself with the big problems that face the nation." And added that "Domenici is of New Mexico. ... He is at ease rubbing shoulders with his friends from all walks of life in New Mexico." "Not since the days of Senator Clinton P. Anderson has a New Mexican been so esteemed both in his home state and on the national scene," wrote the *Santa Fe New Mexican.* Nationally, "he is an acknowledged expert on the intricacies of the federal budget and its relationship to the national economy. [Locally] a secret of his success is that he is low key ... and keeps in touch with New Mexico through many visits and advisers." Pride and respect for his national stature and accomplishments were complemented by satisfaction and comfort with his local attachments.

Not surprisingly, on November 6, 1990, Pete Domenici was reelected to a fourth term by another record-breaking margin of 73 percent to 26 percent.

TABLE A-1   1981 First Budget Resolution for Fiscal 1982, 1983, 1984 (in billions of dollars)

	President	Domenici	Senate Budget Committee	Senate passed
		Fiscal 1982		
Defense	226.3 (+7%)	225.4 (+7%)	225.4	226.2
Total revenues	650.3	650.3	650.3	650.3
Total outlays	695.3	704.1	699.1	700.8
Deficit	45.0	53.8	48.8	50.5
		Fiscal 1983		
Defense	259.6	258.8	254.3	254.3
Total revenues	709.1	709.1	709.1	709.1
Total outlays	732.0	761.3	730.5	730.5
Deficit	22.9	52.2	21.4	21.4
		Fiscal 1984		
Defense	294.9	294.0	289.2	289.2
Total revenues	770.7	770.7	770.7	770.7
Total outlays	770.2	815.4	770.7	770.7
Deficit	+.5	44.7	0.0	0.0

Sources: President column, *Congressional Quarterly Weekly Report,* May 9, 1981 (defense item from Senate Budget Committee report). Domenici and Budget Committee columns, Senate Budget Committee reports. Senate passed column, House-Senate conference committee report.

TABLE A-2   1981 Second Budget Resolution for Fiscal 1982, 1983, 1984
(in billions of dollars)

	President	*Domenici*	*Senate Budget Committee*	*Senate passed*
Fiscal 1982				
Defense	218.6	218.7	226.2	226.2
Total revenues	666.2	665.5	657.8	657.8
Total outlays	709.3	722.1	695.5	695.5
Deficit	43.1	66.6	37.7	37.7
Fiscal 1983				
Defense	249.6[a]	243.7	257.0	257.0
Total revenues	714.1	710.9	713.2	713.2
Total outlays	748.7	759.4	732.3	732.3
Unspecified cuts	11.7			
Deficit	22.9	48.5	19.1	19.1
Fiscal 1984				
Defense	282.9[a]	271.1	292.1	292.1
Total revenues	771.0	794.2	774.8	774.8
Total outlays	794.0	793.4	773.8	773.8
Unspecified cuts	23.0			
Deficit	0.0	+.8	+1.0	+1.0

Sources: President column, *Congressional Quarterly Weekly Report,* May 26, 1981. Domenici and Budget Committee columns, Senate Budget Committee reports. Senate passed column, House-Senate conference committee report.
[a] President's defense request is estimated.

TABLE A-3   1983 Budget Resolution for Fiscal 1984, 1985, 1986
(in billions of dollars)

	President	Senate Budget Committee	Baker-Domenici[a] (May 6)	Senate passed
Fiscal 1984				
Defense	280.5 (+10%)	267.0 (+5%)	275.0 (+7.5%)	270.7 (+7.1%)
Total revenues	659.7	685.6	658.0	671.1
Total outlays	848.5	848.9	850.4	849.7
Deficit	188.8	163.3	192.4	178.6
Fiscal 1985				
Defense	329.4	299.5	304.3	301.0
Total revenues	724.3	762.6	729.2	743.1
Total outlays	918.5	909.6	915.5	910.8
Deficit	194.2	147.0	186.3	167.7
Fiscal 1986				
Defense	364.3	334.8	—	333.1
Total revenues	841.9	830.8	—	836.0
Total outlays	989.6	964.0	—	966.1
Deficit	147.7	133.2		130.1

Sources: President column, *Congressional Quarterly Weekly Report,* February 2, 1983. Budget Committee column, Senate Budget Committee report. Baker-Domenici column, *Congressional Record,* May 6, 1983. Senate passed column, House-Senate conference committee report.
[a] Baker-Domenici estimated only for two years.

TABLE A-4   1983 Revenue Proposals, Fiscal 1984 Budget Resolution (in billions of dollars)

	President	Senate Budget Committee	Baker-Domenici	Senate passed	House passed	Final
Fiscal 1984						
Increase in revenues	+11.2	+30.2	+2.6	+9.9	+35.2	+12.0
Fiscal 1985						
Increase in revenues	+11.3	+39.1	+5.7	+13.7	+48.1	+15.0
Fiscal 1986						
Increase in revenues	+15.3 (+46 contingency)	+51.9	—	+51.0	+58.0	+46.0

Sources: President column, *Congressional Quarterly Weekly Report,* February 5, 1983. Budget Committee column, Senate Budget Committee report. Baker-Domenici column, *Congressional Record,* May 6, 1983. Senate, House, and Final columns, House-Senate conference committee report.

TABLE A-5   1984 Budget Resolution for Fiscal 1985, 1986, 1987
(in billions of dollars)

	President	*Domenici compromise*	*Senate Budget Committee*	*Senate passed*
Fiscal 1985				
Defense	313.4 (+13%)	299.0 (+5.4%)	299.0	299.0
Total revenues	745.1	743.7	743.7	743.8
Total outlays	925.5	924.4	924.4	925.5
Deficit	180.4	180.7	180.7	181.7
Fiscal 1986				
Defense	359.0	333.7	333.7	333.7
Total revenues	814.9	811.0	811.0	810.8
Total outlays	992.1	996.6	996.6	998.0
Deficit	177.1	185.6	185.6	187.2
Fiscal 1987				
Defense	389.1	372.0	372.0	372.2
Total revenues	887.8	882.6	882.6	882.3
Total outlays	1,068.3	1,086.1	1,086.1	1,086.3
Deficit	180.5	203.5	203.5	204.0

Sources: President column, *Congressional Quarterly Weekly Report,* February 4, 1984. Domenici and Budget Committee columns, Senate Budget Committee reports. Senate passed column, House-Senate conference committee report.

TABLE A-6   1984 Revenue Proposals, Fiscal 1985 Budget Resolution
(in billions of dollars)

	President	Domenici compromise	Senate Budget Committee	Senate passed
		Fiscal 1985		
Increase in revenues	+7.9	+10.7	+10.7	+10.8
		Fiscal 1986		
Increase in revenues	+11.6	+16.1	+16.1	+15.9
		Fiscal 1987		
Increase in revenues	+14.2	+19.1	+19.1	+18.8

Sources: President column, *Congressional Quarterly Weekly Report*, February 4, 1984. Domenici and Budget Committee columns, Senate Budget Committee reports. Senate passed column, House-Senate conference committee report.

TABLE A-7   1985 Budget Resolution for Fiscal 1986, 1987, 1988
(in billions of dollars)

	President	Domenici	Senate Budget Committee	Dole compromise	Senate passed
		Fiscal 1986			
Defense	322.2 (+5.9%)	302.5 (+0%)	302.5 (+0%)	312.8 (+3%)	302.5 (+0%)
Social Security/ pension programs COLA	3%	freeze	freeze	2%	freeze
Total revenues	793.7	793.8	793.8	793.6	793.6
Total outlays	973.7	966.1	964.4	969.0	965.0
Deficit	180.0	172.3	170.6	175.4	171.4
		Fiscal 1987			
Defense	363.4 (+5.9%)	323.4 (+3%)	323.4 (+3%)	334.9 (+3%)	323.4 (+3%)
Social Security/ pension programs COLA	3%	3%	3%	2%	3%
Total revenues	861.7	866.6	866.6	866.3	866.3
Total outlays	1,026.6	1,011.5	1,010.0	1,013.0	1,011.1
Deficit	164.9	144.9	143.4	146.7	144.8
		Fiscal 1988			
Defense	411.7 (+5.9%)	346.8 (+3%)	346.8 (+3%)	359.6 (+3%)	346.8 (+3%)
Social Security/ pension programs COLA	3%	3%	3%	2%	3%
Total revenues	950.4	956.2	956.2	955.9	955.9
Total outlays	1,094.8	1,058.0	1,058.5	1,055.1	1,060.2
Deficit	144.4	101.8	102.3	99.2	104.3

Sources: President column, *Congressional Quarterly Weekly Report*, February 9, 1985. Domenici and Budget Committee columns, Senate Budget Committee reports. Dole column, *Congressional Record*, April 25, 1985. Senate passed column, House-Senate conference committee report.

TABLE A-8   1986 Budget Resolution for Fiscal 1987, 1988, 1989
(in billions of dollars)

	President	Domenici	Senate Budget Committee	Senate passed
		Fiscal 1987		
Defense	320.2 (+8%)	295.1 (+3%)	295.1	300.9
Total revenues	850.4	862.7	862.7	857.2
Total outlays	994.0	1,006.6	1,006.6	1,001.2
Deficit	143.6	143.9	143.9	144.0
		Fiscal 1988		
Defense	341.3	309.0	309.0	312.2
Total revenues	933.2	947.8	947.8	941.2
Total outlays	1,026.8	1,055.7	1,055.7	1,051.2
Deficit	93.6	107.9	107.9	110.0
		Fiscal 1989		
Defense	362.9	323.6	323.6	327.2
Total revenues	996.1	1,020.1	1,020.1	1,011.9
Total outlays	1,063.6	1,088.7	1,088.7	1,084.0
Deficit	67.5	68.6	68.6	72.1

Sources: President column, *Congressional Quarterly Weekly Report,* February 8, 1986. Domenici and Budget Committee columns, Senate Budget Committee reports. Senate passed column, House-Senate conference committee report.

TABLE A-9 1986 Revenue Proposals, Fiscal 1987 Budget Resolution
(in billions of dollars)

	President	Domenici	Senate Budget Committee	Senate passed
Fiscal 1987				
Increase in revenues	+5.9	+18.7	+18.7	+13.2
Fiscal 1988				
Increase in revenues	+7.1	+26.8	+26.8	+20.2
Fiscal 1989				
Increase in revenues	+8.6	+28.8	+28.8	+20.6

Sources: President, Domenici, and Budget Committee columns, Senate Budget Committee reports. Senate passed column, House-Senate conference committee report.

Index